International Macroeconomics and Finance

Edward E. Ghartey

International Macroeconomics and Finance

Exploring Developing Economies

palgrave
macmillan

Edward E. Ghartey
The University of the West Indies
Mona, Jamaica

ISBN 978-3-032-04144-9 ISBN 978-3-032-04145-6 (eBook)
https://doi.org/10.1007/978-3-032-04145-6

This Palgrave Macmillan imprint is published by the registered company Springer Nature Switzerland AG
The registered company address is: Gewerbestrasse 11, 6330 Cham, Switzerland

To: Cecilia, and David

Preface

This book employs economic theory and empirical approach as pedagogies to assist advance undergraduate students, MBA, postgraduate students, and economists in especially developing countries to study international finance, macroeconomics, and monetary economics at the advance level.

The motivation for writing this book stems from the fact that most of the existing standard textbooks on international finance, and macroeconomics have been written with emphasis on addressing theoretical and empirical issues which concern developed countries. We have therefore attempted to fill the missing gap emanating from dearth of books which critically address both international finance and macroeconomics needs of developing countries in the academic literature. We have also addressed the need for instructing with clarity up to date advance empirical analysis of macroeconomics and international finance for honors undergraduate students, postgraduate students, MBA students, and practitioners in government, banking, and financial institutions who work on international finance and macroeconomics issues, and problems in especially developing countries.

The book also employs advance mathematics, which are explained in simplified form for readers, especially students who have less rigorous background in quantitative and analytical methods. We have provided derivation of some theories in the book. We have also solved some problems to enhance students' understanding, and to acquaint them to such related policy problems, and assist them to gain better mastery over the difficult facets of the text.

We have provided a variety of empirical publications which have been explained and discussed in detail for students and readers to familiarize them with topics covered. We have also included problems and solved them as illustrative examples throughout the book. Each chapter of the book includes exercises which students are encouraged to practice by solving them to improve their understanding over difficult topics in the book.

The book is principally written for students and readers who are interested in international finance and macroeconomics of developing countries. Consequently, most of the data and examples provided in the book originate from publications of developing countries, and countries which share in their characteristics. Each chapter is built and progresses on earlier texts and chapters. We have assumed that students and readers have rudimentary knowledge of probability, and single and multivariable calculus. Although we have used basic graphs throughout the book, we have in some cases buttressed our graphic illustration with phase diagrams to lend a visual reinforcement of i.e., dynamic paths of cause and effect of policy instruments on results of targeted variables.

We started the textbook with a brief discussion of national income accounting in Chapter 1. It was followed by a discussion of balance of payments accounting in the second chapter. We then discussed the foreign exchange market in Chapter 3, which is followed by the concept and development of rational expectation, and foreign exchange market efficiency in Chapter 4. We covered functions of money, definitions of monetary aggregates, multiple deposits expansion and contraction, determinants of the money supply, and money demand in Chapter 5.

Chapter 6 provides microeconomic foundation of demand for money in an open economy in a developing country. Chapter 7 comprehensively covers an applied study of money demand for a developing country with its data as an example. This amounts to deriving an error-correction model of demand for money, which is estimated and discussed by using data from a developing country. In this respect, we have discussed the properties of a typical demand for money in an open economy, such as price homogeneity, and unit elasticity of income of the demand for money. We have also tested for weak exogeneity, super exogeneity, and structural stability of money demand in an open economy of a developing country.

The liquidity preference-money supply (LM) curve, which is one of the equations developed by Hicks in his interpretation of Keynes' *General Theory of Employment, Interest and Money* in 1937 for the money market, is saddled with a major problem which mars the utility and application of the famous investment-saving (IS) and liquidity preference-money supply (LM) curves known as the (IS-LM) curves, the work horse of most macroeconomics textbooks for nearly eighty-six years. We have, therefore, tried to correct or expunge the LM curve problem inherent in Hicks' 1937 IS-LM gadget by developing the ultimate aggregate demand (AD) curve without using the LM curve in this textbook[1].

To this end, we have used the monetary policy principle (MPP), which is generally referred to as the Taylor's principle to develop a monetary policy curve (MPC), which captures the relationship between inflation rate and real interest rate in the money market. It is then combined with the IS curve developed in the goods market to construct the AD curve in Chapter 8. See the Appendix of that chapter.

In Chapter 9, we used the Phillips curve (PC), which relates inflation inversely to unemployment and Okun's law, which relates economic growth inversely to unemployment to derive the aggregate supply (AS) curve, which is a direct relationship between price (or inflation) and real output (or economic growth). Effects of easy money under a clean floating exchange rate regime in an open economy for a developing economy are discussed in Chapter 10. Results are also captured in phase diagrams to bring to bold relief the impact of easy money on relevant economic variables such as inflation, interest rate, economic growth, to name a few, in the open economy.

We covered (i) external imbalance models, namely: price-specie flow mechanism, elasticities approach to the balance of payments (BOPs), and absorption approach to the BOPs. We also discussed (ii) the J-curve effect, beachhead effects, currency pass-through, and inflation, among others. We derived the exchange market pressure model and employed it to study monetary approach to the BOPs under flexible and fixed exchange rate. We also covered exchange rate interventions by the monetary authorities to correct under-valued and over-valued exchange rates by using the money supply in Chapter 11.

[1] See the Appendix to Chapter 8 for a Summary of Hicks' (1937) interpretation of the *Generalized General Theory* of Keynes (1936), and problems associated with the LM curve.

Exchange rate regimes such as fixed exchange rate, flexible exchange rate, sterilized and unsterilized interventions using monetary policy to correct undervaluation and overvaluation, capital mobility, and speculation are covered in Chapter 12. Carry trade and associated open economy monetary policy trilemma, and exchange rate regimes such as inflation targeting, dollarization, monetary unions, process of interventions and adjustments under integration, regional currency union and process of adjustment under fixed and flexible exchange rate, international currency area versus interregional currency area, exchange rate targeting, and currency-board are discussed, illustrated, and contrasted with roles of central bank in Chapter 13.

The book has benefitted from ideas and writings of several economists, and comments and suggestions of authors of books and journals, professors, students, participants of various international conferences and academic meetings, and colleagues at banking and tertiary institutions I visited during the tenure of my academic life.

The book was written based on my experience in teaching international finance, money and banking, monetary economics, macroeconomics, and econometrics for postgraduate, undergraduate final year, and advance undergraduate courses at The University of the West Indies at Mona Campus in Kingston, and Howard University in Washington, DC. I am indebted to various people who taught me. I am also grateful for especially feedback and comments I received from postgraduate and undergraduate students I taught money and banking, monetary economics, international finance, and macroeconomics theory and policy, not to mention econometrics. Furthermore, I have benefitted from comments I received from institutions as a visiting scholar during my study and travel vacations, my sabbatical leaves in the US and Ghana, and conferences I attended at especially different central banks in several different countries on the globe.

The path to publication from the conception of an idea is long and windy. However, the destination can be arrived at by dint of hard work of which effort of several people became involved. Unfortunately, space does not permit acknowledgment of all involved, consequently, we have mentioned the editor and publication editor of the Palgrave Macmillan.

Mona, Jamaica — Edward E. Ghartey

Contents

1	**The System of National Income Account (SNIA)**	1
	1.1 Introduction	2
	1.2 GDP from the Production Approach or Domestic Products	2
	1.3 Income Approach	2
	1.4 GNP from the Expenditure Approach	3
	1.5 GDP from the Expenditure Approach	4
	1.6 Gross National Income (GNI) at Market Prices Is the Same as GNP	6
	1.7 Closed Economy or the Private Sector	6
	1.8 Open Economy or the International Sector Economy	7
	1.9 Summary	8
	1.10 Problems	8
	Selected References	11
2	**The Balance of Payments Accounts**	13
	2.1 Introduction	14
	2.2 Uses of the BOPs Data	14
	2.3 The US Balance of Payments Account	14
	2.4 The IMF'S Balance of Payments Account	16
	2.5 The Fundamental Balance of Payments Identity	21
	2.6 The BOPs Transaction	21
	2.7 Residents of a Country Are	22

2.8 *Financial Flows* 22
2.9 *Double-Entry Bookkeeping Account* 24
2.10 *Summary* 26
2.11 *Problems* 27
Selected References 30

3 The Foreign Exchange Market 31
3.1 *Introduction* 32
3.2 *FEM Participants or Players* 32
3.3 *Foreign Exchange Rates* 33
3.4 *The Cross Exchange Rate* 34
3.5 *Arbitrage Trading* 35
3.6 *Spot and Forward Rates* 36
3.7 *Foreign Exchange Swap or Currency Swap* 37
3.8 *Foreign Exchange Futures* 38
3.9 *Foreign Exchange Options* 38
3.10 *Foreign Exchange Risk* 39
3.11 *Hedging* 41
3.12 *Speculation* 42
3.13 *Stabilizing and Destabilizing Speculation* 43
3.14 *Interest Arbitrage* 43
3.15 *Covered Interest Arbitrage Parity (CIAP)* 45
3.16 *Taxation under Interest Parity Regime* 46
3.17 *Summary* 47
3.18 *Problems* 48
Selected References 51

4 Rational Expectation, and Efficient Foreign Exchange Market 53
4.1 *Introduction* 54
4.2 *Adaptive Expectation* 54
4.3 *Rational Expectation* 55
4.4 *Fundamental Theorem of Calculus for Bivariate Model with* r.v. X *and* Y 57
4.5 *Solution Procedure of Rational Expectation Problem* 58
4.6 *The Demand for Currency Asset* 60

4.7 *Interest Rates, Interest Rates Differential, and Exchange Rates Expectation in Carry Trade* 61
4.7.1 *Foreign and Domestic Exchange Rate Schedules* 64
4.7.2 *Effect of Changes in the Current Exchange Rate of ¥ Deposit on Expected Returns of GH₵ Deposit* 68
4.8 *Efficient Foreign Exchange Market (FEM)* 70
4.9 *Prices and Exchange Rates* 72
4.10 *The Law of One Price* 73
4.11 *Purchasing Power Parity (PPP)* 73
4.12 *Absolute PPP and Relative PPP* 74
4.13 *Problems with the PPP Theory* 75
4.14 *Summary* 76
4.15 *Problems* 77
Selected References 78

5 Money, Money Supply, and Money Demand 81
5.1 *Introduction* 82
5.2 *Functions of Money* 82
5.2.1 *A Medium of Exchange* 82
5.2.2 *A Unit of Account* 83
5.2.3 *A Store of Value* 83
5.3 *Measuring Money—Monetary Aggregates* 83
5.3.1 *Reliability of Money Data* 85
5.4 *Multiple Deposit Creation and the Money Supply Process* 86
5.5 *Unsterilized and Sterilized Foreign Exchange Intervention* 90
5.5.1 *Unsterilized Foreign Exchange Intervention* 90
5.5.2 *Sterilized Foreign Exchange Intervention* 91
5.6 *The Money Supply and Determinants* 92
5.7 *The Demand for Money* 93

5.8 *Quantity Theory of Money* 93
5.9 *Fisher's Equation of Exchange* 94
5.10 *Cambridge Equation of Exchange* 95
5.11 *Cambridge Demand for Money* 96
5.12 *Liquidity Preference Money Demand* 96
5.13 *The Square Root Formula of Money Demand* 97
5.13.1 *Derivation of the Square-roots formula of Demand for Money and Illustrative Example* 99
5.14 *Shortcomings of the Square Root (SQRT) Formula of Money Demand* 101
5.15 *Summary* 101
5.16 *Problems* 101
Selected References 103

6 Microeconomic Foundation of Open Economy Money Demand 105
6.1 *Introduction* 106
6.2 *Open Economy Money Demand Model* 107
6.3 *Microeconomic Foundation of Demand for Money* 108
6.4 *Households' Multi-Period Utility Function* 108
6.5 *Scale Variable and Opportunity Cost Measures* 110
6.5.1 *The Scale Variable* 110
6.6 *The Opportunity Cost Variable* 111
6.7 *Inter-Temporal Budget Constraint* 111
6.8 *Medium of Exchange Role of Money in the Shopping Time Model* 112
6.9 *Optimizing Multi-Period Utility Function Subject to Inter-Temporal Budget Constraint* 113
6.10 *Derivation of the Microeconomic Open Economy Money Demand Function* 114
6.11 *Economic Interpretations* 115
6.12 *Summary* 118
6.13 *Problems* 118
Selected References 120

7 **Applied Demand for Money Study in Developing Countries** 121
7.1 Introduction 122
7.2 The Open Economy Money Demand Function 122
7.3 Applied Money Demand Study in the Context of Developing Countries 123
7.4 Derivation of the Error-Correction Model 125
7.5 Tests of Homogeneity, Weak Exogeneity, and Stability of the Demand for Money Function 127
7.5.1 Homogeneity Test Results 128
7.5.2 Weak Exogeneity Test Results 130
7.6 Further Test of Exogeneity 132
7.6.1 Super Exogeneity Test 132
7.7 Structural Stability of the Money Demand Model 134
7.8 Summary 138
7.9 Problems 138
Selected References 140

8 **The IS and MP Curves, and Aggregate Demand Curve** 141
8.1 Introduction 142
8.2 The IS Curve 142
8.3 Consumption Sector 142
8.4 Business Investments Sector 144
8.5 Government Sector 145
8.6 Foreign Sector 146
8.6.1 Derivation of the Keynesian multiplier and the IS curve 146
8.7 Factors that Shift the IS Curve 149
8.8 The Monetary Policy Curve (MPC) 150
8.9 Monetary Policy Response and Influence on Inflation 153
8.10 The Aggregate Demand Curve 154
8.10.1 Effectiveness of Exchange Rate Targeting Policy Versus Interest Rate Targeting Policy 157
8.11 Factors that Shift the AD Curve 161
8.12 Summary 161

Appendix 162
Derivation of the LM Curve 162
Limitations of the LM curve 165
Problems 166
Selected References 169

9 The Aggregate Supply (AS) Curve 171
9.1 Topics Covered 172
9.2 Learning Outcomes 172
9.3 Introduction 173
9.4 The Phillips Curve 173
9.5 Okun's Law 174
9.6 Aggregate Supply 176
9.7 Dynamics of AD and AS Curves 176
9.8 Factors which Shift the AS Curve in the Short Run 178
9.9 Factors Which Shift the LRAS Curve 182
9.10 Summary 184
9.11 Problems 185
Selected References 187

10 Effect of Easy Money in an Open Economy 189
10.1 Topics Covered 190
10.2 Learning Outcomes 190
10.3 Introduction 190
10.4 Central Bank's Implementation of Easy Money or Expansionary Monetary Policy 191
10.5 Effect of Easy Money in the Market 195
10.6 Effect of Easy Money in the Open Market under Flexible Exchange Rate 195
10.7 Phase Diagrams Summary 197
10.8 Macroeconomic Policy Lessons 200
10.9 Appendix 201
10.10 Summary 202
10.11 Problems 202
Selected References 203

11 External Imbalance Models 205
11.1 Introduction 205
11.2 Price-Specie Flow Mechanism 206
11.3 Monetary Approach to the Balance of Payments and Exchange Rate 207
11.4 The Exchange Market Pressure (EMP) Model 208
11.5 Derivation of the EMP Model 209
11.6 Monetary Approach to the Balance of Payments Under a Fixed Exchange Rate 212
11.7 Monetary Approach to Exchange Rate 214
11.8 Elasticities Approach to the Balance of Payments (BOPs) 215
11.9 Illustrative Example 216
11.10 Application in a Developing Economy 218
11.11 Response Policy Lag 219
11.12 Other Lags 220
11.12.1 Median Lag 220
11.12.2 Mean Lags 220
11.12.3 Income and Price Elasticities 220
11.12.4 Impact Effect 220
11.13 The J-Curve Effect 220
11.14 Exchange Rate or Currency Pass-Through and Inflation 223
11.15 Beachhead Effect 224
11.16 Absorption Approach and Balance of Trade 225
11.17 Summary 226
11.18 Problems 227
Selected References 229

12 Exchange Rate Regimes, Interventions, and the Money Supply 231
12.1 Introduction 232
12.2 The Foreign Exchange Market Intervention Physiology and the Money Supply 232

12.2.1 *The Case of Unsterilized Foreign Exchange Intervention* 232
12.3 *The Case of Sterilized Foreign Exchange Intervention* 234
12.4 *Operation of the Fixed Exchange Rate Regime* 236
12.5 *Over-Valued Exchange Rate and Its Correction under a Fixed Exchange Rate Regime* 237
12.6 *Under-Valued Exchange Rate and Its Correction under a Fixed Exchange Rate Regime* 239
12.7 *Foreign Exchange Rate and Policy* 240
12.8 *Caveat: Role of Perfect Capital Mobility and Speculation* 241
12.9 *Perfect Capital Mobility* 241
12.10 *Speculation* 242
12.11 *Summary* 244
12.12 *Problems* 244
Selected References 246

13 The Open Economy Trilemma and Exchange Rate Regimes 247
13.1 *Introduction* 248
13.2 *The Impossibility Trinity* 248
13.3 *Exchange Rate Regimes* 252
13.4 *Inflation Targeting* 253
13.5 *Features of Inflation Targeting* 253
13.6 *Advantages of Inflation Targeting* 254
13.7 *Dollarization* 255
13.8 *Advantages of Dollarization* 256
13.9 *Disadvantages of Dollarization* 257
13.10 *Currency or Monetary Union* 258
13.11 *Types of Currency Areas* 259
13.12 *Illustrative Hypothetical Examples* 259
13.13 *Adjustment Process in the International Currency Area with Fixed Exchange Rates* 260
13.14 *Adjustment Process in the Interregional Currency Area with a Common Single Currency* 261

13.15 Summary 262
13.16 Currencies of Countries under Flexible Exchange Rates 262
13.17 Regional Currency Areas under Floating Exchange Rates 264
13.18 Exchange Rate Targeting 266
13.19 Advantages of Exchange Rate Targeting 266
13.20 Disadvantages of Exchange Rate Targeting 268
13.21 The Currency-board 269
13.22 Features of Currency-Board 270
13.23 Fractional-Reserve Operation of Currency-Board 273
13.24 Contrasting Currency-Board versus Central Bank 275
13.25 Summary 278
13.26 Problems 281
Selected References 282

Bibliography 285

Index 291

About the Author

Edward E. Ghartey holds BA Combined Honors, MA, and a PhD. from Dalhousie University in Halifax. He taught for more than five years at Howard University in Washington, D.C. before joining The University of the West Indies at Mona Campus in Kingston in 1993. His main research and teaching interests are in international finance and trade, macroeconomics, monetary economics, and econometrics. He taught macroeconomics, monetary theory and policy, international finance, and econometrics. He has published extensively in these areas with major emphasis on applied empirical analysis in the context of developing countries. He has presented several papers at international conferences and academic meetings in North America, South America, Latin America and Caribbean, Africa, Europe, and Asia. He is a columnist who contributes to current economic policy topics which deal with macroeconomic issues on exchange rates, inflation, fiscal deficit, and stabilization problems of mostly developing countries.

CHAPTER 1

The System of National Income Account (SNIA)

Learning Outcomes

Readers of Chapter 1 will be expected to have acquired knowledge and clear understanding to do the following, among others:

(a) Define and calculate absorption, gross domestic product (GDP), gross national product (GNP), national income (NI), net national product (NNP), and differentiate them.
(b) Describe, distinguish, and analyze taxes, subsidies, and transfer payments; define social insurance, unilateral transfers, indirect business taxes; calculate net foreign assets, private saving, public saving, and GDP by using the value-added method.
(c) Explain, calculate, and collect data on net unilateral transfers from abroad, net factor income from abroad, net current transfer abroad, current account balance.
(d) List the constituents of compensation of employees, gross operating surplus of enterprises, gross domestic fixed investments, and disposable income.
(e) Explain, calculate, and demonstrate value added, double counting, budget deficits and surplus.

E. E. Ghartey, *International Macroeconomics and Finance*, https://doi.org/10.1007/978-3-032-04145-6_1

1.1 Introduction

The System of National Income Accounting provides an internationally recognized system for organizing a continuous flow of information to the performance of a country. There are 5 main sectors or groups of economic agents. These are (i) households, (ii) enterprise, (iii) financial intermediaries, (iv) the government, and (v) non-residents.

1.2 GDP from the Production Approach or Domestic Products

Output ≡ the value of all goods and services produced in an economy. The problem associated with computation of output of the economy is double counting.

Example of double counting is when wheat is counted in the production of flour and counted again in the production of bread or the value of bread as a final output.

Value Added (VA) ≡ the value of output—the value of intermediate consumption. The VA is not subject to the double counting problem. The VA is the contribution of labor and capital to the production process.

Gross Domestic Product (GDP) ≡ The sum of the gross value added to all resident sectors engaged in production + any taxes—any subsidies on products not included in the value of their outputs.

Social insurance is protection of the individual against economic hardships/hazards, (i.e., unemployed, old age, or disability).

1.3 Income Approach

GDP is Domestic Income. It is the sum of income generated by resident producers.

$$\mathrm{GDP} \equiv \mathrm{W} + \mathrm{GOSE} + \mathrm{TMSPM} \tag{1.1}$$

where,

W is compensation of employees. It includes wages and salaries in cash or kind plus social insurance contributions payable by employees.

GOSE is gross operating surplus of enterprises (which includes profits, rents, interests, and depreciation).

TMSPM is taxes minus subsidies on products and imports.

The National Income Accounting records all the expenditures that contribute to a country's income and output.

Gross National Product (GNP) is the value of all final goods and services produced by their factors of production and sold on the markets at a given time or period.

1.4 GNP from the Expenditure Approach

$$GNP \equiv C + I + G + CAB \quad (1.2)$$

where,

C is the amount of final goods and services consumed by private domestic residents.

I is gross private domestic investment, which is the amount set by private businesses and firms to build new plant and equipment for future production. It includes fixed investments (I^f), which comprise of building, construction, machinery, equipment, and transportation, and is also known as gross fixed capital formation, and changes in inventory stocks (Δinv). Thus,

$$I = I^f + \Delta inv$$

G is government expenditure which is the amount of money spent by the government.

CAB is current account balance, and it comprises of net exports, net foreign income from abroad, and net current transfer from abroad. The net exports are the difference between X which is the amount of money received from exporting to foreigners, and IM which is the amount of money spent on imports from foreigners.

Equation 1.2 is referred to as national income identity (NII) for the open economy.

GNP does not take into consideration the economic loss resulting from the tendency of machinery and structures to wear and tear out as they are used. This is known as depreciation or capital consumption allowance which is the wears and tears associated with production of machinery, structures, equipment, etc. It reduces income of capital owners and must be accounted for in the national income account. Hence the need for Net National Product (NNP).

$$NNP \equiv GNP - Depreciation \quad (1.3)$$

GNP may include gifts from residents of foreign countries known as unilateral transfers which also include pension payments to retired citizens living abroad, reparation payments and foreign aid such as relief donated to countries that are stricken by natural disasters such as hurricanes, etc.

Net unilateral transfers must be added to the GNP or national income. This is because although it is not part of the country's products, it is part of a country's income. They must therefore be added to the NNP in the calculation of national income (NI) of a country.

$$\begin{aligned} \text{NI} = \text{GNP} - \text{Depreciation} + \text{Net Unilateral Transfers} \\ -\text{Indirect Business Taxes} \end{aligned} \tag{1.4}$$

Indirect Business Taxes are amount of tax wedges. It results from the fact that national income depends on prices producers receive for their goods whereas the GNP depends on the prices buyers pay for goods.

To the extent that prices buyers pay is different from prices producers receive for their goods, because of sales taxes or general consumption taxes (GCT), buyers pay more for their goods and services whereas sellers receive less from their sales, the GNP overestimates NI. Consequently, there is a need to subtract the tax wedge amounts like sales taxes known also as indirect business taxes from the GNP to arrive at the NI.

Note that NI $\neq$ GNP because of Depreciation, Net Unilateral Transfers, and Indirect Business Taxes since the latter variables are not zero or insignificant. Nonetheless, macroeconomic analysis tends to use the NI, NNI, and GNP interchangeably, in its analysis, although they are conceptually and significantly different when there is a need to do so.

1.5 GDP from the Expenditure Approach

$$\text{GDP} = \text{C} + \text{I} + \text{G} + \text{X} - \text{IM} \tag{1.5}$$

$$\text{CAB} \equiv \text{X} - \text{IM} + \text{NFIFA} + \text{NCTFA} \tag{1.6}$$

where,

GDP is the sum of all the final uses of output or the volume of production within a country's border, and NX = X—IM, where NX is net exports or balance of trade and IM is import of foreign goods and services. NFIFA is net factor income from abroad or net primary income, and NCTFA is net current transfer from abroad which is a net secondary income from abroad. The primary factor incomes from abroad are loans and investments. They comprise of repayments and dividends from loans and investments. Primary incomes are compensations of employees and property incomes from abroad. However, in current transfers, the originator does not receive 'quid pro quo' in return. For instance, recipients of remittances of workers, gifts, aid relief, etc., do not make any payments in return.

Alternatively, the GDP can be explained as expenditures on all domestically produced goods and services for consumption, investment, government expenditures, and exports. This is written as follows:

$$GDP = C^{D} + I^{D} + G^{D} + X \tag{1.6a}$$

where,

C^{D} (C^{IM}) = consumption of all domestic (foreign) produced goods and services.

I^{D} (I^{IM}) = investments of all domestic (foreign) produced goods and services.

G^{D} (G^{IM}) = government expenditures of all domestic (foreign) produced goods and services.

X = export of domestic produced goods and services

$$C = C^{D} + C^{IM}$$

$$I = I^{D} + I^{IM}$$

$$G = G^{D} + G^{IM}$$

Thus, by substituting the above definitions into eq. (1.6a), we obtain the GDP as follows:

$$GDP = \left(C - C^{IM}\right) + \left(I - I^{IM}\right) + \left(G - G^{IM}\right) + X$$

Or

$$GDP = C + I + G + X - \left(C^{IM} + I^{IM} + G^{IM}\right) = C + I + G + X - IM \tag{1.6b}$$

where,

$$IM = C^{IM} + I^{IM} + G^{IM}$$

1.6 Gross National Income (GNI) at Market Prices Is the Same as GNP

$$GNI \equiv GDP + NFA \tag{1.7}$$

where,

Net Foreign Assets (NFA) is defined as NFA = NFIFA + NCTFA

$$\text{Gross National Disposal Income (GNDI)} = GNP - NTX \tag{1.8}$$

$$GNDI = C + S^P \tag{1.9}$$

where,

S^P = gross private national saving, and NTX is net taxes.

Net Receipts of Factor Income from Abroad ≡ Income domestic residents earn on their assets/wealth held outside the country (or abroad)—Payments domestic residents make to foreign owners of assets/wealth located at their home country.

Most countries use the GDP as a primary measure of their national income activity but in 1991 the US began to follow the practice of using the GDP as a primary measure of its national income.

Earnings of National Commercial Bank in Port of Spain, Trinidad-Tobago, which is owned by Jamaican businesses and shareholders, will be included in Trinidad-Tobago's GDP, but they are part of the GNP of Jamaica. Goods and services which Dangote cement factory located in Nigeria provides in Ghana, are a service exports from Nigeria. They are therefore added to the GDP of Nigeria in calculating the GNP of Nigeria. On the other hand, Jamaica's GNP will include its GDP minus service imports from Trinidad-Tobago. Although both GDP and GNP move in parallel, GNP is used often because it tracks the national income better than the GDP. Additionally, welfare of nations depends more on national income than domestic product. If GNP > GDP, then NFA > 0 which means Ghana's residents are earning more abroad than foreigners are earning in Ghana.

1.7 Closed Economy or the Private Sector

Given that Y = GNP, I = Gross Private Domestic Investments, G = Government Expenditure, and A = Absorption.

Closed economy without government roles:

$$\text{Expenditure} : Y = C + I \tag{1.10}$$

$$\text{Income} : Y = C + S^P \tag{1.11}$$

Closed economy with the public sector or government roles:

$$\text{Expenditure} : Y = C + I + G = A \tag{1.12}$$

1.8 Open Economy or the International Sector Economy

$$\text{Expenditure Approach} : Y = C + I + G + X - IM + NFIFA + NCTFA \tag{1.13}$$

$$\text{Income Approach} : Y = C + S^P + NTX \tag{1.14}$$

NTX = Total Taxes—Transfer Payments, and Total Taxes = Total Direct Taxes + Total Indirect Taxes.

At equilibrium, expenditure is equal to income which results from eqs. 1.13 and 1.14 being expressed as

$$C + I + G + CAB \equiv Y \equiv C + S^P + NTX \tag{1.15a}$$

$$I + CAB \equiv S^P + NTX - G = S^P + BS \tag{1.15}$$

where,

budget deficit (BD) = G—NTX, and budget surplus (BS) = NTX—G.

$$\text{Private Saving}\left(S^P\right) : S^P = Y - NTX - C \tag{1.16}$$

$$\text{Government Saving}\left(S^G\right) : S^G = NTX - G \tag{1.17}$$

National Saving (S):

$$S = S^G + S^P = NTX - G + Y - NTX - C = Y - C - G \tag{1.18}$$

$$S = C + I + G + CAB - C - G = I + CAB \tag{1.19}$$

From eq. 1.15,

$$S^P = I + BD + CAB \tag{1.20}$$

1.9 Summary

The system of national income account is covered by accounting for the five sectors or agents of the economy. The GDP and GNP is presented by pointing out the problem of double counting and briefly demonstrating how the method of value-added resolves the double counting problem.

We have also shown that using the GNP as a measure of total output in the nation is fraught with problem. This problem is corrected to obtain national income by including net unilateral transfer and excluding indirect business taxes and capital consumption allowance from the GNP in the country.

It is further demonstrated that the total output of the country can be computed from expenditure approach and income approach. We address the role of foreigners and government in accounting for the total output.

We also examine the total output of the country from the private sector which is the closed economy without the role of government and foreigners. We also include in the private sector model fiscal spending which comprises of government spending excluding net taxes. We further extend the model by including the foreign sector which is captured by current account balance.

1.10 Problems

(1.1) Using the system of national income identities in the chapter, discuss the effect of increase in a country's current account surplus on its I, BD, and S^P.

(1.2)Using the National Income Accounting identities for an open economy with the role of Government, derive a relationship between GNP and GDP. Explain what condition will cause the GDP to be greater that the GNP.

(1.3) Define and/or explain the following terms and concepts in international finance:

(i) Current account balance	(ii) Absorption
(iii) national income	(iv) primary income
(v) GDP from income approach	

(1.4) (a) Using the national income accounting identities, derive a relationship among private saving, current account, domestic investment, and budget deficit.

(b) Explain the effect of higher tariffs on imports on private saving, gross private domestic investment, and government budget deficit.

(1.5)

	GFKF	*CIS*	*GNP*	*X*	*IM*	*C*	*NTX*	*G*
2007	235,106	1587	829,925	337,188	534,658	725,283	209811.2	248011.6

Sources Statistical Digest, 2008 and International Financial Statistics, 2009.

where, GFKF is gross fixed capital formation, CIS is changes in inventory stock.

X is exports, IM is imports, C is consumption, NTX is net taxes, and G is government expenditures.

Compute a time series of the following:

(i) Investment (I) known as Gross Private Domestic Investment,
(ii) Budget Deficit (BD), (iii) Current Account (CA), and (iv) Private Saving (S^P) for 2007.

(1.6) Table of national income account of Jamaica is summarized as follows:

	2002	*2003*	*2004*	*2005*	*2006*	*2007*
GFKF	127,865	142,024	164,173	186,210	220,384	235,106
CIS	774	876	578	64	2708	1587
GNP	438,602	510,354	584,591	652,424	747,773	829,925
X	154,163	199,364	233,772	246,212	311,933	337,188
IM	230,971	280,625	322,377	371,727	468,051	534,658
C	349,505	406,285	467,078	537,645	611,693	725,283

(continued)

(continued)

	2002	2003	2004	2005	2006	2007
NTX	100,613	113189.3	149315.4	167319.1	185967.0	209811.2
G	123,804	149029.1	178732.2	199487.8	207724.1	248011.6

Sources Statistical Digest, 2008 and International Financial Statistics, 2009.

where, GFKF is gross fixed capital formation, CIS is changes in inventory stock, X is exports, IM is imports, C is consumption, NTX is net taxes, G is government expenditures.

Compute a time series of the following: Investment (I) known as Gross Private Domestic Investment, Budget Deficit (BD), Current Account (CA), and Private Saving (S^P) for 2002, 2005 to 2007.

(1.7)

	GFKF	CIS	GNP	X	IM	C	NTX	G
2007	235,106	1587	829,925	337,188	534,658	725,283	209811.2	248011.6

Sources Statistical Digest, 2008 and International Financial Statistics, 2009.

where, GFKF is gross fixed capital formation (I^f), CIS is changes in inventory stock, X is exports, IM is imports, C is consumption, NTX is net taxes, and G is government expenditures Compute a time series of the following:

(i) Investment (I) known as Gross Private Domestic Investment,
(ii) Budget Deficit (BD), (iii) Current Account (CA), and (iv) Private Saving (S^P) for 2007.

(1.8) Can a country which is experiencing balance of trade deficit register current account surplus? Hypothetically, explain your answer with some figures for the current account, net factor income from abroad, net current transfer, export and import of goods and services.

(1.9) Consumption, $C = 10 + YD$, where disposable income, $YD = Y—tY$, and t is the tax rate.

Given that income, Y = J$100 and government spending, G = 40

(i) Calculate the private savings before and after the tax cut if the tax rate is cut from 0.10 to 0.09, and comment on your finding.

(ii) Calculate the budget deficit before and after the tax cut, and comment on your finding.

(1.10) If the government increases spending and concurrently raises taxes to balance the budget, what will be the effect on aggregate demand?

Selected References

Paul R. Krugman, Maurice Obstfeld (2000), *International Economics: Theory and Policy*, (New York: Addison-Wesley Longman, Inc.).
International Financial Statistics (2009).
Institute for Capacity Development (2013), *Financial Programming and Policies*, International Monetary Fund.
Robert C. Feenstra and Alan M. Taylor (2008), *International Macroeconomics*, New York: Worth Publishers.
Statistical Digest (2008), Statistical Institute of Jamaica, Kingston.

CHAPTER 2

The Balance of Payments Accounts

Learning Outcomes.

Readers of Chapter 2 will be expected to have acquired knowledge and clear understanding to do the following, among others:

(a) Define or explain the BOPs account, debt forgiveness, current account balance, capital account, primary income, secondary income, special drawing rights, free on board, brownfield investments, greenfield investments, accommodating transaction, and autonomous transaction, among others.
(b) List the items constituting the IMF's balance of payments account and current account, the US' current account and financial accounts; and other transfer of wealth which are non-market activities.
(c) List three types of residents of a country and three uses of the BOPs data.
(d) Differentiate capital accounts from financial accounts, and secondary income from primary income; explain the fundamental BOPs identity.
(e) Set up the BOPs account table of the US and that of the IMF.
(f) Explain, analyze, and illustrate the BOPs transaction with examples using the T-account.

E. E. Ghartey, *International Macroeconomics and Finance*,
https://doi.org/10.1007/978-3-032-04145-6_2

2.1 Introduction

The balance of payments (BOPs) is a summary statements in which in principle, all transactions of the residents of a nation with the residents of all other nations are recorded during a particular period.

The BOPs of a country measure the international flow of goods, services, and capital during a one-year period. As a flow concept, the BOPs data is typically collected yearly, although in some developed countries it is collected quarterly.

2.2 Uses of the BOPs Data

1. It informs governments of the international position of a country.
2. It provides information to assist governments to formulate monetary, fiscal, and trade policies.
3. Countries employ the BOPs information to find their stance with their trading partners to inform their policy decisions.
4. It is indispensable to banks, firms, and individuals who are directly and indirectly involved in international trade and finance.

2.3 The US Balance of Payments Account

Balance of payments accounts record both payments to a country's residents and receipts from foreigners. Transactions which result in payments to foreigners are entered as a debit or negative (−) and transactions which result in receiving payments from foreigners are entered as a credit or positive (+).

There are three types of transactions recorded in the BOPs account. These are (i) Current Account, (ii) Capital Account, and (iii) Financial Account. The third transaction includes three transactions, namely: (iv) Financial Derivatives, (v) Official Reserve Assets, and (vi) Statistical Discrepancy.

The International Monetary Fund (IMF) sets up their BOPs account tables quite different from that of the US. Nonetheless, both BOPs tables basically capture the three broad categories of the BOPs account.

A. Current Accounts

Current accounts include trade in (i) Goods, (ii) Services, (iii) Primary Incomes or Investments, (iv) Secondary Income or unilateral transfers.

B. Capital Accounts

Capital accounts record transfer of capital. They are different from financial account transaction. These are other transfer of wealth between countries which result from non-market activities. Examples are (i) Debt forgiveness, (ii) Gifts migrant workers carry to their home countries, (iii) Investments grants to build roads, hospitals, (iv) Non produced intangible assets such as patents, copyrights, trademarks, and franchises, and (v) Non produced and non-financial assets such as land and subsoil resources.

C. Financial Accounts

Financial accounts record all the international purchases or sales of assets. Financial account balance is the difference between exports of assets minus imports of assets. They comprise of (i) Direct Investments, (ii) Portfolio Investments, (iii) Derivatives, (iv) Other Investments, and (v) Reserves and Related Asset Flows.

D. Net Errors and Omissions

These are residual of all the BOPs accounts. It is equal to the sum of all the other entries with the sign reversed to bring the sum of credits and debits to zero. It brings credit errors to offset debit errors.

The BOPs account tables are presented differently by the IMF and the US. In the above tables are the setups of the BOP account tables of the US and IMF which are reported in Tables 2.1 and 2.2, respectively.

Net international investment position (NIIP) is the difference between a country's residents assets held abroad minus foreigners or the rest of the world's (ROW) assets held in the country at a point in time. It can also be defined as a country's assets with foreign countries or ROW minus the ROW's assets in the country at the end of the period. If the country's assets held abroad is greater than the ROW's assets held in the country, then the NIIP is in a surplus and the country can be said to be a creditor country. If the NIIP is negative, then the country is said to be a

Table 2.1 The BOPs Account of the US

A: Current account
(1) exports of: Goods
Services
Income receipts (primary income)
(2) imports of: Goods
Services
Income receipts (primary income)
(3) net unilateral Transfers (secondary income)
Balance of Current Account = Exports (1)—Imports (2) + Net Unilateral Transfers (3)
B: Capital Account
(4) capital account
C: Financial account
(5) domestic-own financial assets abroad with the exclusion of derivatives
(6) foreign-own financial assets in domestic country with the exclusion of derivatives
D: (7) financial derivatives
Net financial flows = (5)–(6) + (7)
E: Official reserves and other related assets
F: Statistical discrepancy
BOPs ≡ balance of current account + balance of capital account—Net financial flows ≡ 0
Current account + capital account ≡ net financial flows account
≡ exports of assets—Imports of assets

debtor country. The NIIP is also known as the balance of international indebtedness, and it is a stock concept.

2.4 The IMF'S Balance of Payments Account

A: Current Account.

The Current Account records exports of goods and imports of goods. The IMF calculates exports and imports at free on board (f.o.b.) which include only transportation cost, as the cost of freight and insurance are excluded from the cost of exports which are calculated at cost of transportation, insurance, and freight (c.i.f.) in the US.

A1: Services include: (i) transport and insurance of goods (ii) transport fares paid by travelers, (iii) tourist services which includes hotels, restaurants, and health-related services, (iv) telecommunication, (v) computer and information services, (vi) construction, (vii) government purchases

Table 2.2 The IMF's BOPs Account

A: Current account
Goods: (1) exports of currently produced goods calculated at f.o.b.
(2) imports of currently produced goods calculated at f.o.b.
A1: Balance of trade on goods ≡ (1)–(2)
Services: Credit (+)
Debit (−)
A2: Balance of trade on goods and services
A3: Primary and secondary incomes: Credits (+)
Debits (−)
Balance of current account
Balance of trade on goods, services, and flows of primary and secondary incomes
B: Capital account
Credit (+)
Debit (−)
B1: Balance of capital account
C: Financial account
Direct investments: Abroad (−)
In the nation (+)
Portfolio investment assets: Equity securities (+)
Debt securities (−)
Portfolio investment liabilities: Equity securities (+)
Debt securities (−)
Financial derivatives: Assets (+)
Liabilities (−)
Other investments
C1: Balance of financial account
D: Net errors and omissions = C—B—A—E
E: Reserves and related items: Reserve assets

associated with embassies, etc. Goods for processing are also recorded as a service in situations where the manufacturing is undertaken by an entity that does not own the goods and is paid a fee by the owner. These services are referred to as manufacturing services on physical inputs owned by other countries.

A2: Primary incomes include: (i) labor income, these are compensation of employees or wages paid to employees living in foreign countries but are considered as residents of their home country, (ii) renting of natural resources, (iii) income from financial assets or liabilities, (iv) investment incomes are receipts and payments of interests on financial assets or liabilities, dividends on corporate stocks and re-invested earnings, (v) interest payments or earned on debt, reserved assets, and loans to foreigners.

A3: Secondary incomes which are also known as current transfers in the BOPs account include:

(i) cash transfers or remittances, usually in the form of funds sent by workers residing abroad to their families back home,
(ii) gifts in kind such as food and medicines sent back home by residents in foreign countries,
(iii) taxes on incomes and wealth or assets,
(iv) social security contributions and benefits,
contributions member governments pay to international organizations they hold membership. They exclude contributions that give rise to equity or shares.

B: Capital Accounts.

They record capital transfers which are generally large and infrequent. They can be in cash, as evidenced in investment grants to build roads, schools, or hospitals. They can also be in kind such as debt forgiveness. They can also be delivered as government or official transfers and private transfers. Investment grants are often delivered in the form of specific projects which obligate the recipients (either the general government or private sector) to use the funds for fixed capital formation. Debt forgiveness is the voluntary cancellation of all, or part of a debt specified by a contractual arrangement by an official creditor. Capital transfers also include (i) acquisition or disposal of non-produced, and non-financial assets such as land and subsoil resources, and (ii) non-produced intangible assets such as patents, copyrights, trademarks, and franchises, and leases or other transferable contracts .

C: Financial Accounts.

The financial account includes (i) Direct Investments, and (ii) Portfolio Investments.

C1: Direct Investments are flows which arise when an investor resident of say country A makes an investment in say a foreign country B that gives her/him control or significant degree of influence on the management of an enterprise there (Table 2.3).

Table 2.3 Jamaica's Balance of Payments Account in the first quarter of 2021 in millions of US dollars

	2020	*2021*	*Change*
A: Current account			
(1) exports of goods and services			
Credits	1461.9	854.7	−607.2
Debits	1783.2	1559.1	−224.0
Goods	−834.7	−770.1	64.5
Exports	354.9	354.6	−0.3
Imports	1189.6	1124.8	−64.8
Services	513.4	65.7	−447.7
Credits	1107.0	500.1	−606.9
Debits	593.6	434.3	−159.2
(2) primary income	−200.5	−158.2	42.3
Credits	−77.1	83.2	42.3
Debits	277.6	241.5	−36.2
(3) secondary income	577.8	816.6	238.8
Credits	640.5	879.6	−606.9
Debits	62.8	63.1	0.3
A1: Current account balance	56.0	−46.1	−102.1
Credits	2.7	3.6	0.9
Debits	12.2	12.2	0.0
B: Capital account			
Credits	2.7	3.6	0.9
Debits	12.2	12.2	0.0
B1: Capital account balance	−9.5	−8.6	0.9
Capital and current accounts balance or net borrowing (−)/lending (+) (A1 + B1)	46.5	−54.7	−101.2
C: Financial account			
(4) net lending (+) or net borrowing	321.9	122.4	−199.4
(i) Direct investments	−99.9	−17.1	82.7
Net financial assets acquired	2.6	33.5	30.8
Net liabilities incurred	102.5	50.6	−51.9
(ii) portfolio investments	37.3	218.2	181.0
Net financial assets acquired	−222.7	197.9	420.6
Net liabilities incurred	−260.0	−20.3	239.7
(iii) financial derivatives	16.8	0.0	−16.7
Net financial assets acquired	2.2	54.1	51.9
Net liabilities incurred	−188.1	31.9	220.0
(iv) reserve assets	57.4	162.4	105.1
(v) Net errors and omissions	275.4	177.2	−98.2

Source Bank of Jamaica's BOPs quarterly of March 2021 compiled with the sixth edition BOP manual

Inward Direct Investment—It occurs when a foreign investor buys an existing domestic financial or non-financial firm. It is sometimes known as Brownfield Investment. However, if the investor uses its funds to build a new firm in the home country, it is known as a Greenfield Investment.

Outward Direct Investment: It is the direct acquisition of controlling interest or a significant degree of influence in a foreign company or the use of the domestic investor's funds to create a subsidiary in a foreign country. It is also the reinvestment of retained earnings in a foreign firm that is controlled by a domestic firm.

C2: Portfolio Investment is purchasing of tradeable equity and investment fund shares, and debt securities that do not give the buyer substantial control rights, such as management. It covers the purchasing or selling of stocks, bonds, and money market debt instruments.

C3: Derivatives or financial derivatives such as currency and interest rate swaps.

C4: Other Investment comprises of (i) trade credits and advances, (ii) loans, (iii) insurance, (iv) pensions, etc.

D: Net Error and Omissions are residual of all BOPs accounts. It is equal to the sum of all the other entries in the BOPs with the sign reversed to bring the sum of credits and debits to zero. It uses credit errors to offset debit errors.

E: Reserves and Related Asset Flow. These are changes in the country's holdings of official monetary reserves. Reserves or Official reserves are external assets controlled by monetary authorities. They include (i) the country's gold holdings, (ii) foreign currency, deposits, and securities in US dollars and other hard currencies, (iii) Special Drawing Rights (SDRs), which are international reserves created by the IMF to enable its members to withdraw literally their gold deposit with them. They are also known as 'paper gold,' (iv) the country's reserve position in the IMF, (v) the IMF's credit and loans, and (vi) Exceptional financing.

We have included Bank of Jamaica's compiled quarterly data on balance of payments to provide clarity and familiarity on the BOPs subject for readers.

2.5 The Fundamental Balance of Payments Identity

Current Account Balance + Capital Account Balance ≡ Financial Account or Net Foreign Assets or Official Reserve Transaction Balance or Net Change in Government International Reserves.

Accommodating transactions are transactions that are undertaken to balance international transactions or officially taken to manage international payments.

Official reserve transactions are short-term capital flows that are undertaken in response to expectations of interventions.

Autonomous transactions are undertaken not to manage international payments but for purely business reasons and are independent of unilateral transfers.

The BOPs identity shows the importance of the current account in the news. A current account surplus shows that the country is increasing its claims on foreign wealth or assets. A current account deficit shows that the country is reducing its claims on foreign wealth or assets. A current account balance indicates that the government and private sector have no claims on foreign wealth or assets.

The BOPs deficits occur if the net private capital inflow is less than the sum of the country's current account and capital account deficits. It is covered by a net credit balance on official (or Monetary Authorities') reserve transactions.

2.6 The BOPs Transaction

Every international transaction automatically enters the BOPs accounts twice. Once as a credit and once as a debit. This is known in the BOPs account as double-entry bookkeeping account or principle.

Illustration:

If a resident of country A buys a home in country B, the transaction enters the BOPs account of country A as a debit on its financial account. However, the resident of country A can make payment either (1) by paying into the seller of the home's foreign bank account in country A or (2) by paying into the foreign bank account of the seller in country B. This results in the buyer of the home losing money in the amount of the value of the home, which is outflow of fund from country A to country B. However, the payment to the foreign seller results in the buyer of the foreign bank account increasing in country A which results in capital inflow. Thus, a single transaction in the BOPs account results as both a debit and a credit in country A of the buyer, and reverse single transaction occurs in country B of the seller.

The BOPs accounts include transactions of the residents of a nation with the rest of the world (ROW), the BOPs also include some transactions which do not involve foreign residents directly.

Illustration:

If the central bank of country A sells a fraction of its foreign currency holdings or net international reserve (NIR) to the commercial banks in the same country, the BOPs account is affected, although the transaction does not directly involve foreign countries.

2.7 Residents of a Country Are

1. Diplomats, military personnel, tourists, and temporarily workers who migrate to foreign countries (sugar cane farmers in the US or Canada, etc.) are residents of the nation they hold citizenship and not the country they are temporarily working.
2. A corporation is the resident of the nation in which it is incorporated. However, its foreign branches and subsidiaries such as Toyota in the US or KFC franchise in Jamaica are not.
3. International institution such as the IMF, the UN, the World Bank, WTO, etc., are not residents of the nation in which they are located. The workers are residents of the country they hold its passport.

2.8 Financial Flows

Financial Inflow:

(A0) It occurs if there is an increase in foreign assets in country A or a reduction of country A's assets abroad. See Fig. 2.1 for illustration of financial inflow.

Illustrations.

(1.01) When a citizen of country A buys country B's stock, foreign assets in country A increases.

This results in capital inflow to country B, and it is a credit in country B's BOPs, as it receives payments from foreigners or country B's citizens.

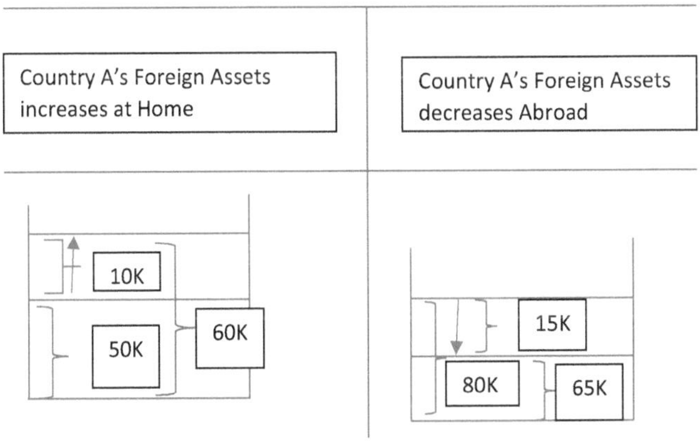

Fig. 2.1 Illustration of financial inflow

(B0) It also occurs when there is a reduction in country B's assets abroad.

(1.02) When a country B's citizen sells his foreign stocks, country B's assets abroad decrease, and it results in capital inflow to country B as capital in country B increases.

Financial Outflow:

(A1) It occurs when there is either an increase in country A's assets abroad or a reduction in foreign assets in country A. Note that in both cases country A makes payment to foreigners.

Illustrations.

(1.01) When a citizen of country A sells country B's stock, foreign assets in country A decreases.

This results in capital outflow of country A, and it is a debit in country B's BOPs, as it receives payments from foreigners or country B's citizens (Fig. 2.2).

(B1) It also occurs when there is a reduction in country B's assets abroad.

(1.02) When a country B's citizen sells his foreign stocks, country B's assets abroad decrease, and it results in capital outflow to country B as capital in country B increases.

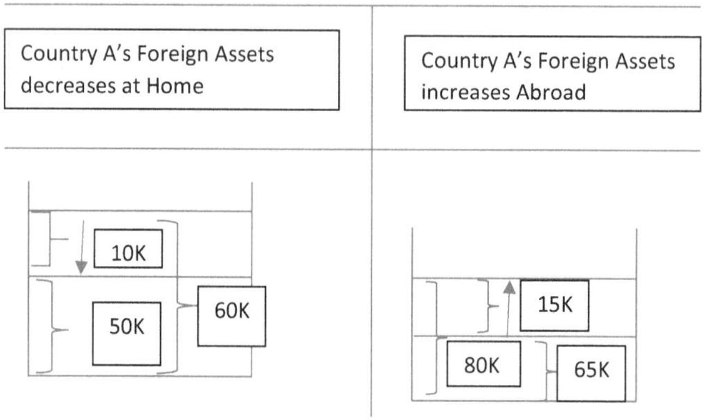

Fig. 2.2 Illustration of financial outflow

2.9 Double-Entry Bookkeeping Account

Examples.

(1.01) Suppose a Jamaican business exports goods worth $1000 abroad. The payment the exporter of the good receives is credited to Jamaica at the value of $1000, and this results in financial inflow to the exporter's country and is entered as a credit in the BOPs account of Jamaica.

The importer of the good can pay from its foreign bank account in Jamaica, the country of the exporter or pay into the foreign bank account of the exporter in abroad. In both cases the activity results in financial outflow of the exporter and is entered as a debit in the BOPs account of Jamaica.

The transaction can be summarized as.

Activities in Jamaica's BOPs account	*Credit (+)*	*Debit (−)*
Financial inflow/exported good receipt	$1000	
Financial outflow/importer's payment		$1000

(1.02) Suppose a Ghanaian tourist visits Canada and spends $200. The $200 expenditure of the Ghanaian tourist will require payment to foreigners (Canada). It can be likened to a Ghanaian importing $200 services or good from Canada. It will therefore enter Ghana's BOPs account as a debit.

The Ghanaian tourist payment can be made either by using his foreign bank account which will cause that account to reduce or by paying into the Canadian foreign bank account in Ghana which will result in that account increasing in Ghana. In both cases, the activity will result in a financial inflow as foreign bank account deposit in Ghana increases and will be entered as a credit.

The transaction is summarized as.

Activities in Ghana's BOPs account	*Credit (+)*	*Debit (−)*
Financial outflow/spending abroad		$200
Financial inflow/tourist payment abroad	$200	

(1.03) Suppose the UK government gives an aid of $600 to Nigeria as a relief assistance.

The UK's unilateral transfers of $600 gift to a foreign country will be entered as a debit to UK. The UK government can make payment of this $600 to Nigeria by either paying the $600 into the foreign bank account of Nigeria in UK or by reducing the UK's foreign bank account in Nigeria by the said amount to pay the gift to Nigeria. In both cases, it will be entered as credit to UK.

The transaction is expressed as.

Activities in UK's BOPs account	*Credit (+)*	*Debit (−)*
Financial outflows/UK'S foreign aid abroad		$600
Financial inflows/Payment from UK'S account abroad	$600	

(1.04) Suppose a Jamaican buys a foreign stock for $500 from Barbados and pays for it by increasing foreign bank balances in Jamaica. The purchase of the foreign stock will cause Jamaica's assets abroad to increase. This will result in financial outflows from Jamaica and will be recorded as a financial debit of $500 in Jamaica's BOPs account. The payment made by increasing the foreign bank balances in Jamaica is an increase in foreign financial assets in Jamaica or a financial inflow to Jamaica. It is entered as a credit in Jamaica's BOPs.

Similarly, the Jamaican resident can pay for the foreign stock by reducing his bank balances abroad or in Barbados. This will result in Jamaica's assets abroad reducing and Jamaica experiencing a financial inflow and is entered as a credit to its BOPs account.

The transaction is summarized as follows:

Activities in Jamaica's BOPs account	*Credit (+)*	*Debit (−)*
Financial outflow/purchasing foreign stock		\$500
Financial inflow/paying foreign bank stock abroad	\$500	

(1.05) Suppose a Chinese buys \$400 T-Bills from Philippines and pays from it by drawing money from his bank balances in China.

The purchase of \$400 T-Bills from Philippines increases foreign assets in China which is a financial inflow to China and is recorded as a credit in China's BOPs account.

The payment of the Philippines' T-Bills by China can be paid by either reducing foreign bank account in China or increasing foreign bank account in Philippines.

The transaction is summarized as.

Activities in China's BOPs account	*Credit (+)*	*Debit (−)*
Financial inflow/buying T-bills	\$400	
Financial outflow/paying from bank account		\$400

2.10 Summary

The BOPs account is defined as a flow concept data typically collected yearly. The uses of the data are expounded. The US BOPs account is discussed, and the framework is set up in a table format. Similarly, the IMF BOPs account is also discussed, and its framework is also set up in a table format.

The current account, capital account, and financial account are discussed in detail. Items constituting services, primary incomes, and secondary incomes in the current account are listed and examples are provided.

The capital account which is a transfer of wealth between countries originating from non-market activities is discussed with examples. Items in the financial account such as direct investments, portfolio investments, derivatives are expounded.

Items in reserves and related flow assets are listed. We have explained special drawing rights, exceptional financing. The fundamental BOPs identity is presented and discussed. Its relation pertaining to the fact that every international transaction enters the BOPs account twice is illustrated with examples by using the double-entry bookkeeping account.

2.11 Problems

(2.1) Explain how the following transactions generate two entries in the balance of payment bookkeeping account:

(2.1a) (i) The Russian government gives a $200 food and medical aid to Syria to assist Aleppo residents.

(ii) The NCB exchanges J$1000 worth of euros for Jamaican dollars at the BOJ.

(iii) A Bahamas-owned factory in France uses local earnings to buy additional machinery.

(2.1b) Set up a framework for the IMF's Balance of Payments accounts.

The following are items in the balance of payments. Arrange them in accordance to the IMF's balance of payments account by including them in their appropriate balance of payments categories such as current account: secondary incomes, primary incomes, etc., and capital account, etc.

(i) Debt forgiveness.
(ii) Migrant Worker in Jamaica's wages.
(iii) Food and medicines received by a hurricane devastated island.
(iv) Interest on loans to a foreigner.
(v) remittances.
(vi) Funds a migrant worker sends to family in Jamaica.
(vii) Contributions St Lucia pays to the CARICOM and Organization of American States.

(2.2a) What are balance of payments accounts? Provide distinctive uses of the balance of payments data.

(2,2b) (i) Explain how the following transaction generates two entries in the balance of payments account bookkeeping: NCB exchanges J$10,000 worth of euros for Jamaican dollars at the BOJ.

(ii) The current account deficit in the nation of Timbuktu was $1 billion and its non-reserve financial account surplus was $1.6 billion in 2016. What was the balance of payments of Timbuktu in 2016? What happened to the country's net foreign assets?

(2.3a) (i) Using the national income accounting identities, derive a relationship among private saving, current account, domestic investment, and budget deficit.

(ii) Explain the effect of higher tariffs on imports on private saving, gross private domestic investment and government budget deficit.

(2.3b) (i) Explain how financial inflows occur.

(ii) Explain how financial outflows occur.

(2.4) In 2012 Jamaica's international transactions recorded the following information:

> compensation of employees was $32.3m, travel expenses was $1877m, transportation was -$614m, investment income -$436m, exports at f.o.b. was $1667m and imports at f.o.b. was $5806m, remittances received from foreign companies was $1754m, remittances received from other foreign sources was $288m, total remittances paid to foreign countries was $266m, gross foreign assets was $1981m and foreign liabilities was $855m. All in US dollars ($), and m denotes millions.

(i) What is the meaning of the term current account?
(ii) Did Jamaica record a current account deficit or a surplus in 2012?
(iii) What was the size of the country's net financial flows?

Calculate the following:

(iv) Balance on current account
(v) Balance on goods and services.

Set a balance of payment account for Jamaica from the information provided under the assumption that they described completely Jamaica's international transactions for 2012.

(2.5a) If nominal interest rates in Jamaica fall but real interest rates rise, predict what will happen to the exchange rate in Jamaica? Use diagrams to illustrate your answer.

(2.5b) Explain how the following transactions generate two entries in the balance of payments accounts in a double-entry bookkeeping:

(i) The Russian government gives a $200 million food and medical aid to Syria to assist Aleppo residents.
(ii) The NCB exchanges J$10,000 worth of euros for Jamaican dollars at the BOJ.
(iii) A Bahamas-owned factory in France uses local earnings to buy additional machinery.

(2.6a) The IMF officials often assert that devaluation or depreciation of a country's currency is a sure requirement for a country either to improve its current account deficit position or experience a current account surplus. Assuming that your classmate who is now the Minister of Finance has sought your opinion on the effect of depreciation on the current account. Write a detail report on what the country should expect from depreciating the national currency.

(2.6b) Set up a framework for the IMF's Balance of Payments accounts.

(2.7) Can a country which is faced with current account surplus also be experiencing a balance of payments deficit at the same time? Explain your answer by including hypothetical figures for the current account, and non-reserve capital account. Include the possible implications for official international reserve flows.

(2.8) The following are items in the balance of payments account. Arrange them according to the IMF's Balance of Payments account by including them in their appropriate balance of payments categories such as current account: goods and services, secondary incomes, primary incomes, etc.; capital account, etc.; financial account: portfolio investments, other investments, etc.

(i) Trade credits and advances.

(ii) UK's investment grants to build prisons in Jamaica.
(viii) Compensations of sugar workers from Bahamas in the US.
(ix) Social security contributions and benefits.
(x) Renting of natural resources.
(xi) Guyana's rice exports to Barbados.

(2.9) Provide reasons to support why a government might be concern about a large current account deficit or surplus? Explain why a country might be concern about its official settlements balance, otherwise known as the balance of payments?

(2.10) Why is it that the trade balance of every nation sums up to be a nonzero world trade balance? Do you expect the trade balance to be positive or negative? Explain your answer with some reasons.

Selected References

Institute for Capacity Development (2013), *Financial Programming and Policies*, International Monetary Fund.

Paul R. Krugman, and Maurice Obstfeld (2000), *International Economics: Theory and Policy*, (New York: Addison Wesley Longman, Inc.).

Paul R. Krugman, Maurice Obstfeld, and Marc J Melitz (2015), *International Economics: Theory and Policy*, (New York: Pearson).

Dominick Salvatore (2010), *International Economics*, (New York: John Wiley & Sons Inc.).

Steven Husted and Michael Melvin (1993), *International Economics*, (New York: Harper Collins College Publishers).

CHAPTER 3

The Foreign Exchange Market

Learning Outcomes

Readers of this chapter will be expected to have acquired knowledge and clear understanding to among others do the following:

(a) Define and explain foreign exchange rates, cross exchange rate, spot rates, forward rates, foreign exchange swap, forward contract, real exchange rate, vehicle currency, nominal effective exchange rate, seigniorage, depreciation, revaluation, arbitrage, translation exposure, call option, put option, foreign exchange risk, and hedging, among others.
(b) List factors that cause shift in demand for and supply of foreign currencies, types of foreign exchange risk. Derive covered interest arbitrage parity condition.
(c) Demonstrate the activities of speculation and hedging; solve problems involving forward contracting, speculation, and hedging; derive the role of taxes on interest parity condition.

E. E. Ghartey, *International Macroeconomics and Finance*,
https://doi.org/10.1007/978-3-032-04145-6_3

3.1 Introduction

The foreign exchange market (FEM) is the market where individuals, firms, and banks buy and sell foreign currencies or foreign exchange. Market where exchange rates are determined. Most countries have their own foreign currencies. Jamaica has the Jamaican dollar, Trinidad-Tobago has the Trinidadian dollar, Ghana has the cedi, Nigeria has the naira, Brazil has the Brazilian real, European Monetary Union has the euro, the US has the dollar, UK has the pound sterling, China has the yuan renminbi, etc.

Foreign exchange trade involves the mutual exchange of different currencies (or bank deposits denominated in Jamaican dollars and other foreign currencies) between countries. When a Jamaican buys foreign goods, services, and financial assets, Jamaican dollars (bank deposits denominated in Jamaican dollars) must be exchanged for foreign currencies (or bank deposits denominated in foreign currencies).

The FEMs are monetary centers which are connected electronically. They are not conducted in specific locations. They are traded over the counter. The FEMs are not formally organized at a specified place for face-to-face meetings of buyers and sellers. They are traded over computer- and telephone-based networks which are connected to trading desks at major banks with each other and with brokers at *cambios*. They are also conducted through direct telephone, fax, and internet links among major foreign exchange trading centers. Foreign currency trading among banks is very common inter-bank trading.

3.2 FEM Participants or Players

Transactors or participants of foreign currencies are:

(1) Traditional users who include tourists, importers, exporters, investors, individuals, etc.
(2) Commercial Banks which serve as clearing houses between users (or buyers of foreign currencies) and earners (suppliers) of foreign currencies.
(3) Non-bank financial institutions such as foreign exchange brokers or *cambios*, etc. They are foreign exchange brokers who serve as a conduit between commercial banks and the traditional users. They are the wholesale or inter-bank market in the FEM.

(4) Corporations
(5) Central Banks which serve as the seller and buyer of last resort. They engage in buying foreign exchange surplus and selling foreign exchange when there are deficits in foreign exchange earnings. They sell foreign exchange from the national reserves when there is foreign exchange shortage in the nation and buy foreign exchange to pile up the NIR when there is surplus in foreign currencies.

Vehicle Currency

A vehicle currency is the currency that is widely used to conduct both domestic and international contracts between parties that reside in different countries. The US dollar is an example of a vehicle currency as it can be used by other countries to conduct their domestic business as well as international businesses.[1]

Reserve Currency

Reserve currency is a foreign currency which is used by other countries as their reserve currencies to conduct international transactions, investments, and settle debt obligations. The US dollar, UK pound sterling, European Monetary Union's euro, and Chinese yuan are examples of reserve and vehicle currencies.

Seigniorage

Is the benefit a country receives when its currency is used as a vehicle currency. It amounts to the country receiving a free interest loan from the country which is using its vehicle currency. Thus, if Ghana uses the US dollar as a vehicle currency in its international transaction, investment, and debt obligation, then it amounts to Ghana extending a free interest loan to the US. It is also explained as the difference between the face value of a currency note net of its production (or printing) cost.

3.3 Foreign Exchange Rates

The exchange rate is the price of one currency in terms of another currency. The exchange rate (XR) between the Jamaican dollar (*J*\$) and the pound sterling (£) is equal to the number of *J*\$s required to buy £1. This is known as the bilateral XR.

[1] See Magee and Rao (1980) for information on vehicle currency.

Thus, the XR = $J\$/£$ (domestic currency per foreign currency)
So, if XR = $J\$/£ = 1$, then it means one $J\$$ is required to buy one £.
If XR = $J\$/£ = 2$, then it means two $J\$$s are required to buy £1.
Thus, if £ = 1, then XR = $J\$2$, so $J\$2$ are required to buy £1.

Generally,

Increase (↑) in XR or ↑XR means it requires more $J\$$s to buy £1 so the $J\$$ is said to have depreciated.

Depreciation is an increase in domestic price of a foreign currency. The reverse of depreciation is appreciation.

Appreciation is a decrease in the domestic price of the foreign currency. ↓XR means it requires less $J\$$s to buy, foreign currency, £1.

If XR = $J\$/£$, then 1/XR = $£/J\$$ which is the number of foreign currencies required to buy one domestic currency.

Example 3.1 If in 2012 \$1 = $J\$100$ and in 2013 \$1 = $J\$107$, then the $J\$$ has depreciated by [(107 − 100)/100]*100% = 7%. However, \$ has appreciated by [(0.009 − 0.01)/0.01] = 10%.

3.4 The Cross Exchange Rate

If XR = $J\$/£$=2, and the XR = $J\$/€ = 3$, then the exchange rate calculated between £ and € is cross exchange rate. It is expressed as XR = (£/€), where € is the euro.

Example 3.2 If XR = $J\$/£ = 2$ and XR = $J\$/€ = 3$, then XR = £/€ = $(J\$/€)/(J\$/£) = (J\$/€)^*(£/J\$) = 3/2 = 1.5$.

Effective exchange rate is the weighted average of the exchange rates between the domestic currency ($J\$$) and that of its most important trading partners, where the weights are given by the relative importance of the nation's trade with each trade partner.

Nominal effective exchange rate (NEXR)

It is the index which measures the average change of a country's nominal exchange rate against number of other currencies during a given period. It compares domestic currency against a basket of major foreign currencies.

$$\mathrm{NEXR}_t = 100 \sum w_i (\mathrm{XR}_{i0}/\mathrm{XR}_{it}), \forall i \in 1, \ldots, n$$

where, n = number of major trading foreign countries; w_i = weight of currency between domestic country and its trading foreign country; S_{nit} = nominal exchange rate for the ith foreign currency at time t; $1/S_{nit}$ measures the domestic currency value in terms of foreign currencies.

A NEER coefficient greater than unity means that the domestic currency is worth more in value than the currencies in the foreign countries' basket. A NEER coefficient less than unity means the domestic currency is worth less than the currencies in the foreign countries' basket.

Real Exchange Rate (RXR)

$$\text{RXR} = q = \left[\left(\text{XR}_{J\$/£} * P^{£}\right)/P^{J\$}\right]$$

where, q is the $J\$$ value of the UK's price level divided by the Jamaican price level.

3.5 Arbitrage Trading

Arbitrage—is the purchase of a currency from a monetary center where it is cheaper for immediate sale at a center where it is more expensive to lock up a profit.

Types of Arbitrage Trading

Two-point arbitrage—It involves two currencies, and two monetary centers. Example is shown above.

Example 3.3 Suppose the US dollar price of the £ is \$1.60 in London and \$1.70 in Frankfurt. The arbitrageur will buy the £ for \$1.60 in London and sell it immediately in Frankfurt for \$1.70 to earn \$0.10 profit. Thus, with \$100,000 transactions, the arbitrageur can make \$10,000 profit in a few minutes. Arbitrage trading can therefore result in a substantial profit even after bearing the electronic transfer and other associated cost.

Arbitrage trading brings the \$ price of £ in both centers to an equilibrium. It increases the demand for £ in London and reduces the demand for £ in Frankfurt by increasing the supply of £ there.

Three-point or triangular arbitrage—It involves three currencies, and three monetary centers.

Example 3.4 Suppose there are three monetary centers and three currencies. The exchange rates are as follows: *J*\$100 = \$1 in Kingston; \$1 = £0.65 in New York; and £0.65 = *J*\$100 in London.

The cross rates are £0.65 = $1 = *J*$100. If, however, the exchange rate is *J*$96 = $1 in Kingston with the other exchange rates remaining the same, then it will be better to use *J*$96 to buy $1 in Kingston, use $1 to buy £0.65 in New York, and use the £0.65 to buy *J*$100 in London to make a profit of *J*$4.00.

On the other hand, if *J*$104 = $1 in Kingston, then use *J*$100 to buy £0.65 in London, and use £0.65 to buy $1 in New York, and sell $1 in Kingston for *J*$104 in Kingston to make *J*$4.00 profit. Thus, arbitrage eliminates profit to equalize cross rates between countries or international money in centers.

3.6 Spot and Forward Rates

Spot exchange rate is the foreign exchange rate where two parties exchange bank deposits and the transaction are executed immediately. The spot trading of exchange rate is termed spot transaction, and the exchange rate is known as spot exchange rate or spot rate. Note that even though the transaction is referred to as spot transaction, it takes two days for the transaction to be effective. The two days originate from the fact that it takes two days for payment instructions and checks to clear through the banking system. Only transactions between Canada and the US are executed within a day. Example $1 = *J*$107.80 is a spot rate.

Forward exchange rate is the exchange rate that occurs in a forward transaction which involves an agreement today to buy or sell a given amount of a foreign currency at a specified future date further than two days: example 30 days, 90 days, 180 days and in some instances even several years at an agreed upon rate today known as forward exchange rate or forward rate. The common forward rate is a 30-day forward rate.

Illustration

A 30-day forward transaction entered to buy £100 at a forward rate say £1 = *J*$180 will not require payment of any money at the time of signing the transaction. The buyer will be required to pay only 10% normal security margin. However, after 30 days from the date the transaction is signed, the buyer will obtain £100 and be required to pay *J*$18,000 for it irrespective of the prevailing spot rate at that time.

Forward contracts are usually not very long because investors do not like great uncertainties associated with longer contracts. Forward contract can be renegotiated by the other party or seller and the buyer has no choice but to honor it, although it is not common. Forward rates and spot rates are not necessarily equal, but they move closely together. They are highly correlated. They can be equal or vary from each other. They are typically used by importers and exporters to hedge against risks from foreign exchange speculation.

Example 3.5 Suppose the spot rate (SR) is *J*\$100 = £1. If the 3-month forward rate (FR) is *J*\$95 = £1, it means that the £ is at a 3-month forward discount of *J*\$5 with respect to the £ or at a 20% forward discount (FD) per year.

On the other hand, if the 3-month forward rate is *J*\$105 = £1, it means that the £ is at a 3-month forward premium (FP) of *J*\$5 or 5% for 3 month or 20% per year.

FD/FP = [(FR–SR)/SR]*100% for a 3-month FR Or FD/FP = [(FR–SR)/SR]*100%*4 for a 12-month (or a year) FR.

FD occurs if FR < SR, and FP occurs if FR > SR.

$$
\begin{aligned}
Thus,\ FD &= [(95-100)/100] * 100\% * 4 \text{ for a year} \\
&= -20\% \text{ for a year} \\
\text{and FP} &= [(105-100)/100] * 100\% * 4 \text{ for a year} \\
&= 20\% \text{ for a year.}
\end{aligned}
$$

3.7 Foreign Exchange Swap or Currency Swap

It is a spot sale of currency combined with a forward repurchase of the same currency in a single transaction. The swap fee is cheaper than the fees incurred by brokers when they sell the currency in the spot market and repurchase the same currency at a forward rate in two separate transactions.

Example 3.6 Citibank has just received *J*\$1 m from clients and would like to invest it for 30 days when its savers will have to be paid their investment. Assume that the £ is more likely to be stable or even appreciate in 30 days. A 1-month swap of *J*\$1m in £ may result in lower broker's fees than two separate transactions of selling *J*\$1m for spot £ and selling the £ for *J*\$s in the forward market.

The swap rate is the difference between the spot and forward rates in the currency swap. It is usually expressed on a yearly basis. Swaps dominate foreign exchange trading next to spot trades.

3.8 Foreign Exchange Futures

They are a promise that a forward contract for a standardized foreign currency amount bought today will be delivered on a specified date in the future. The standard currencies traded are yen, Canadian dollar, British pound, Swiss franc, The Australian dollar, the Mexican peso, euro, etc.

Trading in foreign exchange futures date back from the establishment of International Money Market of Chicago Mercantile Exchange (CME) in 1972. The futures market is different from the forward market. It trades in (a) only few currencies, (b) which are issued in standardized contracts, and (c) are for only a few specific delivery dates.

Both futures and forward contracts of currencies must be exercised on the delivery dates, but while forward deal must be fulfilled, in a futures contract, the contract can be sold in an organized future exchange before the delivery date to make a profit. A forward contract ensures that you receive the same amount of foreign currency on the delivery or maturity date.

3.9 Foreign Exchange Options

They give the owner of the contract the right to buy or sell a specified amount of foreign currency at a specified price at any time up to a specified expiration date.

A call option of a foreign exchange is a contract which gives the buyer the right but not the obligation to buy a standard amount of a traded currency on a stated date (the European option) or at any time before a stated date (the American option) and at a stated price (the strike or exercise price). The buyer of the call option has the choice to buy or forego the purchase if it turns out to be unprofitable.

A put option of a foreign exchange contract gives the seller the right to sell a standard amount of a traded currency on a stated date (the European option) or any time before a stated date (the American option) and at a stated price. The seller of the option must fulfill the contract if the buyer so desires. The buyer pays the seller a premium (the option price) which ranges from 1% to 5% of the value of the contract. Forward contracts are more flexible than option contracts, although option contracts are sometimes very useful.

Example 3.7 Suppose a Jamaican businessman wants to buy a hotel in Trinidad-Tobago (TT). He may make his bid to pay for the hotel by buying option for the required amount of TT dollars needed to pay for the hotel. Since he is not sure whether he will be successful in his bid as there may be other competitors, by buying the amount of TT dollars in an option contract, he will exercise his option to buy the required TT dollars if his bid is successful. If, however, his bid fails, he may choose not to exercise his call option to buy the amount of TT dollars. By so doing, he minimizes foreign currency or exchange risk in his bid.

3.10 Foreign Exchange Risk

Foreign exchange risk occurs because of shifts in demand and supply fluctuations in exchange rates which cause frequent fluctuations and variations in the spot and forward rates. Alternatively, foreign exchange risk is the risk which occurs because foreign goods and transactions are priced in foreign currency and not in domestic currency.

Factors that cause shifts in demand for and supply of foreign exchange rates over time are (i) changes in taste for domestic and foreign products in the nation and abroad, (ii) different growth and inflation rates in countries, (iii) changes in relative rates of interest, (iv) changing expectation, etc.

Illustration

Define exchange rate (XR) as the *J*\$ value or price of the foreign currency. So ↑XR which means an increase in *J*\$ value of foreign currency means depreciation of the *J*\$.

Thus,

↑ in taste of foreign goods result in increase in demand of foreign currencies which will result in depreciation of the *J*\$s.

↓ in rate of inflation in Jamaica relative to foreign countries will result in Jamaica's products becoming cheaper for foreigners. The resulting increase in demand for Jamaica's products will result in increase in the supply of foreign currencies in Jamaica which cause the ↓XR or appreciate.

Example 3.8 Suppose a Ghanaian importer buys £100,000 worth of products from UK to be paid in 3 months in £s. If the SR is £1

= GH¢180 at present, it means that in 3 months s/he must pay GH¢180*100,000 = GH¢18m. But in three months, the spot rate could be £1 = GH¢200 which will make the GH¢18m inadequate to pay for the £20m in three months. Thus, the importer faces foreign exchange risk. It occurs whenever a future payment is to be made or received in a foreign currency. Hence it involves foreign exchange risk which is also known as open position because of sudden changes in spot rates over time.

1. Types of Foreign Exchange Risk
   (1) Transaction (short-term) Exposure

   It occurs from transactions involving future payments and receipts in foreign currency such as imports and exports. "It refers to the risk associated with the change in exchange rate between the time a firm begins a transaction and settles it."

   (2) Translation or Accounting Exposure

   It occurs because firms need to value inventories and assets held abroad in terms of domestic currency to ensure that they are included in their consolidated balance sheets accounts (or combined accounts of the entire groups of companies of the firms). It is the extent at which changes in the exchange rate influence a firm's financial report.

   (3) Economic (long-run) Exposure

   It is known as forecast risk. It occurs when the domestic currency value of the future profitability of the firm is estimated because of unexpected fluctuations in the exchange rate. Alternatively, we can adduce that it occurs when the market value of the firm is affected by the present value of the future cash flows or unexpected exchange rate fluctuations. It can be managed by outsourcing or pricing or branding. The risk is associated with the fact that long-run future knowledge of exchange rate is unknown.

   (4) Contingent Exposure

   It is the foreign exchange risk which is contingent on the outcome of a firm or an investor's bidding for a project or negotiating contracts or foreign direct investment.

3.11 Hedging

Covering an open position to avoid a foreign exchange risk or protecting oneself against foreign exchange risk.

Example 3.9 Suppose the importer borrows £100,000 at the current spot rate of £1 = GH¢10 or (SR = GH¢10/£1) to use to pay for the imported product in three months. Doing so will mean that even if interest rate on £ is very small the importer will have to save at that rate so that he can use it to pay off the imports and forego the higher interest rate he could have earned by saving in GH¢s to convert into £s in three months. S/he may choose to take this stance because s/he wants to avoid foreign exchange risk in 3 months from now.

However, covering the foreign exchange risk as discussed above has serious disadvantage. To avoid tying up his/her funds by buying £100,000 now to be used in three months, the importer can avoid this by hedging in the forward market which will not require borrowing £100,000 now and tying it up for three months. The importer can do this by buying £100,000 forward to be delivered in three months at today's forward rate.

If the £ is at a 4% per year forward premium now, then in three months the importer will have to pay £101,000 (GH¢1.01m) for the £100,000 imports in three months. This hedging therefore has cost the importer £1000 or 1% of £100,000 for the 3-months imports.

If, however, the £ is at a three-month forward discount of 8% per year, the importer will receive £98,000 (or GH¢9.8m) in three months to pay for the £100,000 import in three months, which is 2% of £100,000 or £2000.

In the above case, the forward premium or discount is known with certainty, so exchange rate risk is eliminated. The importer has three months to find the £2000 to ensure that he can completely pay off the £100,000 imports. Additionally, s/he will require GH¢s at the spot rate of £1 = GH¢10 to cover the three months payments of the imports.

Advantages

The advantages of hedging in a world of foreign exchange uncertainty are that traders and investors through hedging can increase their participation in international trade and investments. The absence of hedging will reduce international capital flows, specialization, and the benefits derived from trade. A large corporation can hedge its net open position in dealing with its numerous payments in the same foreign currency at the same time in the future. Banks tend to employ hedging to close most of their open position in foreign currency with other banks. They then use the spot, futures, and option markets to close their remaining open position.

3.12 Speculation

It is undertaking a foreign exchange risk to make a profit if the anticipatory change is correct. Speculation, like hedging, takes place in the spot, forward, futures, or option markets, although it is most common in forward market. A speculator who thinks the *J*$ at the spot market will depreciate vis-a-vis the pound, will buy pounds now, save it, and resell it later when the *J*$ has depreciated to make profit.

If a speculator believes that the spot rate of a foreign currency will appreciate in the future, s/he will borrow the currency and if his/her hunch is correct, s/he will pay for the loan after selling the borrowed currency at the appreciated spot rate in the future, at a lower spot rate.

In both cases of speculating in the spot market, by buying or borrowing at the spot rate and turning around in the future date to sell or pay off at the appreciated spot rate, the speculator will have to either tie up his/her own funds or borrow to speculate. If the spot rate rises (or depreciates) contrary to the anticipation of the speculator, s/he will make a loss.

To avoid tying up of his/her own funds, the speculator can participate in the forward market.

Illustration

If the FR = *J*$190/£1 for 3 months, and SR = *J*$150/£1 in 3 months, the speculator who anticipates appreciation of *J*$s will sell £s forward for delivery in 3 months. After 3 months, if s/he is correct as anticipated, s/he will buy the £ in the spot market at SR = *J*$150/£1 and immediately turn around and resell the £ at the agreed forward rate of *J*$190/£1 to earn a profit of *J*$40 per £.

Long Position and Short Position

A speculator can take a long position or a short position to make profit.

Long position occurs when a speculator buys a foreign currency on either the spot or forward or futures markets or buys option to buy (or a call option) a foreign currency in the expectation of reselling it at a higher future spot rate for profit.

Short position occurs when the speculator borrows or sells forward a foreign currency in the expectation of buying it at a future lower price to repay the foreign exchange loan or honor the forward resale contract or option for profit. Thus, the speculator sells forward now what s/he does not have to buy it later at a cheaper price to make profit.

3.13 Stabilizing and Destabilizing Speculation

Speculation can be either stabilizing or destabilizing.

Stabilizing Speculation—is buying foreign currency when the exchange rate (domestic price of foreign currency) is low or falls in the expectation that it will soon rise so that you can sell it to make profit. It can also mean selling foreign currency when the exchange rate is high or rising in the expectation that it will soon fall, so that you can turn around and buy it to make profit.

Destabilizing speculation—is selling foreign currency when the exchange rate is falling or is lower in the expectation that it will fall even further in the future so that you can buy it back to make profit. It can also mean buying foreign currency when the exchange rate is rising or high in the hopes that it will rise even higher in the future so that you can sell it to make profit.

Stabilizing speculations reduce or moderate fluctuations in exchange rates over time, so it is a useful activity. Destabilizing speculation magnifies fluctuations in exchange rate. It is a harmful activity. Generally, speculation is a very risky activity which results in huge losses.

3.14 Interest Arbitrage

It is the international flow of short-term liquid capital to earn higher returns abroad.

Interest Parity Condition

It is the condition that the expected returns on deposits of any two currencies are equal when measured in the same currency. It implies that foreign currencies are considered as substitutes or equally desirable from the standpoint of potential holders of foreign currency.

Deriving Covered[2] Interest Arbitrage Margin (CIAM)

Assuming that

$i^{GH¢}$ = domestic interest rate/expected return per year

$i^{£}$ = foreign interest rate/expected return per year

SXR = spot exchange rate or XR (domestic currency per foreign currency)

FXR = forward exchange rate (domestic currency per foreign currency)

Q = Amount of investment capital in GH¢s

Both interest rates and foreign exchange rate have the same maturity period of one year, and there is absence of capital gain.

Illustration

One Domestic Cedi = (1/XR).(Foreign Pound)

1GH¢ = (1/XR).UK£

where XR = UK£/GH¢

For annual rate,

$Q + i^{GH¢}.Q$ = investment plus returns in Ghana in GH¢

$[(Q/\text{SXR}) + (i^{£}.Q/\text{SXR})]$ = investment plus return in UK in £

$[(Q/\text{SXR}) + (i^{£}.Q/\text{SXR})].\text{FXR}$ = investment plus return in UK in GH¢s

For arbitrage condition to hold,

$$Q + i^{GH¢} \cdot Q = \left[(Q/\text{SXR}) + \left(i^{£} \cdot Q/\text{SXR}\right)\right] \cdot \text{FXR}$$

$$\left(1 + i^{GH¢}\right).Q = Q.\left(1 + i^{£}\right).(\text{FXR}/\text{SXR})$$

$$\left(1 + i^{GH¢}.\right) = \left(1 + i^{£}\right).(\text{FXR}/\text{SXR})$$

$$\left[\left(1 + i^{GH¢}\right)/\left(1 + i^{£}\right)\right] - 1 = (\text{FXR}/\text{SXR}) - 1$$

$$\left[\left(i^{GH¢} - i^{£}\right)/\left(1 + i^{£}\right)\right] = (\text{FXR} - \text{SXR})/\text{SXR}]$$

$$\text{CIAM} = \left(i^{GH¢} - i^{£}\right) - (\text{FXR} - \text{SXR})/\text{SXR}] = 0 \quad (3.1)$$

[2] The covered interest arbitrage margin becomes uncovered interest arbitrage margin when the forward exchange rate is substituted for by the expected exchange rate. It will be introduced, discussed, and clarified when rational expectation is covered in the Chapter 4.

Covered interest parity condition:

$$i^{GH¢} = i^{£} + \left[(FXR - SXR)/SXR\right] \quad (3.2)$$

Equation (3.1) is non-existing, however in reality CIAM $\neq 0$. It can be either negative (CIAM < 0) or positive (CIAM > 0).

Why is CIAM nonzero? Covered interest arbitrage margin is the percentage gain (or loss) from covered interest arbitrage. There is significant CIAM observed in real life (because non-existing covered interest arbitrage margin does not function) due to the following reasons:

(1) A negative (or positive) CIAM occurs because of higher taxes abroad (or at home) which may prevent arbitrage outflows (inflows). Note that a negative CIAM implies that there is a covered interest arbitrage outflow.
(2) Investors ignore CIAM in determining a monetary center to operate because of the fear that foreign government might default or impose exchange restrictions on the repatriation of profits and principals on foreign investments.
(3) A large CIAM may exist because of lack of information on foreign investments, which may originate from lack of information on foreign investment opportunities in developing countries' financial markets.

3.15 Covered Interest Arbitrage Parity (CIAP)

It occurs when the interest differential is equal to the forward discount or premium on the foreign currency. It is usually expressed on an annual basis. Thus, when ($i^{GH¢}$–$i^{£}$) = –1, then the foreign currency is at a forward discount of 1% per year, and when ($i^{GH¢}$–$i^{£}$) = 1, the foreign currency is at a forward premium of 1% per year. However, the foreign currency is neither at a forward discount or premium when the interest differential ($i^{GH¢}$–$i^{£}$) = 0. This means that the foreign currency is neither at a forward discount or premium. There is CIAP and the forward rate is equal to the spot rate.

Example 3.10 Given that the interest rate on three-month treasury bill is 6% on an annual basis in Nigeria and 10% in the UK, while the spot rate of the pound is N180/£1, and the three-month forward rate on the pound is N160/£1 on an annual basis. What is the CIAM? Explain what it implies.

Solution

Given $i^N = 6\%$, $i^£ = 10\%$, SXR = N180/£1, and FXR = N160/£1

So,

$$\begin{aligned} \text{CIAM} &= \left[\left(i^N - i^£\right)/\left(1 + i^£\right)\right] - (\text{FXR} - \text{SXR})/\text{SXR}] \text{ (On an annual basis)} \\ &= (0.06 - 0.10)/(1 + 0.10) - (160 - 180)/180 \\ &= -0.04/1.1 + 20/180 \\ &= -0.0364 + 0.1111 \\ &= 0.074 \text{ on an annual basis or } 0.0187 \text{ per quarter} \end{aligned}$$

The positive sign implies that there will be a quarterly CIA inflow to Nigeria of 1.87% every quarter.

3.16 Taxation under Interest Parity Regime

In the discussion of the interest parity condition, the income earned from expected return on investing at home and foreign countries was conducted without taking into consideration taxation. However, in real world income earned at home and abroad are taxed. Therefore, there is a need to derive the effect of taxes on interest parity. We have considered two types of taxes, namely: income taxes and capital gain taxes.

The investor who earned $J\$M$ million and invested it in domestic bank at an annual rate of $i^{J\$}$ percent will receive $J\$(M + i^{J\$}\text{M})$ at the close of the year. If the investor invests the same income in a bank in UK, after a year the earned income will be $J\$(M + i^{J\$}M)$.FXR/SXR. Now, assume that the domestic income tax rate is τ_y percent and the capital gain tax on foreign investment is τ_k percent per annum. What will be the interest parity condition after a year's investment?

Solution

Suppose the following:

M = principal capital amount invested in $J\$$ million.
$i^{J\$}$ = domestic annual interest rate in percentages.
$i^£$ = foreign annual interest rate in percentages.
SXR = (spot) exchange rate.
FXR = forward exchange rate.

τ_k = capital gain tax rate percent per annum, $0 < \tau_k < 1$.

τ_Y = income tax rate percent per annum, $0 < \tau_Y < 1$.

$M + i^{J\$}\mathrm{M}$ = investment plus returns in domestic country (Jamaica) expressed in $J\$$.

$(M/\mathrm{SXR} + i^{£}M/\mathrm{SXR})$ = investment plus returns in foreign country (UK) expressed in £s.

$(M/\mathrm{SXR} + i^{£}M/\mathrm{SXR}).\mathrm{FXR}$ = investment plus return in foreign country expressed in $J\$$s.

For arbitrage condition to hold

$$\left(M + i^{J\$}.M\right)(1-\tau_Y) = \left(M + i^{£}.M\right).(1-\tau_Y) + \left(M + i^{£}.M\right).\mathrm{FXR/SXR}.(1-\tau_K) \qquad (3.3)$$

$$\left(1 + i^{J\$}\right).(1-\tau_Y).M = \left(1 + i^{£}\right).(1-\tau_Y).M + \left(1 + i^{£}\right).\mathrm{FXR/SXR}.(1-\tau_K).M$$

$$\left(1 + i^{J\$}\right)(1-\tau_Y) = \left(1 + i^{£}\right).(1-\tau_Y) + \left(1 + i^{£}\right).\mathrm{FXR/SXR}(1-\tau_K) \qquad (3.4)$$

$$\left[\left(1 + i^{J\$}\right) - \left(1 + i^{£}\right)\right].(1-\tau_Y) = \left(1 + i^{£}\right).\mathrm{FXR/SXR}(1-\tau_K)$$

$$\left[(1-\tau_Y).\left(i^{J\$} - i^{£}\right)\right]/\left[\left(1 + i^{£}\right).(1-\tau_K)\right] = (\mathrm{FXR}-\mathrm{SXR})/\mathrm{SXR} \qquad (3.5)$$

If the capital gain tax rate is set equal to the income tax rate or if both tax rates are abolished in the domestic country, we obtain the covered interest parity condition as

$$\left(i^{J\$} - i^{£}\right)/\left(1 + i^{£}\right) = (\mathrm{FXR}-\mathrm{SXR})/\mathrm{SXR}$$

3.17 Summary

The foreign exchange market is defined as market where different exchange rates or foreign currencies are determined and provided examples. Transactors in the FEM are listed. We explain vehicle and reserve currencies and cited the dollar as an example. We define exchange rate and seigniorage.

We explained cross rates and provided several examples to illustrate how they are calculated in a world of different currencies. We also explained nominal effective exchange rate and real exchange rate, and when a rising (falling) real exchange rate connotes depreciation (appreciation).

Arbitrage trading is defined and illustrated with examples. Spot rates, forward rates, forward contract, foreign exchange futures and options are explained with examples. Foreign exchange rate risk is defined, and different types of those risks are discussed with examples.

We also defined hedging as a means of avoiding foreign exchange risk; and explained speculation and illustrated how it can stabilize or destabilize the foreign exchange market. We derived interest arbitrage and discussed when it is covered or uncovered. We discussed why covered interest arbitrage margin is not zero in the world, and how it is influenced by taxation.

3.18 Problems

(1) Given that the one-year forward *J*$/€ exchange rate is *J*$122.85 per euro, and the spot exchange rate is *J*$122.75 per euro. What is the difference between the interest rate on one-year Jamaican dollar deposits and that on one-year euro deposits if there is no political risk? What is the forward premium on euro (or the forward discount on Jamaican dollar)?

(2) The 9-month interest rate is 10 percent in Jamaica, and 12 percent in Barbados. If the current spot rate which is Jamaican dollars per Barbadian dollars is *J*$0.40,

(i) What do you expect the 9-month forward rate to be?
(ii) Is the Barbadian dollar selling at a premium or discount?
(iii) The expected spot rate in 9 months is *J*$0.30, so what is the risk premium or discount?

(3) "In a real world the CIAM is always non-existing or equal to zero." True or False. Provide reasons to justify your answer.

(4) The Jamaican and Trinidad-Tobago dollar price for a unit of the following currencies are as follow:

J\$155.05 = \$1 *J*\$90.25 = CA\$1 *J*\$169.55 = £1 *J*\$122.85 = €1
J\$124.45 = Cayman Island (KY)\$1 TT\$9.70 = £1

Find the following cross rates:
(a) KY\$/£ (b) €/CA\$ (c) €/£ (d) KY\$/TT\$ (e) TT\$/\$

(5) Derive covered interest arbitrage margin. Explain why it is not zero.
(6) "In a real world the CIAM is always non-existing." True or False or Uncertain? Provide reasons to justify your answer.
(7) If the exchange rate moved steadily from \$1 = *J*\$112 to \$1 = *J*\$115 in the last two months, and an investor goes to the forward market and buys US dollars at the FR = *J*\$115.40/\$1 to be delivered in the next three months.

What kind of activity will you say the investor has engaged in? Explain your answer.

(8) The UK pound is currently selling at €2.00, and the 60-day forward premium on the pound is 10 percent. Compute the 2-month €/£ forward rate. What will the expected spot rate be in 60 days if the risk premium is 0.05? Is the expected return from holding a UK bond greater than or less than the expected return from holding a German bond?
(9) Assume that the Jamaican dollar interest rate and the British pound sterling interest rate are the same; both are 10 percent per year.
    (i) What is the relation between the current equilibrium *J*\$/£ exchange rate and its expected future level?
    (ii) Assume also that the expected future *J*\$/£ exchange rate is *J*\$150 per pound and remains the same as Britain's interest rate increases to 15% per annum. If the Jamaican interest rate also remains constant at its initial level, what is the new equilibrium *J*\$/£ exchange rate? Explain.
(10) Suppose an investor enters a 90-day forward transaction to purchase say €10,000.00 at a forward rate of say €1.00 = *J*\$134.35. Explain what this transaction will entail at the signing and closure of the contract.

(11) In third week of April 2018 one US dollar purchased 109.320 Japanese yen, 1.287 Canadian dollar, 0.82 Euros, 125.30 Jamaican dollar, and 6.79 Trinidad-Tobago dollar.

What were the cross exchange rates of (i) Euro/Trinidad-Tobago dollar, (ii) Japanese yen/Jamaican dollar, and (iii) Trinidad-Tobago dollar/ Canadian dollar?

(12) A businessman from The Bahamas spent B$1000 at a restaurant in the Hilton Hotel in Guyana, and bought JMMB bonds at the cost of B$270,000. Set up a double-entry bookkeeping account and explain each transaction.

(13) Exchange rates on Thursday March 12, 2015, are as follow:

$1 = BRL3.17, $1 = €0.94, $1 = Yen 121.39, $1 = CA$1.05, $1 = Mpeso 15.43,

$1 = £0.67, and $1 = *J*$115.35.

Find the cross exchange rates for (a) *J*$ per Mpeso, (b) Yen per £, (c) € per CA$, and (d) *J*$ per BRL.

Note: BRL is Brazilian real, Mpeso is Mexican peso, $ is US dollar, CA$ is Canadian dollar, € is euro, £ is British pound sterling, and *J*$ is Jamaican dollar.

(14) If the exchange rate moved from $1 = *J*$112 to $1 = *J*$115 in the last two months, and an investor goes to the forward market and buys US dollars at the FR = *J*$115.40/$1 to be delivered in the next three months.

What kind of activity will you say the investor has engaged in? Explain your answer.

(15) Define the following concepts:

(i) Foreign exchange rate
(ii) Foreign exchange futures
(iii) Contingent exposure
(iv) Destabilizing speculation

Selected References

Dominick Salvatore. (2010). *International Economics*, (New York: John Wiley & Sons Inc.).

Institute for Capacity Development. (2013). *Financial Programming and Policies*, International Monetary Fund.

Paul R. Krugman, Maurice Obstfeld, and Marc J Melitz. (2015). *International Economics: Theory and Policy*, (New York: Pearson).

Stephen P. Magee and Ramesh K. Rao. (1980). "The evolving world dollar standard: vehicle and nonvehicle currencies in international trade," American Economic Review, 70, (2), 368-373.

Steven Husted and Michael Melvin. (1993). *International Economics*, (New York: Harper Collins College Publishers).

CHAPTER 4

Rational Expectation, and Efficient Foreign Exchange Market

Learning Outcomes

This chapter readers will be expected to have acquired knowledge and clear understanding to do the following, among others:

(a) Define and explain concepts and terms such as: adaptive expectation, rational expectation, efficient FEM, weak-form efficient FEM, random walk, martingale, law of one price, and foreign exchange risk premium.
(b) Derive covered interest rate parity condition, uncovered interest parity condition, and efficient FEM.
(c) Prove that random walk is a universal form of weak-form FEM efficiency. Use foreign expected returns and domestic returns schedule to illustrate the effect of factors such as expectation, fiscal policy, monetary policy, taste for imported goods, foreign income, etc., on the exchange rate.
(d) Discuss purchasing power parity by explaining the law of one price, absolute PPP and relative PPP, and the shortcoming of the PPP.

E. E. Ghartey, *International Macroeconomics and Finance*,
https://doi.org/10.1007/978-3-032-04145-6_4

4.1 Introduction

Expectation is one of the important factors which drives demand for assets. Unfortunately, it is often used heuristically in empirical studies. In economics, attempt has been made to lend scientific formulation to it in the form of rational expectation hypothesis. In this book, we have discussed expectation by building it from adaptive expectation its root. We then adjusted the shortcoming of adaptive expectation by correcting the systematic error problem by developing the concept of rational expectation which requires the use of mathematical concepts. We also included the solution method for solving rational expectation problems.

4.2 Adaptive Expectation

Early form of expectation modeled in economics originated from the study of Phillip Cagan in 1956 on hyperinflation study in seven European countries in the 1920s and 1940s. He introduced expected inflation which he modeled by using what is known as adaptive expectation in time series. The adaptive expectation forms today's expectation about a variable based on past information of the variable itself.

The expectational error in this study can be specified as

$$\pi_t - \pi_{t-1} = \lambda\left[\Delta p_t - \pi_{t-1}\right] \tag{4.1}$$

Then $\pi_t = \lambda\Delta p_t + (1-\lambda)\pi_{t-1}$,
and

$$\pi_t = \lambda\Delta p_t + \lambda(1-\lambda)\Delta p_{t-1} + \lambda(1-\lambda)^2\Delta p_{t-2} + \ldots + \lambda(1-\lambda)^n\Delta p_{t-n} + \ldots \tag{4.2}$$

where, $0 \le \lambda \le 1$; $\lim(1-\lambda)^n\Delta p_{t-n} \to 0$ as $n \to \infty$; $\Delta p_t = p_t - p_{t-1}$; and the weights sum is

$$\lambda + \lambda(1-\lambda) + \lambda(1-\lambda)^2 + \ldots + \lambda(1-\lambda)^n + \ldots = \left(\lambda/[1-(1-\lambda)]\right) = 1$$

π_t is expected inflation or unobserved actual changes in logged prices at time t; Δp_t is growth in actual prices or actual inflation and p_t is actual logged prices at time t; and λ is the coefficient of adjustment which measures the speed of adjustment. $\lambda = 1$ means adjustment is instantaneous, and $\lambda = 0$ means no (or absence of) adjustment.

A shortcoming of the adaptive equation model of inflation is the fact that expectational errors are systematic. Consequently, under-prediction or over-prediction of inflation continues forever on the path of their, respective, directions.

4.3 Rational Expectation

It is in resolving the inherent systematic error in the adaptive expectation formulation that led John Muth (1961) to develop the rational expectation hypothesis. Cf. Robert Lucas (1981), Thomas Sargent (1973), and Benneth McCallum (1989). Muth's rational expectation states that "... in the aggregate, the expected price is an unbiased predictor of actual price." Thus, using the mean of the past actual growth prices to estimate π_t in Eq. (4.2) results in errors systematically different from actual inflation at period $t + 1(\Delta p_{t+1})$. Therefore, instead of using the adaptive expectation specification in Eq. (4.1), we have used an analytic condition which rules out systematic errors as suggested by Muth. The rational expectation assumes that expectations subjectively held by agents are equal to the mean of the probability distribution of the variable being forecast, given all available information.

Thus, at time t, p_{t+1} has a mean of $E(p_{t+1}/\Omega_t)$ which is the mathematical mean of the probability distribution of p_{t+1} given the information Ω_t. The latter notation Ω_t is the set of all available information possessed by the agent at time t. It is expressed as

$$p^e_{t+j} = E(p_{t+j}/\Omega_t) \tag{4.3}$$

where, j is a positive integer, p^e_{t+j} is the subjective expectation (or best guess forecast) held at time t for p_{t+j}, and $E(p_{t+j}/\Omega_t)$ is the objective (mathematical) expectation of p_{t+j} conditioned on Ω_t or the mean (or expectation) of the actual conditional probability of p_{t+j} given Ω_t.

Equation (4.3) is termed as rational expectation by John Muth. The actual probability distribution of say p_{t+j} although unknown can be determined by the model builder who will base it on his/her view of the economy.

Equation (4.3) rules out systematic error, and the expectational errors are independent or uncorrelated with any variable in the economy.

Let $p_{t+j} - p^e_{t+j} = \varepsilon_{t+1}$, be the expectational error at time $t + 1$ or next year from today (t). The average of the expectational error over a large observation is shown as follows:

$$\begin{aligned} E(\varepsilon_{t+1}) &= E\left[p_{t+1} - p^{e}_{t+1}\right] \\ &= E\left[p_{t+1} - E\left(p_{t+1}/\Omega_t\right)\right] \\ &= E(p_{t+1}) - E\left[E\left(p_{t+1}/\Omega_t\right)\right] \\ &= E(p_{t+1}) - E(p_{t+1}) \\ &= \phi,\ QED \end{aligned}$$

The law of iterated expectation, $EE(p_{t+1}) = E(p_{t+1})$, is used. This law states that expectation based on lesser information over expectation based on larger information will be equal to the expectation based on the lesser information. There is no systematic relationship between any variable in the information set and the expectational error. Thus, the covariance between the systematic expectational error and any element belonging to all available information set is zero. This is shown below:

$$\begin{aligned} E\left(x_t{}^{*}\varepsilon_{t+1}\right) &= E\left[x_t{}^{*}\left(p_{t+1} - p^{e}_{t+1}\right)\right] \\ &= E\left[x_t{}^{*}\left(p_{t+1} - E\left(p_{t+1}/\Omega_t\right)\right)\right] \\ &= E\left(x_t{}^{*}p_{t+1}\right) - EE\left(x_t{}^{*}p_{t+1}/\Omega_t\right) \\ &= E\left(x_t{}^{*}p_{t+1}\right) - E\left(x_t{}^{*}p_{t+1}\right) \\ &= \phi,\ QED \end{aligned}$$

Thus, the covariance of expectational error (ε_{t+1}) and any element (x_t) in the information set is zero. There is no systematic relationship between the expectational error and any variable belonging to the information set Ω.[1]

The prove of the law of iterated expectation is also shown below as follows:

$$E\left[E(Y/X)\right] = E\left[\int yf(y/x)dy\right] \text{ for } X \text{ and } Y \text{ random variables } (r.v.)$$

[1] The law of iterated expectation says the unconditional mean of the conditional mean of Υ given X, where X is a random variable, is equal to unconditional mean of Υ itself. This means $E(E[\Upsilon/X]) = E(\Upsilon)$, where X and Υ are random variables.

$$= \iint \left[\int yf(y/x)dy \right] f(x, y)dydx$$

$$= \int \left\{ \left[\int yf(y/x)dy \right] \int f(x, y)dy \right\} dx \quad (4.4)$$

But we know the following:

$$E(Y/X)] = \int yf(y/x)dy; \ \int f(x, y)dy = f(x);$$
$$\int f(x, y)dy = f(y); \text{ and } f(y/x) = f(x, y)/f(x) \quad (4.5)$$

So, equation (4.4) is expressed as

$$\int \left\{ \left[\int yf(y/x)dy \right] \left[\int f(x, y)dy \right] \right\} dx = \int \left[\int yf(y/x)dy \right] f(x)dx$$
$$= \int \left[\int yf(x, y)/f(x)dy \right] f(x)$$
$$= \int y \left[\int f(x, y)dx \right] dy$$
$$= \int yf(y)dy \quad (4.6)$$

Therefore $E[E(\Upsilon/X)] = E(\Upsilon)$, QED

4.4 Fundamental Theorem of Calculus for Bivariate Model with r.v. X and Y

The joint cumulative distribution function (CDF) of X and Υ is $F(x,y)$. $F(x, y) = F(x, \infty) * F(\infty, y)$, where $F(-\infty) = 0$ and $F(\infty) = 1$. Marginal or probability density function of X is $f(x)$. It is the derivative of the cumulative distribution function (CDF) of X, $F(x, \infty)$. So $f(x) = F_1(x, \infty)$, where $f(x) = F'(x) = F_1(x, y) = \partial F(x, y)/\partial x$ is a scalar variable.

$$\int_{-\infty}^{\infty} f(x)dx = \int_{-\infty}^{\infty} F'(x)dx$$

$$= F(\infty) - F(-\infty) = 1$$

and

$$\int_{-\infty}^{\infty}\int_{-\infty}^{\infty} f(x, y)dx.dy = 1$$

Thus, if X and Y are independent or random variables, then we can express the following:

$$f(x, y) = f(x).f(y),\ f(x/y) = f(x),\ \text{as}$$
$$f(y/x) = f(x, y)/f(x) = (f(x).f(y))/f(x) = f(y).$$

$$E(Y) = \int_{-\infty}^{\infty} y.f(x, y).dy;\ \int_{-\infty}^{\infty} f(x, y).dx.dy = 1 \text{ and}$$

$$E(X) = \int_{-\infty}^{\infty}\int_{-\infty}^{\infty} x.f(x, y).dx.dy = \int_{-\infty}^{\infty}\left[\int_{-\infty}^{\infty} f(x, y).dy\right]x.dx = \int_{-\infty}^{\infty} x.f(x).dx.$$

4.5 Solution Procedure of Rational Expectation Problem

The rational expectation concept is used by economic agents to model all kinds of problems to eliminate or minimize committing systematic errors often encounter in daily activities. For instance, stockbrokers, policemen, students, drivers, all and sundry, can utilize the rational expectation concept to minimize or eliminate decision making related problems which originate from systematic error.

However, problems involving rational expectation require special approach to solve. In this book we have explained the rational expectation concept and discussed a basic and apparently easier solution procedure for solving such problems. We have included an illustrative example below which is solved.

Illustrative Example 4.1

Suppose that $p_t = \eta_0 + \eta_1 E_t p_{t+1} + \varepsilon_t$, and ε_t is white noise innovation WN(0, 1). Solve for p_t.

Solution

Let the conjectured solution of p_t be expressed in terms of a constant and ε_t with respective parameters φ_0 and φ_1 as

$$p_t = \varphi_0 + \varphi_1 \varepsilon_t \tag{4.7}$$

At time $t+1$ the solution is

$$p_{t+1} = \varphi_0 + \varphi_1 \varepsilon_{t+1}$$

Taking expectations at time t of the above yields

$$E_t p_{t+1} = \varphi_0 + \varphi_1 E_t \varepsilon_{t+1}$$

$$E_t p_{t+1} = \varphi_0, \text{ Since } E_t \varepsilon_{t+1} = 0 \tag{4.8}$$

So, the problem to be solved is rewritten as

$$\varphi_0 + \varphi_1 \varepsilon_t = \eta_0 + \eta_1 \varphi_0 + \varepsilon_t \tag{4.9}$$

Equating the coefficients of the liked terms of constant and ε_t on the left-hand side to the right-hand side of equation (4.9), we obtain

$$\varphi_0 = \eta_0 + \eta_1 \varphi_0$$

which yield $\varphi_0 = \eta_0 / (1 - \eta_1)$ for the constant term, and $\varphi_1 = 1$ for the error term.

Therefore, the conjectured solution of equation (4.7) in terms of the problem in example 4.1 is as follows:

$$p_t = \eta_0 / (1 - \eta_1) + \varepsilon_t \tag{4.10}$$

4.6 The Demand for Currency Asset

Assets of individuals comprise of stocks, bonds, money, real estates, art works, property, etc. Asset desirability rests on its rate of return, risk, and liquidity, among others. Consequently, we consider its expected rate of return to judge its desirability for the future. The rate of return of an asset is expressed as follows:

$$R_t = C/PB_{t-1} + (PB_t - PB_{t-1})/PB_{t-1}$$

where, R_t is rate of return, C is a fixed annual coupon payment, PB_t is the price of bonds or interest-bearing assets at time t, and t denotes today.

Expected rate of return of asset is as follows:

$$R_t^e = C/PB_{t-1} + \left(PB_t^e - PB_{t-1}\right)/PB_{t-1}$$

In the case of foreign currency, expected rate of return of foreign currency is

$$R_t^e = i_t^f + \left(XR_t^e - XR_t\right)/XR_t$$

where, the maturity period is assumed to be one year; $R^e{}_t = E_{t-1}R_t$, (and expectation is based on all available information at time $t-1$); $i^f{}_t$ = today's interest rate on a one-year \$ (the foreign currency) deposit; $XR_{¢/\$}$ = today's Ghana cedis (¢) per \$ (no. of ¢s per \$1) or spot foreign exchange rate; $XR^e{}_{¢/\$}$ = ¢/\$ exchange rate expected to prevail a year from today (or $XR^e{}_{t+1}$).

Thus, in a carry trade between Ghana, the domestic country and US, the foreign country, the expected returns will be as follow:

In US, expected rate of return measured in ¢s is

$$E\left(R^f\right) = R^e_{\text{USA}} = i_t^f + \left(XR^e_{t+1} - XR_t\right)/XR_t$$

In Ghana, the expected rate of return of one year ¢ deposit is

$$E\left(R^{GH}\right) = R^e_{GH} = i_t^{GH}$$

where, i^{GH} is the rate of return in Ghana, and i^{USA} is the rate of return in the US, and $[(XR^{e}{}_{t+1}-XR_t)/XR_t]$ is expected depreciation of GH₵ against the US \$.

The equilibrium equation relationship between Ghana and the US, $E(R^{GH}) = E(R^{f})$, is referred to as uncovered interest rate arbitrage or currency carry trade or carry trade. See below.

The investor compares expected rate of returns in US, the foreign country, and the home country Ghana, before deciding on where to invest. The expected rate of return difference between Ghana and the US is

$$i_t^{GH} - \left[i_t^{\mathrm{USA}} + \left(XR_{t+1}^{e} - XR_t\right)/XR_t\right] = i_t^{GH} - i_t^{\mathrm{USA}} - \left[\left(\left(XR_{t+1}^{e} - XR_t\right)/XR_t\right)\right]$$

Equilibrium in the Foreign Exchange Market

Interest parity: The basic equilibrium condition, known as interest parity condition, is the condition that the expected return on deposits of any two currencies are equal when measured in the same currency. In the carry trade, equilibrium in the foreign exchange market occurs, when the above equation holds, and it is captured by the following:

Uncovered interest parity condition: $i^{GH} = i^{USA} + [(XR^{e}{}_{t+1}-XR_t)/XR_t]$. See Panel 4.4.

4.7 Interest Rates, Interest Rates Differential, and Exchange Rates Expectation in Carry Trade

In making decisions about where to invest in international trade and finance, the investor of the assets will consider the expected return of the asset in both domestic and foreign markets of both countries. We have hereby discussed how the investor considers the returns of the asset in both countries to determine which country's investment yields the highest rate of expected return, after adjusting for expected rate of depreciation between the two countries, before choosing the profitable investment option.

Thus, an investor in Ghana who makes decision to invest in the US, for instance, will consider the expected rate of returns which will comprise of (a) interest rates on Treasury deposit of the bank of Ghana and the US, and (b) the expected rate of depreciation (or appreciation) of the dollar against viz a viz the cedi in Ghana. The Ghanaian investor's decision to invest in US will require that he/she converts his/her cedis to dollars before investing in the US, and upon the maturity of the US

where, belreer is real effective exchange rate of Belize, jamreer is real effective exchange rate of Jamaica, and ttreer is real effective exchange rate of Trinidad-Tobago.

Data Source: Secondary quarterly data which spans 1995.1 to 2016.2 is sourced from International Standard Organization Country Code Indicators, World Bank.

investment, the investor must convert dollar investment back to domestic cedis. However, if the investor purchases the Treasury bill deposits of Ghana and invests it in Ghana, then there will be no need to convert the cedis investment back to cedis after the maturity period of the investment.

The location which yields the highest expected rate of return either Ghana or the US, the foreign country, will determine the preferred choice of the destination where the investor in the carry trade will invest.

Information in Table 4.1 is provided for an illustrative example of the activities of the investor to determine where he/she invests. Consequently, Table 4.1 has been split into five columns. Column 1 contains cases or type of activities, column 2 contains information on current exchange rates, column 3 contains information on US or foreign interest rates, and column 4 contains information on expected depreciation of the domestic country, and the last column contains information on the expected return of foreign ($) returns expressed in GH₵s.

Category 1: In the penultimate column of the said table, the expected rate of appreciation is approximately −0.003, which means that the expected annual real rate of return on the GH₵ deposit is more than 8 percent higher than that on the dollar. Thus, other things being equal, investors will prefer to invest in Ghana or hold their wealth in GH₵s instead of $s. See Table 4.1.[2]

Additionally, the column 6 of Category 1 in Table 4.2 depicts that the expected appreciation of the cedi which led to rate of return difference

[2] Cf. Table 13.3 of Krugman and Obstfeld (2000), and Table 20.3 of Dornbusch and Fischer (1987, 1990).

Table 4.1 Relating GH₵/$ exchange rate to the expected GH₵ return on $ deposits conditioned on XR^e_{t+1} = GH₵ 10.07 per $ in a carry trade

	Present GH₵/$ Exchange rate	*Interest rate on $*	*Expected GH₵ depreciation of the $*	*Expected GH₵ return on $ deposits =* R^e_{USA}
Categories	XR_t = GH₵/$	i^{USA}	$[(10.07-XR_t)/XR_t]$	$i^{USA} + [(10.07-XR_t)/XR_t]$
1	10.10	0.04	−0.00297	0.03702
2	10.07	0.04	0.00000	0.04000
3	10.04	0.04	0.00298	0.04298
4	10.03	0.04	0.00398	0.04398
5	10.00	0.04	0.007	0.04700

between GH₵ and $ of 8.3 percent, yields the highest return for investing in Ghana.

Category 2: The investors are indifferent as to which country they will invest, judging by the fact that the exchange rate is balanced in the foreign exchange market between both countries. The expected rate of GH₵ depreciation against $ deposits is zero, which means the cedi is equal to the dollar in value, as shown in column 4 of Category 2 of Table 4.1 and

Table 4.2 Relating GH₵/$ exchange rates and returns on Ghana and US deposits per year

Categories	i^{GH}	i^{USA}	*GH₵/$ Exchange rate* XR_t	*Expected rate of ₵ depreciation against $ =* $[(XR^e_{t+1}-XR_t)/XR_t]$ *given that* $XR^e_{t+1} = 10.07$	*Rate of return difference between ₵ and $ deposit =* $i^{GH}-i^{USA}-[(XR^e_{t+1}-XR_t)/XR_t]$
1	0.12	0.04	10.10	−0.00297	0.08297
2	0.12	0.04	10.07	0.00000	0.08000
3	0.12	0.04	10.04	0.00298	0.07702
4	0.12	0.04	10.03	0.00398	0.07602
5	0.12	0.04	10.00	0.00700	0.07300

column 5 of Category 2 of Table 4.2. Thus, the foreign exchange market is in equilibrium. However, the expected return of GH₵ rate in the last column of Category 2 being equal to 4% means investors will deem it profitable to invest in Ghana than in the US, as investing in Ghana in Category 2 earns 4 percent profit without incurring any conversion cost in the foreign currency market. See Table 4.1.

Category 3: Investors will prefer to invest in GH₵ deposit which earns expected GH₵ return on the dollar deposits of 4.3 percent which is higher than returns on $ deposits in US per year. See Table 4.1.

Category 4: The interest rate on GH₵ deposit is 12 percent in Ghana, whereas the interest rate on the same bank of Ghana's (or similar) instrument in the US is 4%. The dollar deposit appreciates against the cedi by almost 0.4 percent. Thus, the expected GH₵ return on $ deposit is almost 4.4 percent which can be observed in the last column of Category 4 in Table 4.1.

Category 5: In the last row of Category 5 in Table 4.1, the interest rate differential between domestic and foreign interest is 8 percent, and the expected rate of depreciation of the GH₵ against the $ is 0.70 percent. This means that the expected GH₵ return on the $ deposit is 4.7 percent, so it is profitable for the investor to invest in Ghana.

4.7.1 Foreign and Domestic Exchange Rate Schedules

The current GH₵/$ exchange rate (XR_t), which is reported in the second column of Table 4.1 and expected GH₵ return of foreign or the US ($) deposit $E(R^f)$, which is reported in the last column of Table 4.1, is plotted in Panel 4.1. It is the relationship between the expected return of foreign currency deposits expressed in terms of domestic currency as function of expected return of domestic currency deposits. in carry trade schedule.

The investor compares expected rate of returns in US, the foreign country, and the home country Ghana, to decide where to invest. The expected rate of return difference between Ghana and the US is

$$i_t^{GH} - \left[i_t^{\text{USA}} + \left(XR_{t+1}^e - XR_t\right)/XR_t\right] = i_t^{GH} - i_t^{\text{USA}} - \left[\left(\left(XR_{t+1}^e - XR_t\right)/XR_t\right)\right]$$

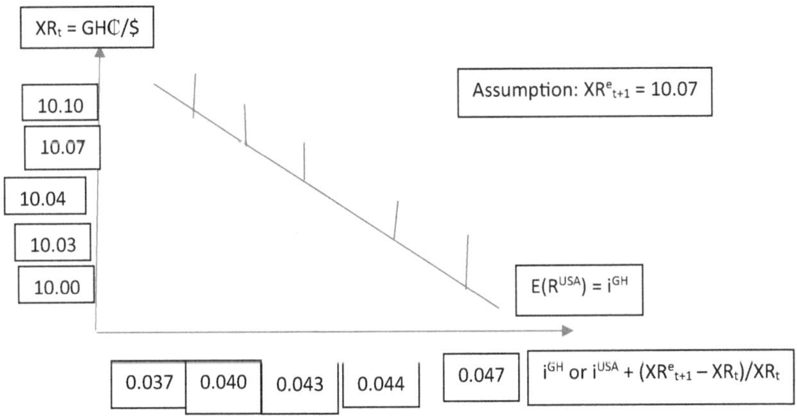

Panel 4.1 Current GH₵/$ exchange rate (XR_t) and expected GH₵ return on $ deposits relationship

Equilibrium in the Foreign Exchange Market

Interest parity: The basic equilibrium condition, known as interest parity condition, is the condition that the expected return on deposits of any two currencies are equal when measured in the same currency. In the carry trade it is captured by the following:

Uncovered interest parity condition: $i^{GH} = i^{USA} + [(XR^e{}_{t+1} - XR_t)/XR_t]$.

Relative Prices (relp) and Exchange Rates of Some Caribbean Countries

Relative prices of Belize, Jamaica, and Trinidad-Tobago are calculated below:

$$\text{relpbel} = \text{belcpi}/\text{uscpi}, \ \text{relpjam} = \text{jamcpi}/\text{uscpi},$$
$$\text{and relptt} = \text{ttcpi}/\text{uscpi}$$

where, relative price of Belize (relpbel) is CPI of Belize (belcpi) as a ratio of uscpi.

relative price of Jamaica (relpjam) is CPI of Jamaica (jamcpi) as a ratio of uscpi, and relative price of Trinidad-Tobago (relptt) is CPI of Trinidad-Tobago (ttcpi) as a ratio of uscpi.

The relative prices data span 1995 to 2016. See the graphs in Panel 4.2. The slope of the graph of relpjam is steeper than that of graph of relptt, and both graphs have positive slope, while the graph of relpbel is relatively stable although it spikes around 2010. Graphs of relative prices indicate that in Jamaica and Trinidad-Tobago their prices have been rising over the years as shown in Panel 4.2.

The real effective exchange rate (reer) graphs of Belize, Jamaica, and Trinidad-Tobago are shown in Panel 4.3. Graphs of the reer of all three countries span 1995.1 to 2016.4. Graphs of the reer of the three countries indicate that over the years, Jamaica and Trinidad-Tobago, especially the latter, has been depreciating, while the graph of relative effective exchange rate of Belize has been relatively stable. Furthermore, the similarities in the slope of graphs of both relative price and relative effective exchange rate suggest the existence of purchasing power parity in Trinidad-Tobago, and Belize.

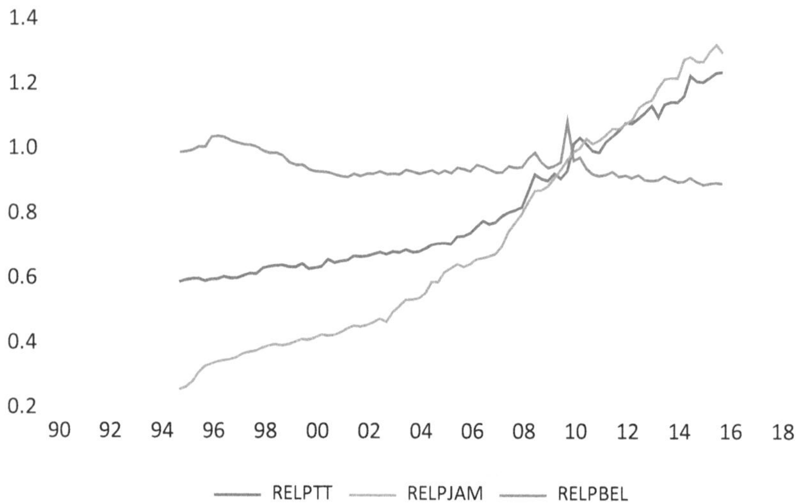

Panel 4.2 Relative prices of Belize, Jamaica, Trinidad-Tobago with US as the foreign country

Panel 4.3 Real Effective Exchange Rate (reer) of Belize, Jamaica, and Trinidad-Tobago

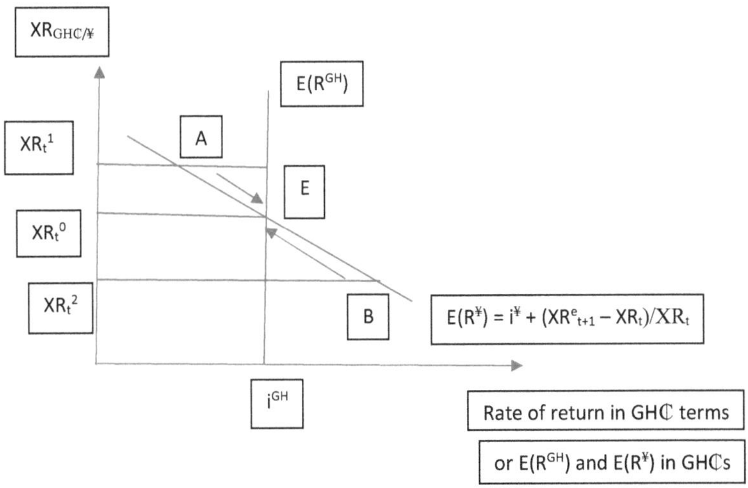

Panel 4.4 Determination of the Equilibrium GH₵/¥ Exchange Rate of Today GH₵

See Dornbusch and Fischer (1987, 1990), and Krugman, and Obstfeld (2000).

4.7.2 *Effect of Changes in the Current Exchange Rate of ¥ Deposit on Expected Returns of GH₵ Deposit*

The current GH₵/¥ exchange rate equilibrium occurs in the foreign exchange market of Ghana when the expected return of domestic deposit is equal to the expected return of foreign deposit expressed in domestic currency such that

$$i^{GH} = E(R^{GH¢}) = E(R^{¥}) = i^{JP} + [(XR^{e}_{t+1} - XR_t)/XR_t]$$

where, i^{GH} is expected return on GH₵ deposit and is equal to the expected return on ¥ deposit which is $(i^{JP} + [(XR^{e}_{t+1} - XR_t)/XR_t])$ expressed in cedis. The equilibrium foreign exchange market in Ghana for current GH₵/¥ deposits are discussed and depicted below in Panel 4.4.

At *A* in Panel 4.4, the rate of return of GH₵ deposit is greater than the rate of return on ¥ deposits at $XR^1{}_t$. Investors holding ¥ deposits will sell them off for more valuable GH₵. Excess demand for GH₵ deposits causes the *XR* to appreciate. No investor is willing to sell GH₵ deposits. Thus, the exchange rate of GH₵ appreciates against the ¥ till it reaches $XR^0{}_t$ at point *E*.

At *B*, the reverse scenario occurs. The rate of return on ¥ deposits is higher than the rate of return on GH₵ deposits. Investors increase their demand for ¥ deposits while shunning GH₵ deposits. Excess demand for ¥ deposits causes the *XR* to depreciate against the ¥. The value of GH₵ continues to depreciate against the ¥ until it reaches *E* where the market settles at equilibrium.

At *E*, the foreign exchange market is in equilibrium. Both holders of GH₵ and ¥ deposits are satisfied. See Panel 4.4.

Given that XR_t = GH₵12.00 and $XR^{e}{}_{t+1}$ = GH₵12.08. What is the rate of expected depreciation? What is the effect of the expected depreciation rate when the increase in expected future exchange rate drops to 12.04?

Solution:

The rate of depreciation is as follows:

$$\left(XR_{t+1}^{e} - XR_t\right) / XR_t = (12.08 - 12.00) / 12.00 = 0.67\% \text{ or } 0.0067$$

However, when the expected future exchange rate rises, the rate of depreciation becomes

$$\left(XR_{t+1}^{e} - XR_t\right) / XR_t = (12.04 - 12.00) / 12.00 = 0.0033 \text{ or } 0.33\%,$$

which is a moderately higher expected depreciation. It results in the foreign exchange schedule shifting moderately upward or rightward. Thus, the exchange rate increases or depreciates by 0.33% at the current expected future rate. See Panel 4.5.

Effect of an Increase in Domestic Interest Rates

An increase in interest rate from $i_0^{GH₵}$ to $i_1^{GH₵}$ results in the exchange rate appreciating from $XR_0^{GH₵}$ to $XR_1^{GH₵}$ along the original foreign exchange schedule as shown in Panel 4.6.

Similarly, an increase in the expected future exchange rate causes an increase in the current exchange rate (or depreciation) which shifts the foreign expected return schedule rightward at the current interest rate as is depicted in Panel 4.5.

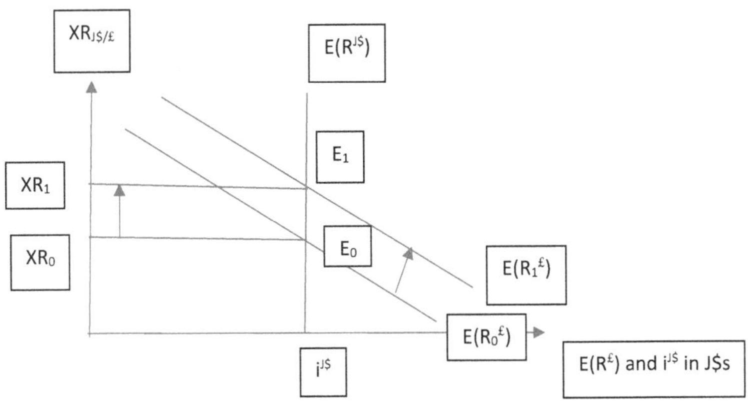

Panel 4.5 The effect of changing expectation on the current future exchange rate $(\uparrow XR^{e}{}_{t+1})$

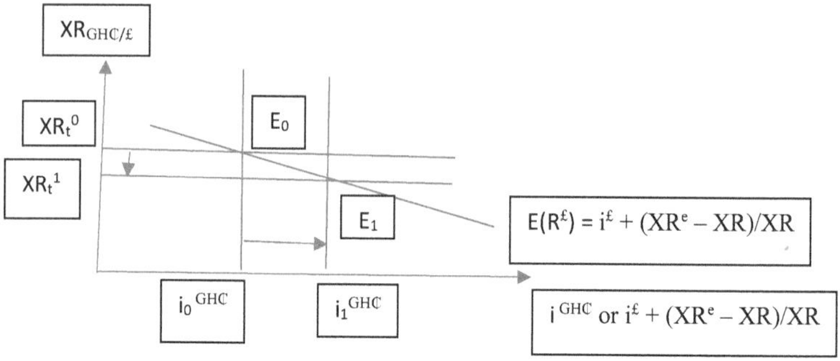

Panel 4.6 The effect of increase in interest rate on GH₵ deposits from i_0 to i_1, where $i_0 < i_1$

Other factors that shift the demand curve for domestic assets and affect the exchange rates are:

(1) domestic interest rate
(2) foreign interest rate
(3) expected domestic price level
(4) expected trade barriers
(5) expected import demand
(6) expected export demand

4.8 Efficient Foreign Exchange Market (FEM)

Efficient foreign exchange market is the market where exchange rates reflect all available information (see Fama 1970). There is no unexploited profit. This can be shown by using the definitions of covered interest rate parity condition (CIRPC) and uncovered interest rate parity condition (UIRPC) with or without risk premium.

$$\text{CIRPC} : (1 + i_t)\Big/\left(1 + i_t^f\right) = f_t^{t+1}\Big/s_t + \rho_t \qquad (4.11)$$

$$\text{UIRPC} : (1 + i_t)\Big/\left(1 + i_t^f\right) = s_{t+1}^e\big/s_t + \rho_t \qquad (4.12)$$

where, ρ_t is time varying risk premium, s_t is spot exchange rate, t denotes time, ${f^{t+1}}_t$ is the forward rate and i_t is domestic interest rate and ${i^f}_t$ is foreign interest rate.

Equating equations (4.11) and (4.12) yield efficient FEM as follows:

$$s_{t+1}^{e} = f_t^{t+1} \tag{4.13}$$

This shows that an efficient FEM is the market where the expected spot rate is equal to the forward rate, and the exchange rate reflects all available information. There is no unexploited profit.

Unfortunately, there are no data on forward exchange rates in most developing countries. This means that efficient FEM cannot be tested empirically for most developing countries. However, it has been shown that even developing countries which do not possess data on forward exchange rates can test for weak-form efficient foreign exchange market. In such situation instead of testing for efficient FEM, the researcher can test for weak-form FEM efficiency, which requires the spot exchange rate to follow or exhibit random walk. See Ghartey (2004).

Proof of Weak-form Efficient Foreign Exchange Market

The weak-form efficient foreign exchange market is proven by using the definition for rational expectation, efficient FEM, and Martingale which have been expressed, respectively, as follow:

Rational expectation:

$$s_{t+1}^{e} = E\left(s_{t+1}/\,\Omega_t\right) = E_t s_{t+1} \tag{4.14}$$

Efficient FEM:

$$E_t s_{t+1} = f_t^{t+1} \tag{4.15}$$

Martingale[3]:

$$E_t s_{t+1} = s_t \tag{4.16}$$

[3] Readers can refer to Edward E. Ghartey (2004) for the prove of the martingale. See also the Appendix.

We first lagged equations (4.15) and (4.16), respectively, to obtain the following:

$$E_{t-1}s_t = f_{t-1}^t \tag{4.17}$$

$$E_{t-1}s_t = s_{t-1} \tag{4.18}$$

We then subtracted s_t from both sides of the equations (4.17 and 4.18)

$$E_{t-1}s_t - s_t = f_{t-1}^t - s_t \tag{4.19}$$

Lagged Eq. (4.16) and unanticipated spot rate are expressed, respectively, as

$$E_{t-1}s_t = f_{t-1}^t = s_{t-1} \text{ and } E_{t-1}s_t - s_t = -v_t,$$

where the v_t is an uncorrelated error term.

Substituting the above equations into Eq. (4.20) result in

$$-v_t = s_{t-1} - s_t \text{ or } s_t = s_{t-1} + v_t \tag{4.20}$$

Thus, when the foreign exchange market is efficient, the spot rate follows or exhibits a random walk behavior, which is a weak-form FEM efficiency. Countries which do not have forward rates can use spot rates to test weak-form FEM efficiency.

4.9 Prices and Exchange Rates

Exchange rates are analyzed in the free market by first examining how they are determined over the long run. The information obtained in determining the exchange rate over the long run is then used to determine the exchange rate in the short run. We shall therefore start the examination of the short-run exchange rate analysis by first establishing proper understanding of the long-run exchange rate from studying the law of one price.

4.10 The Law of One Price

It states that in competitive markets free of transportation costs and official barriers to trade (such as tariffs and quota restrictions), identical goods sold in different countries must sell for the same prices, when those prices are expressed in terms of the same currency.

This means that if a meal deal at the KFC costs \$5 in the US and the exchange rate between GH₵ and \$ is GH₵5 = \$1, then the meal deal should sell at GH₵25 in Ghana. If the exchange rate is J\$145 = \$1, then the same meal deal should cost J\$725 in Jamaica.

Let $XR = \text{GH₵}/\$$

The law of one price can be stated formally as

$XR.P^{US}{}_i = P^{GH}{}_i$ for good i which can be any good.

Thus,

$$XR = P_i^{GH} \Big/ P_i^{US} \text{ for good } i \tag{4.21}$$

4.11 Purchasing Power Parity (PPP)

The theory of PPP states that the exchange rate between two countries' currencies is equal to the ratio of those countries' price levels. The theory was first proposed by David Ricardo among others, but it was popularized by Gustav Cassel who made it an important tenet in the theory of exchange rates.

Thus, the PPP theory can be expressed as

$$XR = P^{JM} \Big/ P^{UK}, \text{ where } XR = J\$/£ \tag{4.22}$$

Additionally,

$$P^{JM} = XR.P^{UK}$$

The right-hand side is the J\$ price of the reference basket bought in UK, while the left-hand side is the J\$ price of the reference commodity basket in Jamaica. Thus, the PPP shows that prices of all countries are equal when measured in terms of the same currencies.

The law of one price and the PPP are different. The law of one price applies to individual commodities (i), while the PPP applies to the general price level of all commodities that are included in the basket of goods that constitute the reference basket of the price index. The PPP is a valid long-run theory, but it does not depend on the law of one price. Even if the law of one price fails for each individual good, prices and exchange rates may result in the PPP holding and assist to eventually equalize a country's purchasing power.

4.12 Absolute PPP and Relative PPP

The absolute PPP states that the exchange rate equals relative price levels. It postulates that the equilibrium exchange rate between two countries is equal to the ratio of the price levels in two nations. Specifically,

$$XR = P^{GH} / P^{JP}$$

where, XR is the exchange rate or spot rate, P^{GH} is domestic or national prices of home country, and P^{JP} is the foreign price level.

The relative PPP theory states that the percentage change in the exchange rate between two currencies over any period is equal to the difference between the percentage changes in national price levels.

Log-linearizing the above equation results as follows:

$$\ln XR_t = \ln\left[P_t^{GH} / P_t^{JP}\right] = \ln P_t^{GH} - \ln P_t^{JP}$$

Differentiate the above equation with respect to time t

$$\begin{aligned}(1/XR_t).(\partial XR_t/\partial t) &= \Delta XR_t/XR_{t-1} \\ &= \left(1/P_t^{GH}\right)\left(\partial P_t^{GH}/\partial t\right) - \left(1/P_t^{JP}\right)\left(\partial P^{JP}/\partial t\right)\end{aligned} \tag{4.23}$$

where,

$(XR_t - XR_{t\text{-}1})/XR_{t\text{-}1}$ is the rate of change or percentage change in the exchange rate at time t.

$(1/P_t^{GH})(\partial P_t^{GH}/\partial t)$ is inflation rate in Ghana at time t.

$(1/P_t^{JP})(\partial P^{JP}/\partial t)$ is inflation rate in Japan, the foreign country, at time t.

Problems with the Absolute PPP

The absolute PPP theory makes sense if and only if the price level estimates on product baskets of the two countries are the same. It does not make sense when the baskets of goods are different between the two countries. In such situations, the different commodity baskets between countries should not be expected to sell for the same price levels, so we do not expect the absolute PPP to hold.

However, under such circumstances, the relative PPP may still be valid so long as the factors causing deviations in the absolute PPP are stable over time, even if the basket of goods is different and invalidates the absolute PPP.

4.13 Problems with the PPP Theory

The PPP theory of exchange rates may not hold because of the following reasons:

(1) Contrary to the assumption of the law of one price, transport costs and restrictions on trade do exist. These trade barriers may be so high to prevent some goods and services from being traded between countries. In such situation the PPP cannot be used to determine the exchange rate.
(2) Monopolistic or oligopolistic practices in goods markets may interact with transport costs and other trade barriers to weaken the link between prices of similar goods sold in different countries. Thus, violating the PPP determination of the exchange rate.
(3) Inflation rate data of different countries may be based on different commodity baskets. There is, therefore, no reason for exchange rate changes to cancel out official measures of inflation differences in such cases, even where there are no barriers to trade and all products are tradeable.

The Real Exchange Rate (q):

$q = XR.P^{JM}/P^{USA}$ (*JM* is the home country, and *US* is the foreign country).

$\uparrow q$ denotes depreciation, *XR* is the nominal exchange rate, and *P* is price index.

Equation (4.23) can be rewritten as expected relative PPP as follows:

$$
\begin{aligned}
\left(XR^e - XR_t\right)/XR_t &= \left(P^{JMe} - P_t^{JM}\right)/P_t^{JM} - \left(P^{USe} - P_t^{US}\right)/P_t^{US} \\
&= \pi^{JMe} - \pi^{USe}
\end{aligned}
\tag{4.24}
$$

and uncovered interest rate condition is

$$
\left(XR^e - XR_t\right)/XR_t = i^{JM} - i^{US} \tag{4.25}
$$

So, equations (4.25) and (4.24) yield

$$
i^{JM} - i^{US} = \pi^{JMe} - \pi^{USe} \tag{4.26}
$$

where,

P^{JMe} (P^{USe}) is expected price level in Jamaica (*US*) for a year from today, π^{JMe} (π^{Use}) is expected inflation in Jamaica (*US*) from a year from today.

The difference between interest rates offered by the J$ and foreign ($) bank deposits will be equal to the difference between the inflation rates expected over the relevant horizon in Jamaica and in the foreign country to offset the international inflation difference, ($\pi^{JMe} - \pi^{USe}$). The interest rate difference must be equal to the expected inflation difference.

Foreign Exchange Risk Premium

It is defined as the difference between forward exchange rate (FXR) and expected future exchange rate (XR^e). Risk premium = $FXR_t - XR_t{}^e$. In an efficient FEM the risk premium is zero. Hence the forward exchange rate is equal to the expected future exchange rate, or $FXR_t = XR_t{}^e$.

Foreign return (or expected return from holding a foreign bond) is equal to the foreign interest rate (i^F), and the expected change in the exchange rate which is equal to $(XR_{t+1}{}^e - XR_t)/XR_t$.

4.14 Summary

Adaptive and rational expectation are defined and specified mathematically. We discuss their difference. We also discuss that the adaptive expectation is subject to systematic errors, while rational expectation eliminates systematic errors.

We prove mathematically that rational expectation eliminates systematic errors, and it is independent with any variable in the economy. We explained how to use conjectured solution method to solve problems involving rational expectation. We provide examples to assist students and readers to master the solution procedural technique.

We prove that efficient FEM has a zero foreign exchange risk premium. We explain martingale and used it together with rational expectation and efficient market hypothesis to show that in developing countries where there is no forward market, the FEM is weak-form efficient when the exchange rate exhibits a random walk. We also derived interest rate arbitrage.

We also use covered interest rate parity condition and uncovered interest rate parity condition to show that the FEM is efficient if expected exchange rate is equal to forward exchange rate or zero foreign exchange risk premium.

We derived exchange rate schedule which shows a relationship between domestic exchange rate and the domestic value of expected return of foreign currency deposit (or expected return of domestic currency). We used it to determine the exchange rate value when the foreign exchange market is in equilibrium. We demonstrated factors which shift the foreign exchange schedule in the country, namely: changes in expectation, foreign income, foreign inflation, changes in the money supply, government spending, economic growth, and inflation on the country's exchange rate.

We discussed the PPP by explaining the law of one price, absolute PPP and relative PPP, and the shortcomings of the PPP.

4.15 Problems

(1) Prove that the foreign exchange market is efficient.

(2) Prove the proposition "That domestic or national value of earnings from foreign assets (coupon bonds and bank deposits accounts) holdings follow a martingale process."

(3) Is the statement: "An efficient market rules out all opportunities for speculative profits" true or false? Explain your answer.

(4) The supply of cocoa equation is expressed as

$$Q_t = c_0 + c_1 P_t + v_t, \ c_1 > 0$$

and the demand for cocoa equation is captured as

$$Q_t = d_0 + d_1 P_t + d_2 E_t P_{t+1} + \mu_t, \ d_1 < 0 \text{ and } d_2 > 0.$$

Error terms v_t and μ_t are given to be white noise innovations. Solve for P_t.

(5) The money demand for a small island economy in the Caribbean is characterized by the Cagan demand function as

$$m_t - xr_t = \pi + \alpha(E_t xr_{t+1} - xr_t) + u_t$$

where u_t is a white noise innovation.

The money supply (m_t) is created by the Central Bank according to the following relation:

$$m_t = \lambda_0 + \lambda_1 m_{t-1} + v_t$$

where v_t is a white noise innovation. Calculate the exchange rate (xr_t) and comment on its behavior.

Selected References

Cagan, Phillip (1956), "The Monetary Dynamics of Hyperinflation," in *Studies in the Quantity Theory of Money*, edited by Milton Friedman (Chicago: University of Chicago Press).

Dornbusch, Rudiger and Stanley Fischer (1987, 1990), Macroeconomics, (New York: McGraw-Hill, Inc.).

Fama, E.F. (1970), Efficient Capital Market: A Review of Theory and Empirical Work, Journal of Finance, 25, 383–416.

Ghartey, Edward E. (2004), "Random Walk as a Universal Test of Weak-Form Foreign Exchange Market Efficiency: A Proof," *Frontiers in Finance and Economics*, 1 (1): 37–45.

Husted, Steven and Michael Melvin (1993), *International Economics* (New York: Harper Collins College Publishers).

Institute for Capacity Development (2013), *Financial Programming and Policies*, International Monetary Fund.

Krugman, Paul R. and Maurice Obstfeld (2000), *International Economics: Theory and Policy* (New York: Addison-Wesley, Inc.).

McCallum, Bennett T. (1989), *Monetary Economics: Theory and Policy*, New York, Macmillan Publishing Company.

Lucas, Robert E. Jr., (1981), *Studies in Business-Cycle Theory* (Cambridge: Mass.: The MIT Press).

Muth, John F. (1961), "Rational Expectations and the Theory of Price Movements," *Econometrica*, 29, 315–35.

Sargent, Thomas, J. (1973), "Rational Expectations, the Real Rate of Interest, and the Natural Rate of Unemployment," *Brookings Papers on Economic Activities*, 2, 429–72.

Salvatore, Dominick (2010), *International Economics* (New York: John Wiley & Sons Inc.).

CHAPTER 5

Money, Money Supply, and Money Demand

Learning Outcomes

By the close of this chapter, readers will be expected to have gained mastery over the topics covered to proficiently do the following:

(a) Define money supply, automatic transfer from saving, float, monetary base, sterilize intervention, etc.
(b) Derive the Cambridge and square root formula for money demand; write different types of money supply. Explain factors that shift the demand for money.
(c) List different functions of money. List all monetary aggregates, central bank's assets and liabilities. Describe the characteristics of a commodity which functions as money.
(d) Discuss the determinants of the money supply, and show which factors shift the money demand function.

E. E. Ghartey, *International Macroeconomics and Finance*,
https://doi.org/10.1007/978-3-032-04145-6_5

5.1 Introduction

Money is generally known as the money supply. It is defined as anything that is generally accepted in payment for goods, services, and in repayment of debts. It is usually considered as coins and bills. However, it is commonly mistaken on the streets as income and wealth. Money is not income which is a flow of earnings per unit of time. It is neither wealth which is a list of all the assets in ones' portfolio such as bonds, common stocks, art works, land, furniture, cars, houses, to name a few.

5.2 Functions of Money

There are three basic functions of money which serves as its identifiers. These are medium of exchange, a unit of account, and a store of value.

5.2.1 A Medium of Exchange

Assets that function as a typical medium of exchange are currency and checks. This role of money spurs economic growth by promoting specialization and division of labor. It also generates economic efficiency, as it minimizes the time spent in exchanging goods and services. It eliminates barter economy where goods and services are exchanged for other goods and services.

A commodity which functions effectively as money in an economy minimizes transaction cost by exhibiting the following characteristics: These are as follow:

(i) homogenous which makes it easier for its value to be ascertained,
(ii) widely acceptable because it has value,
(iii) divisible which makes it easier to make a change,
(iv) portable as it is not bulky and heavy and can be easily carried around, and
(v) durable and can be stored easily for future use without deteriorating.

5.2.2 *A Unit of Account*

Money is used to measure value of goods and services in the economy. This function is best understood if it is contrasted with a barter economy. For two goods economy, the price for trading is one. Thus, if there are goods A and B, the price for trading is AB, which is one. If there are four goods A, B, C, and D the number of prices will be AB, AC, AD, BC, BD, and CD, which is six. Using combination, N goods will require $[N(N-1)]/2$ prices which means the number of prices is obtained by pairing the goods. It is important to note that unlike permutation, order does not matter in this case. With the introduction of money, the number of prices required in the economy for N goods is N, and for one good is one for each good, unlike barter which has $[N(N-2)]/2$ prices.

$$C_2^N = [N(N-1)(N-2)!]/[2(N-2)!] = [N(N-1)]/2, \text{ where } 0! = 1.$$

5.2.3 *A Store of Value*

Money serves as a repository of purchasing power over time. The commodity regarded as money must be liquid. It must be relatively easy and rapid to convert into other forms of assets or a medium of exchange. The asset must withstand inflation.

5.3 Measuring Money—Monetary Aggregates

The general definition that money is anything that is widely accepted as a means of payment of goods and services and to settle debt suggests that money is defined by people's behavior. Over the years, different commodities have been used as money in different societies. Thus, commodities such as cowries, gold, currencies, checks, and e-money such as bitcoin have served as money, and some are still serving as money.

Which asset should we regard as money based on people's behavior?

Different central banks have used different measures of money in their studies. The Federal Reserve System (FRS) in the US has obtained different measures of money which are based on different studies done in the country. These standard measures of money have been modified by different countries to capture the behavior of their citizens. The standard

FRS measures of money commonly referred to as monetary aggregates are as follows:

$$M1 = \text{Currency} + \text{Traveler's Checks} + \text{Demand Deposits} + \text{Other Checkable Deposits} \quad (5.1)$$

where,

Other Checkable Deposits consist of Negotiable Order of Withdrawals (NOW) and Automatic Transfers from Savings (ATS). The ATS is savings account that can be automatically transferred into checking account and has check writing privileges.

Currency is paper money or bills and coins in the hands of nonbanking public. It is currency in circulation and excludes currency in automatic teller machines (ATMs) and currency in central bank's vaults.

Traveler's Checks include traveler's checks not issued by banks.

Demand Deposits are business checking accounts that do not bear interest and traveler's checks issued by banks.

Other Checkable Deposits are all other checkable deposits held by households that pay interest, Before the mid-1970s only Commercial Banks were authorized to issue checks which pay interests. Since then, Savings & Loans Associations, Mutual Saving Banks, and Credit Unions (Thrift Industry) have been authorized to also offer checking accounts. Dating back from 1986 banking institution also offer NOW accounts and ATS accounts which are checkable deposits that pay interest on their balances.[1]

$$\begin{aligned} M2 = M1 &+ \text{Small-denomination Time Deposits} \\ &+ \text{Savings Deposits} + \text{Money Markets Deposits} \\ &+ \text{Money Market Mutual Funds Shares (retail).} \end{aligned} \quad (5.2)$$

where,

Small-denomination time deposits are CDs that can be easily turned into cash at a little cost. They are less than \$100,000 and can be redeemed upon fixed maturity date without a penalty.

[1] Most central banks in developing countries define M1 and M2 differently. The following are definitions used in Ghana and Jamaica, respectively: $M1$ = Currency + Demand Deposits, and $M2 = M1$ + Time Saving Deposits + Foreign Currency Deposits. Belize's $M2$ = Currency + Demand Deposits + Time Saving Deposits.

Saving Deposits are non-transaction deposits that can be added to or withdrawn from at any time.

Certificate of Deposits (CDs) are negotiable bank certificates of deposits which are debt instruments sold by banks to depositors that pay annual interest.

Money Market Deposits are Certificate Deposits (CDs) issued by banks. They are very similar to money market mutual fund shares except that they are issued by banks. Interest rates they earned are higher than saving deposits but less than CDs.

Mutual Funds are financial intermediaries which acquire funds by selling shares to several people and using the proceeds to purchase diversified portfolio of stocks and bonds. It allows shareholders to pool their resources so that they can take advantage of lower transaction cost when buying large blocks of stocks and bonds.

Money Market Mutual Fund Shares (MMMFS) are retail accounts which allow households to write checks on. The check writing privileges are limited. They are not covered by depository insurance. They are open-ended.

As of 2006, the FRS has ceased reporting $M3$. It is however defined as follows:

$$\begin{aligned} M3 = M2 &+ \text{Large Denomination Time Deposits} \\ &+ \text{Term Repurchase Agreement} \\ &+ \text{MMMFS (Institutional)} + \text{Term Eurodollar.} \end{aligned} \tag{5.3}$$

The choice of a desirable monetary aggregate depends on how stable it is. Thus, if $M1$ and $M2$ move in the same direction, then the choice is solely dependent on which of the two is more stable. If, however, they move in the opposite direction, then the choice is much difficult.

5.3.1 Reliability of Money Data

Monetary aggregates data undergo frequent changes over the short term. This is because small depository institutions tend to report their data to central banks infrequently because of floats resulting from the fact that small banks may be at rural areas which make daily reporting of small banks data to central banks impossible. Consequently, central banks use estimates as substitutes for the short-term unreported data which are replaced in the long run when they receive actual data from those small banks. This makes long-run data more reliable than short-term data. Thus, money data are also reported as seasonally adjusted data, and non-seasonally adjusted data.

5.4 Multiple Deposit Creation and the Money Supply Process

The main players in the money supply process are central banks, banks, borrowers, and depositors. Central banks are banks or agencies of government which oversee the banking system of nations and conduct their monetary policy. They influence the behavior of banks, and clear checks by transferring funds between banks. They also set rules and regulations which govern banks behavior.

Banks are depository institutions which make loans and accept deposits from individuals and institutions and make loans. They constitute commercial banks, savings and loans associations, mutual saving banks, and credit unions.

Depositors are individuals and institutions which hold deposits in banks, and borrowers are individuals and institutions which borrow from depository institutions that issue bonds which are sold to depository institutions.

The balance sheet of a central bank consists of assets and liabilities. It is from the difference between assets and liabilities that monetary base, an important component of the money is obtained. These assets include government securities, discount loans, gold and Special Drawing Rights (SDR) certificates, coins, cash item in the process of collection, and other assets of the central bank such as international reserves and equipment, etc. The liabilities of the central bank include reserves, bank deposits, governments treasury deposits, foreign and other deposits, deferred availability cash items, and other central bank liabilities and capita account.

Central Bank's T-account:

Assets (A)	*Liabilities (L) & Net Worth (NW)*
Government Securities	Central Bank Notes Outstanding
Discount Loans	Bank Deposits
Gold and SDR certificate	Treasury Deposits
Coins	Foreign and Other Deposits
Cash items in process of collection	Deferred availability cash items
Other Central Bank's assets	Other Central Bank's liabilities and Capital account

$$
\begin{aligned}
\text{Monetary Base (MB)} &= \text{Currency in circulation}(C) + \text{ Reserves } (R) \\
&= \text{Government Securities} + \text{Discount Loans} \\
&+ \text{Gold and SDRs} + \text{Treasury Currency (Coins)} \\
&+ \text{Cash items in the process of collection} \\
&+ \text{Other Central Bank's assets} \\
&- [\text{Treasury Deposits} + \text{Foreign and Other Deposits} \\
&+ \text{Deferred availability cash items} \\
&+ \text{Other Central Bank's liabilities and Capital accounts}].
\end{aligned}
$$

where,

> MB = Central Bank's monetary liabilities (Currency in circulation + Reserves) + Central Government monetary liabilities known as Treasury currency in circulation which are primarily coins.
> Reserves = Deposits with central bank + vault cash (currency held at banks).
> Currency = Central Bank's notes + Treasury currency.
> Float = Cash items in the process of collection – Deferred availability cash items.

$$
\begin{aligned}
&\text{CMB} = \text{Government Securities} + \text{Discount Loans} + \text{Gold and SDRs} + \text{Float} + \text{Other CB's assets} - \\
&\text{Treasury Deposits} - \text{Foreign Deposits and Other Deposits} - \text{Other Central Bank's liabilities and} \\
&\text{Capital accounts} = C + R
\end{aligned}
\tag{5.4}
$$

The monetary base can be split into

$$MB = BMB + NBMB \tag{5.5}$$

where, BMB is borrowed MB also known as Discount Loans (DL) which is controlled by the Central Bank's discounting process, and NBMB is non-borrowed MB which is controlled by open market operations. Other factors that affect the MB but are not controlled by central Banks are float, Treasury Deposits, and foreign exchange market dictated by the government.

Float occurs during the check clearing process, where a bank that is to receive a check has its reserves increased immediately, while the bank which is issued the check against is debited after the check clearing in two days period. Consequently, the bank from which the check is being paid from has its reserves reduced after the official check clearing period. This results in a float which results in a temporary increase in MB during the two days before the check is cleared. The float last longer when there is poor weather which delays banks from presenting their checks for clearance by central banks.

Treasury Deposit occurs when the Minister of Finance withdraws money from banks and deposits it with the Central Bank as Treasury deposits. Thus, causing bank reserves to decrease which also reduces the MB.

Foreign exchange market interventions following government's instruction to the central bank to intervene in the foreign exchange market affect the MB. The government holds foreign exchange stabilization fund with the Minister of Finance and the central bank, from which the latter uses on behalf of the government to intervene the foreign exchange market.

Suppose the central bank sells its foreign assets of say GH¢10m to the public, the public can pay for it with either checks or currency. How the payment is made by the public has different effect on the reserve but the effect is the same on both MB and money supply.

Illustration using the central bank's T-accounts.

Case 1: Payment made with currency by the public.

Central Bank's T-account	
Assets	*Liabilities & Net Worth*
Foreign assets/international reserves –GH¢10m	Currency in circulation –GH¢10m

$$MB = C + R$$

$$\Delta MB = \Delta C$$

$$= -\text{GH₵}10\text{m}$$

Thus, currency in circulation falls, reducing the MB by the same GH¢10m. There is no effect on reserves, although only the currency and monetary base drop by –GH¢10 m.

Case 2: Payment with checks

$$MB = C + R$$

$$\Delta MB = \Delta R$$

$$= -\text{GH₵}10\text{m}$$

Thus, reserves in the banking system drops by –GH¢10m, and both monetary base and reserves fall by the same amount causing the money supply to fall by –GH¢10m.

Illustration using the central bank's T-accounts.

Central Bank's T-account	
Assets	*Liabilities & Net Worth*
Foreign assets or international reserves –GH¢10m	Reserves (Checks or deposits with central bank) –GH¢10m

Thus, reserves which are checks or deposits with the central bank fall, reducing the MB by the same GH¢10m. The net effect of the government selling foreign assets or international reserves to the public on the money supply is the same, irrespective of how the public pays for it. The MB and the money supply contract by the same amount.

5.5 Unsterilized and Sterilized Foreign Exchange Intervention

5.5.1 *Unsterilized Foreign Exchange Intervention*

The effect of the government instructing the central bank to sell (or buy) foreign assets to (from) the public decreases (or increases) the MB and the money supply. It is known as unsterilized intervention as its effect on the MB or the money supply is one-to-one. Both foreign assets and the MB change in the same direction by either decreasing by –GH¢10m (or increasing by GH¢10m).

Example 1: The government has instructed the central bank to buy foreign assets which is worth GH¢100m

Illustration

$$\text{MB} = C + R$$

Central Bank's T-account for the unsterilized foreign exchange interventions.

Assets	*Liabilities & Net Worth*
Foreign assets or international reserves purchase GH¢100m	MB (Currency or Reserves) GH¢100m

$$\Delta \text{MB} = \Delta R$$

$$= \text{GH₵}100\text{m}$$

The net effect of unsterilized foreign exchange intervention is GH¢100m.

and since $M1 = \text{mm}\cdot\text{MB}$

we obtain

$$\Delta M1 = \text{mm}\cdot\Delta\text{MB} = \text{GH₵}100\text{m}$$

Thus, the net effect of government instructing the central bank to buy foreign assets is to increase both monetary base and money supply by GH¢100m each.

5.5.2 *Sterilized Foreign Exchange Intervention*

Sterilized intervention can also be described as the unsterilized foreign exchange intervention which is reversed with open market operations to net out the initial effect on the MB and the money supply.

Example 2: The government has instructed the central bank to sell foreign assets which is worth GH¢10m and offset the sale with open market purchase of Treasury bonds of the same amount GH¢10m.

Illustration

Central Bank's T-account for sterilized foreign exchange interventions

Assets	*Liabilities & Net Worth*
Foreign assets or international reserves sale –GH¢10m	MB (Currency or Reserves) –GH¢10m
Treasury Bonds Purchased +GH¢10m	MB (Reserves) +GH¢10m

$$\begin{aligned} \text{MB} &= C + R \\ &= \Delta\, C + \Delta R \end{aligned}$$

Sale of foreign assets

$$\Delta M1 = -\Delta \text{MB} = -\text{GH₵10m} \qquad \text{(I)}$$

Repurchase of foreign assets

$$\Delta M1 = \Delta \text{MB} = \text{GH₵10m} \qquad \text{(II)}$$

Sterilized intervention: MB Sum = (I) + (II) = - GH₵10m + GH₵10m

= 0

The net effect of sterilized foreign exchange intervention is zero. The sale of the foreign exchange intervention results in a decrease in MB of –GH¢10m, while the purchase of the Treasury bonds results in an increase in MB of +GH¢10m. These two activities net out to zero reserves.

5.6 The Money Supply and Determinants

The money supply is principally determined by the monetary base (MB). It can be expressed as being proportional to the monetary base (MB). The different definition of the money supply can be used to derive the money supply. We have simplified the derivation of money supply by using $M1$.

$M1$ is directly proportional to MB

$$M1 = mm \times \mathrm{MB}$$

where the money multiplier (mm) is a constant of proportionality, and * denotes product sign.

$M1$ is then simplified as

$$M1 = C + DD, \text{ and } \mathrm{MB} = C + R$$

R is total reserves. It can be split up into required reserve (RR) and excess reserve (ER) and is expressed as

$$R = \mathrm{ER} + \mathrm{RR}$$

So,

$$\mathrm{MB} = C + \mathrm{RR} + \mathrm{ER}$$

$$\mathrm{MB}$$

$$= (\mathrm{C/DD} + \mathrm{RR/DD} + \mathrm{ER/DD}) \times \mathrm{DD} \text{ and } M1 = (\mathrm{C/DD} + 1) \times \mathrm{DDBut\ DD}$$

$$= [1/(c + \mathrm{rr} + \mathrm{er})]\mathrm{MB}, \text{ where } c = C/\mathrm{DD}, \ \mathrm{rr} = \mathrm{RR/DD} \text{ and } \mathrm{er} = \mathrm{ER/DD}$$

So $M1$ can be rewritten as

$$M1 = [(c + 1)/(c + \mathrm{rr} + \mathrm{er})] \times \mathrm{MB} \qquad (5.6)$$

where,

$$\mathrm{mm} = [(c+1)/(c + \mathrm{rr} + \mathrm{er})]$$

mm is the money multiplier, c is currency (C) ratio, rr is required reserve (RR) ratio, er is excess reserve (ER) ratio, and DD is demand deposits.

The er is a negative function of inter-bank interest rate (iir) and market interest rate (i). The er is banks' insurance against deposit outflows. Banks tend to pile up more excess reserves when inter-bank interest rates are low, and loan out more excess reserves when the inter-bank interest rate is high. The inter-bank interest rate and the market interest rate are therefore inversely related to the er. The FRS started to pay interest on excess reserves of banks in October 2008 during the 2007–2008 financial meltdown. Thus, Eq. (5.6) can be expressed as

$$M1 = [(c + 1)/(c + \mathrm{er(iir)} + \mathrm{rr})] \times \mathrm{MB} \tag{5.7}$$

where,

The $M1$ decreases when c, rr and er increase, *all other things being equal*. Increase in iir causes banks to hold low excess reserves as they decide to loan out deposits to take advantage of the higher iir. This results in a fall in er which then causes the mm to rise and the $M1$ to increase, all other things being equal.

Equation (5.6) can be generalized as

$$M1/\mathrm{MB} = q(iir;\ c,\ rr),\ q_1 > 0,\ q_2 < 0 \text{ and } q_3 < 0 \tag{5.8}$$

5.7 The Demand for Money

Monetary Theory is the study of the effect of money and monetary policy on the economy. Considering that we have covered the money supply, we will now focus on the demand for money. The demand for money has evolved over the years from the Quantity Theory of Money, the Keynesian theory of money demand, to the Modern Quantity Theory of Money developed principally by Milton Friedman.

5.8 Quantity Theory of Money

The classical theory was independently developed by Irving Fisher, Alfred Marshall, A.C. Pigou, to name a few. The quantity theory of money explains how the nominal value of aggregate income is determined. It explains how much money is held for transactions or a given amount of income. The theory does not find any effect of interest rate on money demand. Their main determinant of money was transaction which is captured by income. Irving Fisher (1911) in his Purchasing Power of Money expounded the classical Quantity Theory of Money. He examined the connection between total quantity of money and transactions. Total quantity of money is the money supply (M), and transaction is captured by the total amount of spending on final goods and services produced in the economy. This latter variable is captured by aggregate income (or GDP) which is denoted by Y.

5.9 Fisher's Equation of Exchange

Fisher, originally, related the money demand to transactions in what is termed as transaction demand for money. He linked the transaction demand for money with what is termed transaction velocity of money (V_T). Transactions (T) conducted per year is measured by income since there is no data on it, and both are found to be directly related. His equation of exchange is expressed as

$$M \times V_T = p \times T$$

However, because of absence of data on transaction, he substituted income for transaction, and his equation of exchange is rewritten as

$$M \times V_Y = Y \text{ and } Y = y \times p$$

where,

M is either $M1$ or $M2$. Y is nominal GDP which is a product of real GDP (y) and price (p). Thus, the equation of exchange becomes as follows:

$$M \times V_Y = p \times y \tag{5.9}$$

$$V_Y = p \times y/M$$

V_Y is the income velocity of money. It is the number of times money changes hands in transactions. It is also the average number of times (or turnover) that a dollar is spent in buying the total amount of goods and services produced in the economy per year.

Illustration

$$\text{If } M = 1000 \text{ and } Y = 3000, \text{ then } V_Y = 3000/1000 = 3$$

This means that on the average a dollar is spent 3 times in buying goods and services produced in the economy per year.

Again, if $M\uparrow$ to 2000, and Y$\uparrow$ to 3000, then $V_Y = 3000/2000 = 1.5$; if $M\downarrow$ to 500, and Y = 3000, then $V_Y = 3000/500 = 6$.

Generally, for a given income, an increase ($\uparrow$) in money supply results in a decrease ($\downarrow$) in income velocity of money. Thus, $\uparrow M \rightarrow \downarrow V_Y$ and $\downarrow M \rightarrow \uparrow V_Y$ for a given Y (3000).

According to Fisher, V_Y is determined by institutions and technological features of the economy. However, these institutions and technological features of the economy change slowly so they are reasonably constant in the short-term. Hence, by the classical economists' assumption that the economy is always operating at full employment; V_Y and y^f are fairly constants. Thus, an increase in M results in an increase in Y, and the converse holds true. Additionally, the money supply is procyclical in Fisher's Classical Quantity Theory of Money.

However, at the full employment level real income (y^f) and V_Y is fixed so

$$\uparrow M \rightarrow \uparrow Y \rightarrow \uparrow p \times y^f \rightarrow \uparrow p \text{ as } k = \left(y^f / V_Y\right) \text{ is constant}$$

Thus, the Quantity Theory of money also predicts that increase in money supply causes increase in prices or simply inflation.

5.10 Cambridge Equation of Exchange

The proponents of the Cambridge or Marshallian equation of exchange are Alfred Marshall and A.C. Pigou, to name two. Their thesis is that people hold a fraction of their wealth demand for money as income. Thus, although they, like Fisher assumes that money is held for transactions, but unlike the latter, their model also assumes that money is held for other purpose. The fact that people hold a fraction of their demand for money on transactions also suggest that if interest rates of bonds increase, they will hold a lesser fraction of their incomes for transaction, and the rest on bonds. This is because in the time of their writing only money and bond which is interest-bearing assets constitute the wealth in investors' portfolios. This reasoning was interpreted to mean that the Cambridge or Marshallian equation of exchange realizes the role of interest rate in the demand for money.

5.11 Cambridge Demand for Money

$$M^D = k \times Y = k \times p \times y \tag{5.10}$$

k is constant of proportionality, M^D is quantity of money demand which is equal to the quantity of nominal money stock, with all the other notations maintaining their definitions. Comparing Fisher's Eq. (5.9) to the Cambridge Eq. (5.10), $k = 1/V_Y$ is Cambridge or Marshallian constant, which is named after Alfred Marshall or Cambridge university. At equilibrium where $M = M^S = M^D$, an increase in the money supply will cause an increase in prices or inflation. The money supply (M^S) is also procyclical and income velocity of money is constant in the Cambridge equation. However, in the real world,

$$k = M^{D/}/p \times y = M/p \times y = M/\text{GDP} = 1/V_Y$$

However, both developed and developing countries data for $M1$, $M2$, and GDP or M/GDP data is volatile and not constant. In Ghana, Jamaica, Mexico, and the US, to name a few, $M1$ and $M2$ data have been unstable. The volatility in velocity from real world data is the reason central banks all over the world have ceased to target monetary aggregates as a reliable guide for monetary policy. This has led to the search of other theories of money demand and other targets of monetary policy.

5.12 Liquidity Preference Money Demand

John Keynes attempted to develop the role of interest rate in money demand in his *General Theory of Employment, Interest and Money*. His approach was to pose a question: why do people hold money? He answered the above question by stating three reasons for holding money. The first reason for holding money is for transaction purpose, and the variable that captures transaction best is real income. The second reason for holding money was for precautionary purposes. This ensures that when there are any unforeseen exigencies before pay day it can be met. The primary variable for capturing such behavior is again real income.

It is obvious that had Keynes ended his thesis here, his contribution would have been the same as the classical economists like Alfred Marshall, A.C. Pigou, Dale Robertson, to name a few. But he ventured a third reason for holding money which is for speculation purpose. He argued that the wealth of an individual comprises of money which earn zero interest rate, and bonds which earn interest. Some authors have suggested that it is better to use the term an interest-bearing asset rather than bonds because it widens the number of assets investors can trade in than using bonds which is limited investment instrument. For the simple reason that indeed during Keynes writing there was only bonds which served as a good substitute or competing asset to money, however, this is not the case anymore in our world now. Keynes argued that the variable which captures the speculative behavior is interest rate (Panels 5.1 and 5.2).

Thus, two variables capture his three purposes for holding money which he termed as liquidity preference (or demand for money) function, and it is denoted as $L(y, r)$. He posed the question: what do people hold money to achieve? His answer was to purchase real goods and services which he captured by the ratio of money demand to price ratio (M^D/p). He combined these two functions to obtain what he termed as real cash balances where at equilibrium the money supply ($M1$ or $M2$) is equal to money demand, and he expressed it as

$$M^D/p = L(y, r),\ L_y > 0 \text{ and } L_r < 0 \tag{5.11}$$

where,

(M/p) is real cash balances, y is real income, r is real interest rate; $L_y = \partial L(y, r)/\partial y$ captures the responsiveness of money demand in response to change in real income, $L_r = \partial L(y, r)/\partial r$ captures the responsiveness of money demand in response to change in real interest rate; $L_y > 0$ and $L_r < 0$.

5.13 The Square Root Formula of Money Demand

The lack of sound microeconomic foundation in Keynesian demand for money led to development of the transaction demand for money or square root formula for money demand, shopping time model, cash in advance model, to name a few. The square root formula of demand for money was first developed by Maurice Allais (1947) and independently developed later by William Baumol (1952) and James Tobin (1956). It assumes that when people are paid, their salaries are lodged directly into their bank account. An individual goes to the bank to withdraw income to buy his goods and services at the beginning of each payday. Any money lodged in a bank is paid an interest.

One trip to the bank:

Average income = (Y + 0)/2 = Y/2

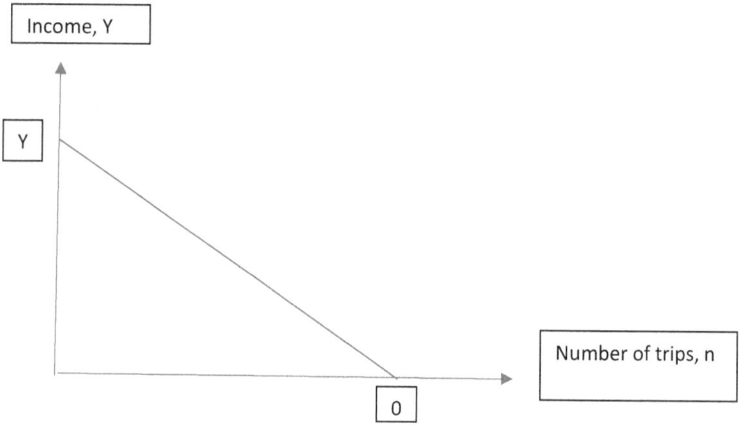

Two trips to the bank:

Average income = (Y/2 + 0)/2 = Y/4

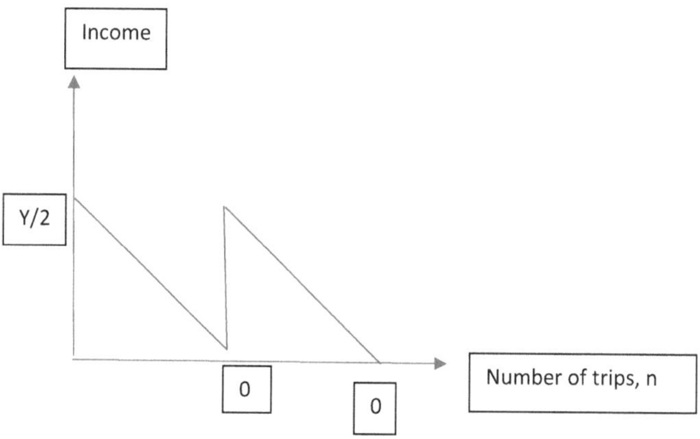

Panel 5.1 Number of trips to the bank for withdrawal of money

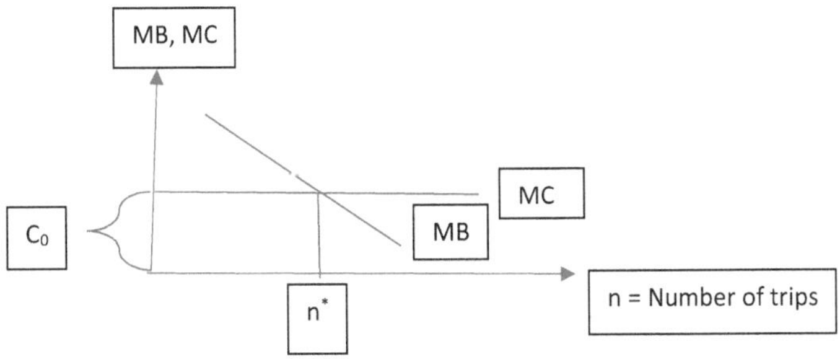

Panel 5.2 Optimal number of trips (n^*) when marginal benefit (MB) equals marginal cost (MC)

If an individual makes one trip to the bank and withdraws all his salary or income (Y) at the beginning of each month and spends it down evenly, the average income is Y/2. It is the average of the withdrawn income Y at the beginning of the month, which is spent down evenly, and zero income is left at the close of the month. If the individual makes two trips to the bank, his average income is Y/4 which is equal to average income of (Y/2) at the beginning of the month which is spent down evenly, and zero income is left at the close of the month. If he makes n trips to the bank and withdraws the same income on each trip, his average income is $Y/2n$. This average income for each trip which is spend down evenly will comprise of the individual's withdrawn income Y/n at the beginning of each trip and zero which is the income at the end of each trip.

5.13.1 *Derivation of the Square-roots formula of Demand for Money and Illustrative Example*

Derivation of the square-roots formula of demand for money and illustrative example is provided below as follows:

For two trips to the bank:

$$\text{Average income} = (Y/2 + 0)/2 = Y/4 = Y/2(2)$$

For n trips to the bank:

$$\text{Average income} = (Y/n + 0)/2 = Y/2n$$

The average income of each withdrawal for n trips

$$= (Y/n + 0)/2 = Y/2n = M$$

The cost of n trips at a fixed cost C_0[2] for each trip = $n^* C_0$.
The interest rates the bank pays is i, so m deposits interest cost = $i^* m$

$$\text{TC} = n \times C_0 + i \times m \tag{5.12}$$

where,
$m = M/p$ is real cash balances, $Y = y^* p$ is real income, * is product sign, and total cost of managing the portfolio is TC.

But average income of the entire n trips made to withdraw income from the bank is equal to real cash balances,

$$y/2n = m \tag{5.13}$$

Substituting for m into Eq. (5.12) we obtain

$$\text{TC} = n \times C_0 + i \times (y/2n)$$

Optimizing by finding the optimal number of trips (n^τ) to the bank for withdrawals we obtain

$$\partial\text{TC}/\partial n = C_0 - (i \times y)/2n^2 = 0$$

$$n^{\tau 2} = (i \times y)/2C_0$$

substituting n^τ into Eq. (5.13) yield

$$m^2 = \left[y^2 \times 2C_0\right]/[4 \times i \times y] = y \times C_0/2i$$

So

$$m = \text{SQRT}[(y \times C_0)/2i] \text{ or } M/p = \text{SQRT}[(y \times C_0)/2i] \tag{5.14}$$

[2] C_0 is the fixed cost of changing or transferring wealth from interest bearing asset to money as a liquid asset.

5.14 Shortcomings of the Square Root (SQRT) Formula of Money Demand

The shortcomings are many, but we have mentioned a few here. The Baumol and Tobin model which is based on the inventory rule model is simple and grossly specific. Not everybody is paid directly into their bank account. The self-employed may either receive payments daily or even not at all. The notion that an individual withdraws the same fraction of income and spends it evenly after each trip is artificial and unrealistic. The model is also subject to integer constraint. The elasticity of the number of trips to the bank is also subject to integer constraint.

The income elasticity of demand for money ranges from 0.5 to 1.0, and the interest elasticity of demand for money ranges from −0.5 to zero. However, there are other models of money demand which are not subject to restrictive assumptions and yet provide a more realistic results, such as the shopping time model, and the cash in advance (CIA) demand for money. We have provided a detailed derivation of the shopping time model in the ensuing chapter.

5.15 Summary

Money is defined and its functions are discussed. Monetary aggregates are discussed in the contest of developed and developing countries. We discussed how the balance sheet of central banks influences the money supply through the monetary base. The T-account is used to show the effect of unsterilized and sterilized foreign exchange intervention on both monetary base and the money supply. Money supply is derived, and its determinants are briefly pointed out.

The money demand is derived in the context of the classical economists, the liquidity preference model of Keynes, and the square root formula. The shortcomings of the square root formula are briefly discussed in the chapter.

5.16 Problems

(1) Assume that the required reserve ratio on checkable deposits is 20%, banks do not hold on to excess reserves, and the public do not change their holdings of currency. If the BNS sells \$10 million of bonds to the BOJ to pay back its \$10 million discount loans

it owes, what will this effect have on checkable deposits, and the monetary base? Will this activity affect reserves and/or currency in circulation? Explain.

(2a) Which of the following three expressions uses the definition of money by economists?

(i) "How much money did you earn last month?"
(ii) "I always take enough money with me when I go to shop at the mall."
(iii) "The love of money is the root of all evil."

(2b) Explain what will happen to the money supply as results of the following activities:

(i) Increase in illegal activity.
(ii) Increase in the interest rate on checkable deposit.
(iii) Bank panics.
(iv) Increase in expected deposits outflows.
(v) effectively than it can the reserves.

(3) NCB buys \$200 million bonds from the BOJ, the BOJ loans NCB an additional \$300 while depositors lodge \$150 checkable deposits with NCB's account.

(i) What will happen to the money supply and reserves?
(ii) Assume that the required reserve ratio on checkable deposits is 20%, banks do not hold any excess reserves, and the public's holding of currency do not change. Use the T-accounts.

(4a) List the factors that affect demand for money. Show their directional impact that will result in money demand increasing.

(4b) Given that interest rate is zero, if Jack is paid \$6,000 a month, what will be his average income?

(5) Banks in an economy hold discount loans (DL) and total reserves (TL) which can be expressed as

$$(\mathrm{DL}_t/\mathrm{TR}_t) = 10\left(i_t - i_t^D\right)$$

where i_t is interest rate and $i^D{}_t$ is the discount rate (measured in percentages) in time t. In a particular period, required reserves are \$90 billion, non-borrowed reserve are \$85 billion, and the discount rate is 6 percent. What will be the amount of excess reserve if the interest rate is 12 percent?

(6) Suppose the central bank of Trinidad-Tobago increases its lending of TT$250.00 to Royal Bank, and depositors withdraw TT$80.00 and keep it as cash. Show by using the T-accounts to explain your answer what happens to reserve and the monetary base.

(7) The money supply for $M2$ is defined as follows:

$$M2 = C + \text{DD} + \text{TSD} + \text{FXD}$$

where, C = currency in circulation, DD = demand deposits, TSD = time and savings deposits, FXD = foreign currency deposits. Derive the formula for the money multiplier for $M2$.

(8) For each of the following assets, indicate which of the monetary aggregates ($M1$ and $M2$) include them: (i) Currency, (ii) Travelers' checks, (ii) Money market mutual funds shares (institutional), (iii) Small-denomination time deposits, (iv) Large-denomination time deposits, and (v) Other checkable deposits.

Arrange all the assets listed above from the most liquid to the least liquid.

Selected References

Allais, Maurice (1947). E'conomie et interet, Paris: Librairie des publications officielles.

Baumol, William J. (1952). "The Transactions Demand for Cash: An inventory theoretic approach". *Quarterly Journal of Economics*, 66 (4): 545–556.

Ghartey, Edward E. (1998). "Monetary Dynamics in Ghana: Evidence from Cointegration, Error Correction Modelling, and Exogeneity," *Journal of Development Economics*, December, 57 (2): 473–486.

Hicks, John R. (1937). "Mr. Keynes and the 'classics'; A suggested interpretation", *Econometrica*, 5 (2): 147–159.

McCallum, Bennett T. (1989), *Monetary Economics: Theory and Policy*, Macmillan Publishing Company, New York.

Mishkin, Frederic S. (2016), *The Economics of Money, Banking, and Financial Markets*, (New York: Pearson).

Tobin, James (1956). "The interest elasticity of the transactions demand for cash". *Review of Economics and Statistics*, 38 (3): 241–247.

CHAPTER 6

Microeconomic Foundation of Open Economy Money Demand

Learning Outcomes

By the close of this chapter, the reader is expected to gain mastery over the topics covered in the chapter to proficiently do the following:

(1a) Derive households' multi-period utility function, list their associated assumptions, and explain their implications.
(1b) Express the utility function of households as it relates to its principal arguments. Express the multi-period utility function.
(2) Write the equation of leisure as a function of expenditure on goods and services or GDP, real effective exchange rate, and real cash balances.
(3) Explain why the scale variable g is said to capture expenditure on both domestic and foreign goods and services.
(4) Define the money demand function in an open economy to include real effective exchange rate as one of the arguments in the function of leisure, which is used to address foreign transactions. Is this money demand function the same as the money demand function for a closed economy?

E. E. Ghartey, *International Macroeconomics and Finance*,
https://doi.org/10.1007/978-3-032-04145-6_6

(5) Employ the Cobb–Douglas type production function to capture the utility function of households, and appropriate model for leisure to derive the shopping time money demand relation.
(6) Differentiate direct effect of the scale variable gt in the utility function from the indirect effect gt in leisure in the microeconomic foundation model of the shopping time model.
(7a) Explain household's multi-period utility function in terms of expenditure of goods and services, real cash balances, and exchange rate.
(7b) List all the assumptions and respective implications of the multi-period utility function.
(8) Express the utility function of the household and relate it to its principal arguments.
(9) Explain the scale variable? Provide reason why it captures expenditure on both domestic and foreign goods and services.
(10) Write the equation of leisure as a function of expenditure on goods and services, exchange rate, and real cash balances.
(11) Explain why the effect of expenditure on both domestic and foreign goods and services or gross domestic product (g) on leisure is different from its effect on the utility function?

6.1 Introduction

In Chapter 5 we developed a general macroeconomic or monetary economic model of money demand curves or equations from the perspective of the classical economists such as Irving Fisher, Alfred Marshall, and other Cambridge university economists like Dale Robertson and A.C. Pigou, and the perspective of Keynesian economists such as William Baumol and James Tobin's square-roots formula of demand for money. What has been a consistent criticism of the earlier money demand equations derived is the fact that they lack a sound microeconomic foundation, besides being suitable for closed economy.

In this chapter, we have attempted to resolve these shortcomings mentioned above, by developing a money demand function for an open economy model which is built on a microeconomic foundation by using the shopping time model, see Bennett T. McCallum (1989). An alternate to the shopping time model is the cash in advance model, and money in a utility function, see Robert W. Clower (1967), Miguel Sidrauski (1967), and Carl E. Walsh (1998).

6.2 Open Economy Money Demand Model

The traditional money demand function is explained by a scale variable which is captured by real income and opportunity cost measures such as the real interest rate, and other exogenous variables. Mundell (1963, p. 476) identified real interest rate and real income as the sole determinants of demand for money in an open economy. However, studies of demand for money which emphasized their relevance in open economies included uncovered interest rate differential as a substitute for real exchange rate, and real exchange rate as a proxy for currency substitution to address the nature of open economy. See Cuddington (1983), and Ahking (1984).

Studies by Ghartey (1998), Bahmani-Oskooee (1991), and Arango and Nadiri (1981) added real exchange rate to real income and real interest rate, the primary explanatory variables of real cash balances; whereas Heung (1999) and Levantakis (1993) included foreign and domestic interest rate as a substitute of real interest rates to address the open economy feature of the same demand for money.

The greater likelihood of autocorrelation stemming from the fact that domestic interest rates tend to correlate with foreign interest rates has been a bane in including opportunity cost measures in the empirical estimation of demand for money. We have attempted to minimize this type of autocorrelation problem by using real income, real effective exchange rates and domestic interest rate as our standard arguments of the demand for money in open economy in this study.

According to Mundell, increase in the money supply results in reducing interest rate to trigger capital outflow, and the resulting depreciation of the real exchange rate causes surplus in net exports. The resulting net exports lead to further increase in employment and real output through the multiplier effect. When the dynamics of the effect of the increase in the money supply in the economy finally settles down, the resulting increase in real output causes increase in tax receipts and saving to finance the associated net capital outflows.

The effect of increase in money supply under floating exchange rate results in capital outflow to trigger further depreciation which causes foreign assets of banks to increase. Consequently, under floating exchange rate, the stabilization effect of an increase in the money supply renders monetary policy more effective than under a fixed exchange rate. See Mundell (1961, p. 478).

6.3 Microeconomic Foundation of Demand for Money

The microeconomic foundation of demand for money is built by using the multi-period utility function of household which comprises of a scale variable g_t and leisure l_t. The inputs g and l of the utility function is assumed to behave as a Cobb-Douglas production function. The leisure of the household is explained by three arguments, namely: the scale variable g_t, real cash balances, m_t, and the real exchange rate q_t. The three inputs of leisure have indirect effect on the household's utility function. Therefore, by using inter-temporal budget constraint which is based on resources brought into the current period from immediate past and total current expenditures, the demand for money is derived by optimizing the household's multi-period utility function subject to inter-temporal budget constraint. The following sections provide detailed information and analysis of the shopping time money demand function.

6.4 Households' Multi-Period Utility Function

The household utility function is explained by a function comprising of expenditure on goods and services (g) and leisure (l) at period t. The multi-period utility function is as follows:

$$\begin{aligned} &U(g_t, l_t) + \lambda U(g_{t+1}, l_{t+1}) + \lambda^2 U(g_{t+2}, l_{t+2}) \\ &\quad + \ldots + \lambda^j U\left(g_{t+j}, l_{t+i}\right) + \ldots ; j = 1, \ldots , p. \end{aligned} \tag{6.1}$$

Assume that

$$\begin{aligned} &U_1 > 0 \text{ and } l_1 > 0,\ U_2 > 0 \text{ and } l_2 > 0,\ U_{12} > 0 \text{ and } l_{12} > 0, \\ &U_{21} > 0 \text{ and } l_{21} > 0,\ U_{11} < 0 \text{ and } l_{11} < 0,\ U_{22} < 0 \text{ and } l_{22} < 0, \end{aligned}$$

where,

$$\begin{aligned} &\partial U(g_t, l_t)/\partial g_t = U_1,\ \partial U(g_t, l_t)/\partial l_t = U_2,\ \partial^2 U(g_t, l_t)/\partial g_t^2 = U_{11}, \\ &\qquad \partial^2 U(g_t, l_t)/\partial g_t \partial l_t = U_{12}, \text{ and } \partial^2 U(g_t, l_t)/\partial l_t^2 = U_{22}. \end{aligned}$$

The function, $u(g_t, l_t)$, is an increasing function of both g and l, respectively. At time t, the household is concerned about the current and future expenditure on goods and services, and leisure. Thus, the household has positive time preference. The utility function is well behaved so there is no corner solution. Further, the household discount the future time preference of his utility function. This means that if $g_t = g_{t+1}$, $l_t = l_{t+1}$, and $\lambda = 1/(1 + \rho)$ for $\rho > 0$, where ρ is the discount rate because the household discount the future utility. Then,

$$U(g_t, l_t) > \lambda U(g_{t+1}, l_{t+1}) > \lambda^2 U(g_{t+2}, l_{t+2}) > \dots .$$

where,

$$g_t = g_{t+1},\ l_t = l_{t+1},\ U_t = U_{t+1}$$

So, $U_t > \lambda U_{t+1}$

The household prefers current utility (or expenditure on goods and services and leisure) to the future utility. The household's multi-period utility which is expressed in equation (6.1) is the same as equation (6.2) below:

$$U_t + \lambda U_{t+1} + \lambda^2 U_{t+2} + \dots + \lambda^i U_{t+j} + \dots ; j = 1, \dots, p. \quad (6.2)$$

The budget constraint of the household is restricted by the current and future budget or reserves constraint. The household has positive time preference since $0 < \lambda = 1/(1 + \rho) < 1$. The household's time preference, $0 < \lambda < 1$, is stable, and positive, $\lambda > 0$. Households maximize their multi-period utility function which is equation (6.2) subject to their budget or reserve constraints. See R.G. King et al. (1988).

We shall model the role of money in facilitating transactions, by assuming that the purchase of goods and services requires input of transaction services, which is produced by money and time. See Bennett T. McCallum (1989) and Dean O. Croushore (1993).

We derive the empirical money demand function in an open economy by building a shopping time microeconomic foundation model which incorporates the multi-period utility function discussed above. We have decided not to use the two-country portfolios balance money demand which were used in other studies. This is because regressors of the standard demand for money function, namely: real interest rate and real income, address both foreign and domestic expenditures from domestic money on both domestic and foreign spending on domestic goods and services.

6.5 Scale Variable and Opportunity Cost Measures

6.5.1 The Scale Variable

The scale variable, which is the real income (y), addresses the foreign sector or the open economy, and is defined as

$$Y = C^D + I^D + G^D + X \tag{6.3}$$

where,

$$C = C^D + C^{IM},\ I = I^D + I^{IM},\ \text{and } G = G^D + G^{IM},$$

$$\begin{aligned} \text{IM} &= C^{IM} + I^{IM} + G^{IM},\ C^D = C - C^{IM}, \\ I^D &= I - I^{IM},\ \text{and } G^D = G - G^{IM}. \end{aligned}$$

Equation (6.3) can be expressed as

$$\begin{aligned} Y &= C - C^{IM} + I - I^{IM} + G - G^{IM} + X \\ &= C + I + G + X - \left(C^{IM} + I^{IM} + G^{IM}\right) \\ &= C + I + G + X - IM \end{aligned} \tag{6.4}$$

Thus, the gross output scale variable in the demand for money captures the use of domestic expenditures on both domestic and foreign components of consumption (C), gross domestic private investments (I), government expenditures (G), and on domestic exports of goods and services (X) net of imports of goods and services (IM). C^D is domestic or national C, C^{IM} is foreign or imported C, I^D is domestic or national I, I^{IM} is foreign or imported I, G^D is domestic or national G, and G^{IM} is foreign or imported G.

We, therefore, do not find any need to use domestic and foreign components of portfolio balance as was used by Leventakis (1993) and Heung (1999) in defining the money demand function.

6.6 The Opportunity Cost Variable

The opportunity cost variable which is interest rate (i_t) is borrowing or loaning interest rate. It is typically issued at the beginning of each year and matures at the close of the same year as stipulated in the one-year loan agreement. Thus, a loan which is issued at time t-1 in the beginning of that year will mature at the close of the year at time t. Similarly, a loan which is issued at the beginning of the year t, will mature at the close of time t+1.

6.7 Inter-Temporal Budget Constraint

A nominal quantity of one-year loans or bonds (ℓ_t) issued or purchased at time t expire/mature at time t+1. $\ell_t < 0$ will imply households borrowing at time t. Thus, at the beginning of time t, assets of households will sum up to $\ell_{t\text{-}1}$ and $M_{t\text{-}1}$. See Robert J. Barro (2001) on money and budget constraint of household in especially Chapter 4.[1]

The budget constraint of households at time t which is the current period will become as follows:

$$p_t y + M_{t-1} + (1 + i_{t-1})\,\ell_{t-1} = p_t g_t + M_t + \ell_t. \tag{6.5}$$

where,

$p_t y + M_{t\text{-}1} + (1 + i_{t\text{-}1})\,\ell_{t\text{-}1}$ is resources brought into period t from the immediate past, and
$p_t g_t + M_t + \ell_t$ is total expenditures at time t

Notations used are as follow:

y is real income received each year
i_t is interest rate on loans or bonds bought at time t
g_t is consumption goods and services at time t
ℓ_t is nominal quantity of loans or bonds bought at time t
$p_t g_t$ is total consumption expenditure on goods and services at time t
M_t is money balances held at time t

[1] Cf. McCallum (1989) and Hendry and Ericson (1991).

The budget constraint in the successive years ahead for the future can be derived from equation (6.5) as follows:

$$\ell_{t-1} = \left[p_t(g_t - y) + (M_t - M_{t-1}) + \ell_t\right](1 + i_{t-1})^{-1} \tag{6.6}$$

So, at time $t+1$ we shall obtain the following:

$$\ell_t = \left[p_{t+1}(g_{t+1} - y) + (M_{t+1} - M_t) + \ell_{t+1}\right](1 + i_t)^{-1} \tag{6.7}$$

By substituting for ℓ_t in equation (6.7) into equation (6.6) we obtain the inter-temporal budget constraint of households over the entire infinite planning horizon as

$$\begin{aligned} \ell_{t-1} = {} & \left[p_t(g_t - y) + (M_t - M_{t-1})\right](1 + i_{t-1})^{-1} \\ & + \left[p_{t+1}(g_{t+1} - y) + (M_{t+1} - M_t) + \ell_{t+1}\right](1 + i_t)^{-1}] \\ & [1 - (1 + i)^{-1}] + \ldots \end{aligned}$$

Or

$$\begin{aligned} (1 + i_{t-1})\,\ell_{t-1} = {} & \left[p_t(g_t - y) + (M_t - M_{t-1})\right] \\ & + \left[p_{t+1}(g_{t+1} - y) + (M_{t+1} - M_t)\right](1 + i_t)^{-1} + \ldots \\ & \text{limit as } t \rightarrow \infty,\ \ell_t \rightarrow 0. \end{aligned} \tag{6.8}$$

Thus, we note that the present value of ℓ_t in equation (6.8) turns to zero.

6.8 Medium of Exchange Role of Money in the Shopping Time Model

We assume that leisure is a function of consumption of goods and services (g_t), real cash balances (M_t/p_t), and real exchange rate (q_t). This is expressed as

$$l_t = \phi(g_t, q_t, M_t/p_t),\ \phi_1 < 0,\ \phi_2 < 0,\ \phi_3 > 0 \tag{6.9}$$

There is time and energy spent in seeking appropriate goods and services to purchase for consumption. Consequently, an increase in expenditure on goods and services means the household must spend more time and energy, and this will in fact cause a decrease in leisure of the household. Hence $\phi_1 = \partial l_t(.)/\partial g_t, \phi_2 = \partial l_t(.)/\partial q_t$, and $\phi_3 = \partial l_t(.)/\partial M_t$.

The relationship between expenditure on goods and services, and leisure is negative as the more expenditure on goods and services of the household, the lesser the leisure hours of the household, $\phi_1 < 0$. Additionally, the relationship between the real effective exchange rate and leisure is negative. This means that an increase on the real effective exchange rate which emanates from depreciation results in a decrease in the wealth of households, which means households will have to spend more time and energy and hence less leisure to acquire goods and services, and this means that $\phi_2 < 0$.

The larger the real cash balances of the household, the larger the leisure hours available to the household. This results from the fact that an increase in real cash balances can allow households to acquire machines and equipment to do their chores and basic responsibilities for them. On the contrary, expansive ownership of real cash balances empowers households to hire workers, assistants, house helpers, and purchasing gadgets and equipment to increase leisure hours of households, so $\phi_3 > 0$.[2]

6.9 Optimizing Multi-Period Utility Function Subject to Inter-Temporal Budget Constraint

Households maximize their multi-period utility function in equation (6.1) which is expressed as

$$U(g_t, \phi(g_t, q_t, M_t/p_t)) + \lambda U(g_{t+1}, \phi(g_{t+1}, q_{t+1}, M_{t+1}/p_{t+1})) \\ + \cdots + \lambda^j U\big(g_{t+j}, \phi\big(g_{t+j}, q_{t+j}, M_{t+j}/p_{t+j}\big)\big) + \cdots ; j = 1, \ldots, p.$$

subject to their inter-temporal budget constraint shown in equation (6.8) by choosing g_t, M_t, q_t, and l_t at time-period t.

[2] An increase in real cash balances results in increased use or purchase of internet of things which in turn augments the household's leisure hours.

The Lagrangian equation required for the maximization problem is as follows:

$$\begin{aligned}\mathcal{L} &= U(g_t, \phi(g_t, q_t, M_t/p_t) + \lambda U(g_{t+1}, q_{t+1}, M_{t+1}/p_{t+1}) \\ &+ \cdots + \mu_t\{(1 + i_{t+1}) - [p_t(g_t - y) \\ &+ (M_t - M_{t-1})] - [p_{t+1}(g_{t+1} - y) + (M_{t+1} - M_t)](1 + i_t)^{-1} - \cdots\}\end{aligned} \tag{6.10}$$

6.10 Derivation of the Microeconomic Open Economy Money Demand Function

The money demand function is determined for period t by differentiating $\mathcal{L}$ in Eq. (6.10) with respect to μ_t, g_t, q_t, and M_t, and setting them to zero.

$$\begin{aligned}&\partial\mathcal{L}(.,..,.)/\partial\mu_t = 0, \partial\mathcal{L}(.,..,.)/\partial g_t = 0, \\ &\partial\mathcal{L}(.,..,.)/\partial q_t = 0, \text{ and } \partial\mathcal{L}(.,..,.)/\partial M_t = 0\end{aligned}$$

This leads to the following:

$$\begin{aligned}\partial\mathcal{L}(.,..,.)/\partial\mu_t &= (1 + i_{t-1})\ell_{t-1} - \left[p_t(g_t - y) + (M_t - M_{t-1})\right] \\ &- \left[p_{t+1}(g_{t+1} - y) + (M_{t+1} - M_t)\right](1 + i_t)^{-1} = 0\end{aligned} \tag{a}$$

$$\begin{aligned}\partial\mathcal{L}(.,..,.)/\partial g_t &= U_1(g_t, \phi(g_t, q_t, M_t/p_t)) \\ &+ U_2(g_t, \phi(g_t, q_t, M_t/p_t))\phi_1(g_t, q_t, M_t/p_t)) - \mu_t p_t = 0\end{aligned} \tag{b}$$

$$\partial\mathcal{L}(.,..,.)/\partial q_t = U_2(g_t, \phi(g_t, q_t, M_t/p_t))\phi_2(g_t, q_t, M_t/p_t)) = 0 \tag{c}$$

$$\begin{aligned}\partial\mathcal{L}(.,..,.)/\partial M_t &= U_2(g_t, \phi(g_t, q_t, M_t/p_t))\phi_3(g_t, q_t, M_t/p_t))/p_t \\ &+ (1 + i_t)^{-1}\mu_t - \mu_t = 0\end{aligned} \tag{d}$$

Thus, we have the following:

$$U_1(g_t, \phi(g_t, q_t, M_t/p_t)) + U_2(g_t, \phi(g_t, q_t, M_t/p_t))\phi_1(g_t, q_t, M_t/p_t)) = \mu_t p_t \tag{6.11}$$

$$U_2(g_t, \phi(g_t, q_t, M_t/p_t))\phi_3(g_t, q_t, M_t/p_t)) = \left[1 - (1 + i_t)^{-1}\right]\mu_t p_t \tag{6.12}$$

6.11 Economic Interpretations

$$U_1(g_t, l_t) + U_2(g_t, l_t)\phi_1(g_t, q_t, M_t/p_t)) = \mu_t p_t \tag{6.11$'$}$$

$$U_2(g_t, l_t)\phi_3(g_t, q_t, M_t/p_t)) = \left[1 - (1 + i_t)^{-1}\right]\mu_t p_t \tag{6.12$'$}$$

The above results are based on two first-order optimality conditions. In equation (6.11′) μ_t is the net marginal utility of real cash balance, $\mu_t p_t$ is the net marginal utility of nominal cash balance. The first term of the equation is the utility derived from an extra unit of expenditure on goods and services, and the second term is utility derived from an extra unit of leisure as a product of the cost measured in utils of leisure lost in terms of energy and time spent as households increase their expenditures on goods and services.

In equation (6.12′), the interest on the net marginal utility of expenditure on goods and services is equal to the utility of extra unit of leisure times the additions to leisure provided by an incremental unit of real cash balances.

By substituting $\mu_t p_t$ in equation (6.11′) into equation (6.12′), we obtain the following:

$$\begin{aligned} U_2(g_t, \phi(g_t, q_t, m_t))\phi_3(g_t, q_t, m_t)) = \{&U_1(g_t, \phi(g_t, q_t, m_t)) \\ &+ U_2(g_t, \phi(g_t, q_t, m_t)) \\ &\phi_1(g_t, q_t, m_{tt}))\}.\left[1 - (1 + i_t)^{-1}\right] \end{aligned} \tag{6.13}$$

By inspecting equation (6.13), we find that the solution variables include $M_t/p_t, g_t, q_t$, and i_t. By making the real cash balances the subject of the equation, we express the unique solution function as

$$m_t = M_t/p_t = F(g_t, q_t, i_t)$$

The question then is, how do the solutions independent variables g_t, q_t, and i_t relate to the dependent real cash (M_t/p_t) variable? To answer this question, we shall express the utility function of the household by using the Cobb-Douglas function[3] as

$$U(g_t, l_t) = g_t^{1-a} l_t^a \quad (6.14)$$

$$U_1(.) = \partial U(.)/\partial g_t = (1-a) g_t^{-a} l_t^a$$

$$U_2(.) = \partial U(.)/\partial l_t = a g_t^{1-a} l_t^{a-1}$$

$$l_t = \phi(g_t, q_t, m_t) = g_t^{-b}.q_t^c.m_t^b \quad (6.15)$$

$$\phi_3(g_t, q_t, m_t) = \partial l_t/\partial m_t = b.g_t^{-b}.q_t^c.m_t^{b-1}$$

where,

$$\begin{aligned} m_t = M_t/p_{t,}, U_1 > 0 \text{ and } l_1 > 0,\ U_2 > 0 \text{ and } l_2 > 0, \\ U_{12} > 0 \text{ and } l_{12} > 0,\ U_{21} > 0 \text{ and } l_{21} > 0, \\ U_{11} < 0 \text{ and } l_{11} < 0,\ U_{22} < 0 \text{ and } l_{22} < 0, \end{aligned}$$

The utility function of households is explained by goods and services expenditure, and leisure. An increase in expenditure on goods and services, and leisure both independently increase the utility of households. The utility function is expressed in Cobb-Douglass form to maintain the assumptions which suggest that although initial increment in expenditure on goods and services augments households' utility, extra increments in expenditures in goods and services result in households experiencing disutility as can be inferred from equation (6.16).

[3] The Cobb-Douglass function is used because of its constant returns to scale properties.

The households' leisure is explained by expenditure on goods and services, the real exchange rate, and real cash balances. The functional form of leisure indicates that after the initial increment of goods and services expenditure had augments leisure of the households, further extra increment in expenditure of goods and services decreases the households' leisure as shown in equation (6.13). Thus, both utilities and leisure of households are subject to the law of diminishing marginal returns.

We then substitute these microeconomics observations in equations (6.12) and (6.13) into equation (6.11) to obtain the following equation:

$$ag_t^{1-a}l_t^{a-1}b.g_t^{-b}.q_t^c.m_t^{b-1} = \{(1-a)g_t^{-a}l_t^a - abg_t^{1-a}l_t^{a-1}.g_t^{-b-1}q_t^c m_t^b\}.\left[1 - (1+i_t)^{-1}\right] \quad (6.16)$$

By substituting for l_t into the above equation and canceling like terms, we obtain

$$abg_t/m_t = \{(1-a) - ab\}.\left[1 - (1+i_t)^{-1}\right] \quad (6.17)$$

But we know that the following relationship holds:

$$[1 - (1+i_t)^{-1}] \approx i_t$$

Therefore, equation (6.17) can be expressed as

$$abg_t/m_t = \{(1-a) - ab\}.i_t \quad (6.18)$$

So

$$m_t = (ab/[1-a(1+b)]).g_t/i_t or\ M_t/p_t = F(g_t, i_t),\ F_1 > 0,\ F_2 < 0 \quad (6.19)$$

Thus, in an open economy, although the real exchange rate is an important instrument for capturing foreign trade, its effect cancels out in the derived money demand. Consequently, in the derived money demand function, the real cash balance is explained by real expenditure on goods and services or real income as a scale variable, and real interest rate. The real effective exchange rate, which is included in explaining the utility function and leisure, resulted in obtaining a real cash balance which is explained by real income or expenditure on goods and services, and real interest rate which is the standard money demand function.[4]

6.12 Summary

The standard money demand function is explained by real income as a scale variable, real interest rate as an opportunity cost measure, and real effective exchange rate as an exogenous variable, although the latter is seldom included. The dynamics of the effect of increase in money supply in the economy is briefly pointed out in the discussion.

The multi-period utility function of households is explained and expressed in a mathematical model. The scale variable is modeled to show that the transaction variable, which is expressed as a real income, addresses the open economy nature of the traditional or standard money demand function.

The inter-temporal multi-period budget constraint of households in the economy is combined with the multi-period utility function over the entire infinite planning horizon to form a Lagrangian equation. It is then optimized by differentiating the Lagrangian function, with respect to the respective regressors of the standard demand for money function, to obtain two first-order optimality condition equations, which are then interpreted to espouse their economics significance. The two first-order optimality conditioned equations are then solved by making real cash balances the subject of the solution to complete the derivation of the money demand function with a microeconomic foundation.

6.13 Problems

(1) Assuming that the stock of transactions conducted at period t are facilitated by money balances held at period t. This means leisure during time t can be expressed as

$$lt = \phi(g_t, m_t)$$

where $m_t = M_t/p_t$.

[4] The real cash balance is obtained by optimizing multi-period utility function subject to inter-temporal resource constraint.

(a) Specify and explain the significance of the inter-temporal budget or reserve constraint and the multi-period utility function.

(b) Express the Lagrangian utility function and differentiate it with respect to g_t and M_t to obtain $\partial\mathcal{L}_t/\partial g_t$ and $\partial\mathcal{L}_t/\partial M_t$ by maximizing the multi-period utility function subject to the inter-temporal multi-period budget constraint to get the relationship expressed in equation (XI).

(2) Using an appropriate theory or definition show explicitly from equation (XI) the effect of increase in expenditure on goods and service (or transaction) on real cash balances.

(3) What is the elasticity of money demand with respect to a decrease in interest rate? And what is the effect of increase transaction on leisure. Explain your answer in some detail.

(4) Using an appropriate theory or definitions derive an explicit relationship among real cash balances, interest rate, and transaction or real income.

(5) What is the effect of transaction or expenditure on goods and services on leisure and the utility function?

(6) Show that the scale variable or expenditure on goods and services captures both domestic and foreign goods and services.

(7) Express leisure as a function of expenditure on goods and services, exchange rate, and real effective rate. Explain the directional effect of the three variables on leisure.

(8) In the Kingdom of Dom, the transactions at each period are facilitated by only money balances held at the beginning of each period t. This means the households' general specification of leisure at each period t can be expressed as

$$l_t = \varphi(g_t,\ M_{t-1}/P_t).$$

Formulate the Lagrangian (L) expression for the household's multi-period utility function subject to multi-period budget constraint.

Compute the partial derivatives$\partial L_t/\partial g_t$, and $\partial L_t/\partial M_t$. Solve for an expression for M_t/P_t.

Selected References

Ahking, F, W. (1984), "International currency substitution: A reexamination of Brittain's econometrics evidence," *Journal of Money, Credit, and Banking*, 16: 546–556.

Arango, S. and Nadiri, M.I. (1981), "Demand for money in open economies," *Journal of Monetary Economies*, 7: 69–83.

Bahmani-Oskooee, Moshin. T. (1991), "The demand for money in an open economy: The United Kingdom," *Applied Economics*, 23: 1037–1042.

Barro, Robert J. (2001), *Macroeconomics*. New York: The MIT Press.

Clower, Robert W. (1967), "A reconsideration of the Micro-foundations of Monetary Theory," *Western Economic Journal*, 6 (1): 1–9.

Croushore, Dean. (1993), "Money in the utility function: Functional equivalence to a shopping-time model," *Journal of Macroeconomics*, 15 (1): 175–182.

Cuddington, J. T. (1983), "Currency substitution, capital mobility and money demand," *Journal of International Money and Finance*, 2: 111–133.

Ghartey, Edward E. (1998), "Monetary dynamics in Ghana: Evidence from cointegration, error correction modelling, and exogeneity," *Journal of Development Economics*, 57 (2): 473–486.

Hendry, David F. and Neil R. Ericsson (1991), "An econometric analysis of U.K. money demand in monetary trends in the United States and the United Kingdom by Milton Friedman and Anna J. Schwartz," *The American Economic Review*, 8 (1): 8–38.

Heung, Cheung J. (1999), "Money demand in an open-economy shopping time model: An out-of-sample-prediction application to Canada," *Journal of Economics and Business*, (51): 489–503.

King, Robert T., Charles L. Plosser and Rebelo, S. T. (1988), "Production, growth, and business cycles: I. The basic neoclassical model," *Journal of Monetary Economics*, 21, 2–3: 195–232

Levantakis, John A. (1993), "Modelling money demand in open economies over the modern floating rate period," *Applied Economics*, 25: 1005–1012.

McCallum, Bennett T. (1989), *Monetary Economics: Theory and Policy*, New York: Macmillan Publishing Company.

Mundell, Robert A. (1961), "A theory of optimum currency area," *The American Economic Review*, 51 (4): 657–665.

Mundell, Robert (1963). "Capital Mobility and Stabilization Policy under Fixed and Flexible Exchange Rates," *Canadian Journal of Economics and Political Science*, XXIX (4), November, 475–448.

Sidrauski, Miguel (1967), "Rational choice and patterns of growth in a Monetary Economy," *American Economic Review*, 57 (2), Papers and Proceedings of the 79th Annual Meeting of the American Economic Association: 534–544.

Walsh, Carl E. (1998). *Monetary Policy and Theory*, (New York: The MIT Press).

CHAPTER 7

Applied Demand for Money Study in Developing Countries

Learning Outcomes

By the close of the chapter readers and students must gain mastery in the topic to do the following:

(1) Explain the following terms and concepts: (a) price homogeneity and unit income elasticity of demand for money (b) weak-form and super exogeneity of money demand and (c) stability of money demand.
(2) Discuss data for estimating the demand for money in open economy in a developing country of their choice.
(3) Explain in some detail whether the statement "Demand for money and demand for money in an open economy are the same" is true or false or uncertain.
(4) Explain the effect of real exchange rate on demand for money in an open economy.
(5) Explain in some detail why the demand for money derived from the microeconomic foundation in the previous chapter is different from the demand for money specified in Ghartey's (1998) empirical study for Ghana in the JDE?

E. E. Ghartey, *International Macroeconomics and Finance*, https://doi.org/10.1007/978-3-032-04145-6_7

(6) Explain how the error-correction model is used to determine weak-form price homogeneity and unit income elasticity.
(7) Specify a disequilibrium equation of demand for money. Use it to derive the error-correction model of demand for money. [Hint: specify a long-run demand for money in an open economy and a disequilibrium model which captures the short-term dynamic relationship among the standard regressors of demand for money in an open economy.]
(8) Discuss the dynamic stability of the demand for money.
(9) Use the Wu-Hausman method to explain how to conduct weak exogeneity of price and real income in the demand for money in a developing economy.

7.1 Introduction

The demand for money is an important appendage of monetary policy, and demand for money in an open economy. It is also very important for especially developing countries because their economies tend to be more open than developed countries. In this chapter, we have used the demand for money function which we constructed from the microeconomic foundation in the previous chapter, to estimate a demand for money function for a developing country in an empirical study which can be employed to conduct monetary policy in developing countries.

The empirical model is constructed, and it is followed by a discussion of the data and its sources. The empirical estimates of demand for money in an open economy are discussed, and the dynamic stability, price homogeneity, unit real income elasticity, weak-form and super exogeneity properties of demand for money are reported and evaluated. The paper is summarized with conclusion and policy recommendation.

7.2 The Open Economy Money Demand Function

The demand for money equation in an open economy employed is the standard money demand function we discussed in Chapter 6. We have, however, included a real effective exchange rate as one of the explanatory variables of money demand to address the influence of exchange rate on foreign goods and services in the domestic economy. See Sect. 1.7 on GDP from expenditure approach.

The money demand function for an open economy which is used in the derivation of the micro foundation of money demand is expressed as follows:

$$\log(M_t/P_t) = F(\log y, \log i_t, \log q_t) + \varepsilon_t,\ F_1 > 0,\ F_2 < 0,\ \text{and } F_3 > \text{or} < 0 \tag{7.1}$$

The real cash balance (M_t/P_t) is expressed as a function of real income (y_t), real interest rate (i_t), and real effective exchange rate (q_t). The a priori expectation is that the real cash balances are directly increased by increase in real income, decreased by increase in real interest rate,[1] and uncertain by the increase in depreciation of the exchange rate.

The household budget constraint is restricted by current and future budget constraints. In deriving it, we assume that y is the real income or real GDP which is received every year and it is not affected by households' choices and time factor.

7.3 Applied Money Demand Study in the Context of Developing Countries

Empirical studies of demand for money abound for developed countries, although they are few and far between in developing countries. We have discussed an applied study of demand for money in a developing country in this chapter.

We have presented a money demand function which is estimated by using an econometric approach. The model for the applied study is specified to capture features of the demand for money model developed by modifying Eq. (6.19) in the microeconomic foundation in the previous chapter.

The demand for money Eq. (6.19) is specified as

$$M_t/p_t = (ab/[1-a(1+b)]) \cdot g_t/i_t$$

[1] Exchange rate is an important policy instrument which monetary authorities in especially developing countries often implement as a substitute for operating target instrument such as Treasury Bills rates during open market operations. It also provides information on the determination of prices in international traded goods and services in developing countries.

It is log-linearized below to yield

$$\log \cdot M_t - \log \cdot p_t = \log \cdot (ab/([1-a(1+b)]) + \log \cdot g_t - \log \cdot i_t$$

In empirical studies, the demand for money function (M_t/p_t) is explained by a scale variable which is captured by either g_t or real GDP (y_t) or consumption (c_t), opportunity cost measure such as real interest rate (i_t), and an intercept variable. It is expressed as

$$\log \cdot M_t = \log \cdot (ab/[1-a(1+b)]) + \log \cdot g_t - \log \cdot i_t + \log \cdot p_t \quad (7.2)$$

Econometric estimation of the above equation is expressed as

$$\log \cdot M_t = \alpha_0 + \alpha_1 \log \cdot y_t + \alpha_2 \log \cdot i_t + \alpha_3 \log \cdot p_t + \xi_t, \alpha_1 > 0, \alpha_2 < 0, \text{ and } \alpha_3 > 0.$$

In applied econometric study, the inclusion of real interest rate in the regression analysis often results in a serial or autocorrelation problem. This autocorrelation problem often requires the use of Cochran-Orcutt techniques, among other estimation techniques, to correct.

In Ghartey (1998, p. 475), the long-run money demand equation employed was expressed as

$$\log \cdot M_t = \alpha_0 + \alpha_1 \log \cdot y_t + \alpha_6 \log \cdot xr_t + \alpha_3 \log \cdot p_t + \alpha_4 \log \sigma_t^2 + \xi_t \quad (7.3)$$

where,

$\alpha_0 = ab/[1-a(1+b)]$, $\alpha_0 <$ or > 0, $\alpha_1, \alpha_3 > 0$, α_4 and $\alpha_6 < 0$; and ξ_t is the error term.

Thus, the money demand function of Ghana, a developing country, is explained by real income as the scale variable, real effective exchange rate, and foreign exchange risk which is measured by a four-quarter moving variance as opportunity cost variables.[2]

Time series data, typically monthly or quarterly or annual data are used to estimate the money demand function. The a priori expectations are that an increase in a unit change in real income or prices causes an increase in nominal money demand, whereas an increase in exchange rate and exchange rate risk decreases the nominal money demand.

[2] The interest rate variable is dropped from this specification to avoid the serial correlation tendency which it often introduces in such studies. We have dropped seasonal dummies s_2 and s_4 in Ghartey (1998) to simplify the analysis.

7.4 Derivation of the Error-Correction Model

Equation 7.3 is the desired demand for money. In empirical study, the desired demand for money which is expressed in terms of permanent and expected variables are transformed into actual variables by using a partial or adaptive expectation mechanism. However, such transformation introduces a lagged dependent variable as a regressor, which causes autocorrelation problem. To correct the autocorrelation problem, we have used an error-correction model (ECM) which is a two-step procedure developed by Engle and Granger (1987) to capture both the long-run equilibrium relationship known as cointegration estimates, and short-term dynamics among the variables.[3]

The disequilibrium model which captures the short-term dynamic relationship among the variables is expressed as

$$\begin{aligned}\log M_t = {} & \alpha_0 + \alpha_1 \log \cdot y_t + \alpha_1' \log \cdot y_{t-1} + \alpha_6 \log \cdot xr_t \\ & + \alpha_6' \log \cdot xr_{t-1} + \alpha_3 \log \cdot p_t + \alpha_3' \log \cdot p_{t-1} \\ & + \alpha_4 \log \sigma_t^2 + \alpha_4' \log \sigma_{t-1}^2 + \alpha_5 \log M_{t-1} + \xi_t \end{aligned} \quad (7.4)$$

For a stable relationship among the variables, $0 < \alpha_5 \leq 1$, where α_5 is the coefficient of the lagged dependent variable. The ECM is developed by assuming the steady-state condition where $\log y_t = \log y_{t-1}$, $\log xr_t = \log xr_{t-1}$, $\log p_t = \log p_{t-1}$, $\log\sigma_t = \log\sigma_{t-1}$, and $\log M_t = \log M_{t-1}$.

This means Eq. (7.4) becomes as follows:

$$\begin{aligned}(1-\alpha_5)\log \cdot M_t = {} & \alpha_0 + (\alpha_1 + \alpha_1')\log \cdot y_t + (\alpha_6 + \alpha_6')\log \cdot xr_t \\ & + (\alpha_3 + \alpha_3')\log \cdot p_t + (\alpha_4 + \alpha_4')\log \cdot \sigma_t^2 + \xi_t \end{aligned} \quad (7.5)$$

Thus, in the long run the coefficients of the liked variables are equal so

$$(\alpha_1 + \alpha_1') = (\alpha_6 + \alpha_6') = (\alpha_3 + \alpha_3') = (\alpha_4 + \alpha_4') = 1 - \alpha_5 = \lambda$$

and

$$(\lambda - \alpha_1) = \alpha_1', (\lambda - \alpha_6) = \alpha_6', (\lambda - \alpha_3) = \alpha_3', (\lambda - \alpha_4) = \alpha_4', \text{and } \alpha_5 = 1 - \lambda$$

[3] Error-correction model maps cointegration of the endogenous variable one-for-one with regressors to produce a long-run equilibrium relationship among them.

By substituting the above parameters on the right-hand side of respective terms into Eq. (7.4), it becomes as follows:

$$\begin{aligned}\log\cdot M_t &= \alpha_0 + \alpha_1 \log\cdot y_t + (\lambda - \alpha_1)\log\cdot y_{t-1} + \alpha_6 \log\cdot xr_t \\ &\quad + (\lambda - \alpha_6)\log\cdot xr_{t-1} + \alpha_3 \log\cdot p_t + (\lambda - \alpha_3)\log\cdot p_{t-1} \\ &\quad + \alpha_4 \log\sigma_t^2 + (\lambda - \alpha_4)\log\sigma_{t-1}^2 + (1-\lambda)\log M_{t-1} + \xi_t \end{aligned} \quad (7.6)$$

which reduces to

$$\begin{aligned}\log\cdot M_t &= \alpha_0 + \lambda\log\cdot y_{t-1} + \alpha_1(\log\cdot y_t - \log\cdot y_{t-1}) \\ &\quad + \alpha_6(\log\cdot xr_t - \log\cdot xr_{t-1}) + \lambda\log\cdot xr_{t-1} \\ &\quad + \lambda\log\cdot p_{t-1} + \alpha_3(\log\cdot p_t - \log\cdot p_{t-1}) + \lambda\log\sigma_{t-1}^2 \\ &\quad + \alpha_4\left(\log\cdot\sigma_t^2 - \log\cdot\sigma_{t-1}^2\right) + \log\cdot M_{t-1} - \lambda\log\cdot M_{t-1} + \xi_t \end{aligned} \quad (7.7)$$

$$\begin{aligned}\log\cdot M_t - \log\cdot M_{t-1} &= \alpha_0 + \alpha_1(\log\cdot y_t - \log\cdot y_{t-1}) \\ &\quad + \alpha_6(\log\cdot xr_t - \log\cdot xr_{t-1}) \\ &\quad + \alpha_3(\log\cdot p_t - \log\cdot p_{t-1}) \\ &\quad + \alpha_4\left(\log\cdot\sigma_t^2 - \log\cdot\sigma_{t-1}^2\right) - \lambda\log\cdot M_{t-1} \\ &\quad + \lambda\log\cdot y_{t-1} + \lambda\log\cdot xr_{t-1} \\ &\quad + \lambda\log\cdot p_{t-1} + \lambda\log\sigma_{t-1}^2 + \xi_t \end{aligned} \quad (7.8)$$

It is expressed further as an error-correction model as follows:

$$\begin{aligned}\Delta\log\cdot M_t &= \alpha_0 + \alpha_1\Delta\log\cdot y_t + \alpha_6\Delta\log\cdot xr_t \\ &\quad + \alpha_3\Delta\log\cdot p_t + \alpha_4\Delta\log\cdot\sigma_t^2 \\ &\quad - \lambda\left(\log\cdot M_{t-1} - \log\cdot y_{t-1} - \log\cdot xr_{t-1}\right. \\ &\quad \left. - \log\cdot p_{t-1} - \log\sigma_{t-1}^2\right) + \xi_t \end{aligned} \quad (7.9)$$

where, the error-correction (EC_{t-1}) term is $-\lambda \cdot (\log\cdot M_{t-1} - \log\cdot y_{t-1} - \log\cdot xr_{t-1} - \log\cdot p_{t-1} - \log\sigma_{t-1}^2)$, and the dynamic stability of the error-correction model is the coefficient of the EC term, λ. It is determined from the level form estimate of the long-run demand for money or the cointegrated equation. The error term, ξ_t, is a white noise innovation, and the dynamic stability is $-1 \leq \lambda < 0$. The significance of the coefficient of the EC_{t-1} term confirms the existence of cointegration or long-run relationship among nominal money, real income, price, real effective exchange rate, and foreign exchange risk. Thus, the errors resulting from decision on $\Delta\log\cdot M_t$ is corrected by including the error-correction term of the immediate past to minimize the deviation of $\log\cdot M_{t-1}$ line from $\log\cdot y_{t-1}+\log\cdot xr_{t-1}+\log\cdot p_{t-1}+\log\sigma^2_{t-1}$ line. See Hendry and Ericsson (1991).

The error-correction Eq. (7.9) was re-modeled and estimated for Ghana for comparative purpose. Ghartey's (1998) estimated error-correction equation used for comparative study and discussion is reported below as follows:

$$\begin{aligned}\Delta\log\cdot M_t = &-0.175[1.995] + 0.244[1.721]\Delta\log\cdot y_t \\ &+ 0.453[3.496]\Delta\log\cdot p_t - 0.067[2.611]\Delta\log\cdot xr_t \\ &-0.075[1.713]\log EC_{t-1} - 0.002[0.475]\Delta\log\cdot xr_{t-1} \\ &+ 0.032[0.432]\Delta\log\cdot p_{t-1} + 0.051[2.913]s_2 + 0.209[11.725]s_4\end{aligned} \tag{7.10}$$

$$\begin{aligned}&N = 90,\ R^2 = 0.65,\ F(8,81) = 21.734,\\ &DW = 1.837,\ SEE = 0.065,\ \chi^2_{SC}(4) = 6.006,\\ &\chi^2_{FF}(1) = 1.074,\ \chi^2_{N}(2) = 2.273,\\ &\chi^2_{H}(1) = 0.008,\ \text{and}\ EC_{t-1} = m_{t-1} - p_{t-1} - y_{t-1}.\end{aligned}$$

where, t-ratios are reported in square brackets; s2 and s4 are the respective second and fourth seasonal dummies with the rest of the notations maintaining their previously mentioned definitions.

The results are very satisfactory judging by the reported diagnostic results, as there are no autocorrelation and heteroscedasticity problems. Furthermore, the functional form and normality tests are well satisfied.

7.5 Tests of Homogeneity, Weak Exogeneity, and Stability of the Demand for Money Function

Estimation of the demand for money equation after the researcher has derived the model by going through the process discussed in Sect. 7.4, is to identify the variables in the model, namely: the money stock (M1 or M2), price (CPI or GNP-deflator or GDP-deflator), real income (GNP or GDP), real effective exchange rate, and interest rate as an opportunity cost measure (TBR), although the latter is likely to introduce serial correlation problem in regression results. Central banks of countries are often the source of such data, although from pragmatic experience, the IMF's International Financial Statistics and World Bank are excellent sources of such data. It should be noted that both the IMF's and World Bank receive these economic data from the Minister of Finance and central banks of member countries.

Empirically, the acceptable estimated demand for money function must maintain parameter constancy for it to be employed reliably for inference, forecasting, and policy. See Hendry and Ericsson (1991). This constancy property of parameters is tested by using super exogeneity and structural invariance of parameters tests over recent data. Additionally, it ensures that the econometric model is well specified, and there is no shift in fiscal and monetary policy and exchange rate regime changes, and statistical data employed is stable.[4]

The desired long-run demand for money is expressed as Eq. (7.3). However, to specify a money demand function which addresses both short-term and long-run effects, a partial adjustment model is often used. Unfortunately, the conventional partial adjustment demand for money function is too restrictive. It is therefore necessary to specify an error-correction model (ECM) which is a less restrictive lagged structure, and an improvement over the partial adjustment model.

7.5.1 Homogeneity Test Results

The cointegration demand for money function of Ghana is estimated by using a dynamic least squares (DLS) method with xr_t, σ_t^2, m_{t-1}, s2, s4, and intercept term as instrumental variables. The results which are sourced from Table 2 of Ghartey (1998) are reported below as

$$\begin{aligned}\log \cdot M_t = &-2.53[2.00] + 1.00[18.20]\log \cdot p_t + 1.18[5.65]\log \cdot y_t \\ &-0.07[5.65]\log \cdot xr_t - 0.06[3.00]\log \cdot \sigma_t^2 \qquad (7.11)\end{aligned}$$

[4] Non-constancy of parameters of an econometric model can result from misspecification of the underlying model which results from shifting exchange rate regimes, for instance, from fixed exchange rate to floating exchange rate or petroleum crises.

$$N = 90,\ R^2 = 0.995,\ \mathrm{DW} = 0.532,\ \chi^2_{\mathrm{SC}}(4) = 51.142,$$
$$\chi^2_{\mathrm{FF}}(1) = 2.503,\ \chi^2_{\mathrm{N}}(2) = 2.232.$$

Thus, the demand for money function reported in Ghartey (1998) has long-run price homogeneity property and unit income elasticity. The estimated long-run price elasticity is unity, and the real income elasticity is 1.18. Furthermore, the t-ratios of $\log p_t$ and $\log y_t$ regressors are significant which means that the long-run price homogeneity and unit income condition is satisfied.

The Wu-Hausman method is used to test for price homogeneity and unit real income elasticity by remodeling the error-correction Eq. (7.9) to include $\log p_{t-1}$ and $\log y_{t-1}$ as regressors to obtain

$$\begin{aligned}\Delta\log\cdot M_t &= \alpha_0 + \alpha_1\Delta\log\cdot y_t + \alpha_6\Delta\log\cdot xr_t + \alpha_3\Delta\log\cdot p_t + \alpha_4\Delta\log\cdot\sigma_t^2\\ &\quad -\lambda(\log\cdot M_{t-1} - \log\cdot y_{t-1} - \log\cdot xr_{t-1} - \log\cdot p_{t-1} - \log\sigma_{t-1}^2)\\ &\quad + \omega_1\log\cdot y_{t-1} + \omega_2\log\cdot p_{t-1} + \xi_t \end{aligned} \tag{7.11a}$$

Thus, the Wu-Hausman method entails estimating the ECM in Eq. (7.11a) to test long-run price homogeneity and unit income elasticity properties by imposing a joint test of zero restriction on the coefficients of $\log\cdot p_{t-1}$ and $\log\cdot y_{t-1}$ in the estimated Eq. (7.11a), and the significance of the error-correction term as judged by its t-ratio to justify the existence of the estimated ECM.

The ECM of Ghana which was estimated in Ghartey (1998) is used to test price homogeneity and unit income elasticity properties, and it is reported below as follows:

$$\begin{aligned}\Delta\log\cdot M_t = &-0.079[0.369] + 0.241[1.583]\Delta\log\cdot y_t\\ &+ 0.463[3.377]\Delta\log\cdot p_t\\ &- 0.068[2.593]\Delta\log\cdot xr_t\\ &+ 0.052[2.930]s_2 + 0.209[11.810]s_4u\\ &- 0.073[1.582]\log\cdot EC_{t-1} - 0.013[0.448]\log\cdot y_{t-1}\\ &- 0.002[0.528]\log\cdot p_{t-1}\end{aligned} \tag{7.12}$$

$$N = 90,\ R^2 = 0.65,\ F = 21.688,$$

$$\begin{aligned}&DW = 1.844,\ \chi^2_{SC}(4) = 5.951,\ \chi^2_{FF}(1) = 0.951,\\&\chi^2_{N}(2) = 2.054,\ \chi^2_{H}(1) = 0.014,\\&\chi^2_{WS}(1) = 0.346,\ \text{and}\ EC_{t-1} = m_{t-1} - p_{t-1} - y_{t-1}.\end{aligned}$$

The estimated coefficients of regressors p_{t-1} and y_{t-1} are insignificant, which indicate that long-run price homogeneity property and the unit elasticity of real income of the money demand for Ghana are satisfied. See the estimated cointegrated Eq. (7.11) which has a unit price elasticity and a unit real income elasticity of demand for money.

Additionally, the joint test of zero restriction of the long-run price homogeneity property and unit elasticity of real income of the estimated ECM of money demand under the null hypothesis, H_0: $\omega_1 = \omega_2 = 0$, cannot be rejected. Thus, confirming that the long-run price homogeneity and unit real income property are satisfied in the money demand function of Ghana.

7.5.2 *Weak Exogeneity Test Results*

Potential weak exogeneity test is conducted by using two additional methods developed by Wu (1973) and Hausman (1978) methods, and Engle and Granger (1987) method. This is done by generating residuals rlogp_t and rlogy_t, which are computed from regressing logp_t and logy_t independently on their respective money demand instrumental variables, which are listed as logy_{t-1}, logy_{t-2}, logp_{t-1}, logp_{t-2}, log$\cdot M_{t-1}$, log$\cdot M_{t-2}$, and an intercept term. The two residual variables are then included as regressors in the ECM of the demand for money Eq. (7.9) which is expressed as

$$\begin{aligned}\Delta\log\cdot M_t = {} & \alpha_0 + \alpha_1\Delta\log\cdot y_t + \alpha_6\Delta\log\cdot xr_t\\& + \alpha_3\Delta\log\cdot p_t + \alpha_4\Delta\log\cdot\sigma_t^2\\& + \omega_1'\log\cdot ry_t + \omega_2'\log\cdot rp_t\\& -\lambda\big(\log\cdot M_{t-1} - \log\cdot y_{t-1} - \log\cdot xr_{t-1}\\& - \log\cdot p_{t-1} - \log\sigma_{t-1}^2\big) + \xi_t \qquad (7.13)\end{aligned}$$

The estimated coefficients of ω_1' and ω_2' are jointly tested by imposing zero restrictions on them to find their importance in the demand for money Eq. (7.13). If the null hypothesis of joint test of zero restriction (H_0: $\omega_1' = \omega_2' = 0$) is insignificant or failed to be rejected, then it means both price and income are weakly exogenous in the estimated demand for money function.

The estimated ECM of Ghana in Ghartey (1998) which is used to conduct the weak exogeneity test yielded the following results:

$$\begin{aligned}\Delta\log \cdot M_t = & -0.134 - 0.192[0.312]\Delta\log \cdot y_t \\ & + 0.242[0.667]\Delta\log \cdot p_t - 0.062[2.237]\Delta\log \cdot xr_t \\ & + 0.046[2.301]\Delta\log \cdot \sigma_t^2 + 0.258[0.525]\log \cdot ry_{t-1} \\ & + 0.495[0.686]\log \cdot rp_{t-1} - 0.062[1.792]\mathrm{EC}_{t-1} \end{aligned} \tag{7.14}$$

$$\begin{aligned} & N = 88,\ R^2 = 0.645,\ \mathrm{F} = 20.737, \\ & \mathrm{DW} = 1.970,\ \chi^2_{\mathrm{SC}}(4) = 5.317,\ \chi^2_{\mathrm{FF}}(1) = 0.968, \\ & \chi^2_{\mathrm{N}}(2) = 4.037,\ \chi^2_{\mathrm{H}}(1) = 0.005,\ \chi^2_{\mathrm{SIV}}(1) = 0.002. \end{aligned}$$

Wald test of joint test of zero restriction is $\omega_1' = \omega_2' = 0$ and $\chi^2_{\mathrm{WS}}(1) = 0.346$, where WS denotes Wald Statistics (WS). See Table 3 of Ghartey (1998).

The Lagrange multiplier test of serial correlation (χ^2_{SC}), Ramsey's RESET test of functional form using the square of the fitted values (χ^2_{FF}), normality test based on skewness and kurtosis of residuals (χ^2_{N}), heteroscedasticity test based on the regression of squared residuals on squared fitted values (χ^2_{H}), and Sargan's legitimate test of instrumental variables (χ^2_{SIV}). Absolute values of the t-ratios are given in the square brackets.

The results show that real output and price are weakly exogenous. Furthermore, the ECM encompasses short-term and long-run dynamics of the demand for money function. It maps cointegration one-to-one with the endogenous variable and the regressors. Thus, the ECM is used to determine weak-form exogeneity of both regressand and regressors.

7.6 Further Test of Exogeneity

Aside from making an inference of the stability or structural invariance of the demand for money function from inversion of the demand for money equation with price and income as regressors, inversion of respective price and income equations conditional on the money stock as one of the regressors can be used to determine which of the three equations is endogenous, and which of the three variables are regressors in the demand for money equations.

7.6.1 *Super Exogeneity Test*

The estimated ECM of the demand for money function must have coefficients which are constant even when the process of conditional variables changes due to the following three conditions, namely: (1) shift in regimes or economy-wide structural change, (2) super exogeneity of the conditioning variables, and (3) the endogeneity condition of the estimated money demand function. The existence of the above conditions means the estimated money demand function has independent explanatory variables which cannot be inverted because the money stock in the demand for money function is endogenous, whereas the regressors of the demand for money are exogenous.

The ECM of demand for money equation must be invertible to obtain price equation and interest rate equation. Barro (1987) inverted the money demand equation to obtain price equation. See also Hendry and Ericsson (1991). Thus, price inversion and interest rate inversion of the demand for money equation can be used to determine the exogeneity or endogeneity of price equation and interest rate equation in the demand for money equation.

Super exogeneity tests confirm that the ECM of demand for money equation, conditioned on $\Delta\log{\cdot}p_t$ and $\Delta\log{\cdot}r_t$ exists. If it can be inverted to obtain a price equation conditioned on $\Delta\log{\cdot}M_t$, then it will mean that the said demand for money equation is unstable; whereas a test which shows that inverted price or interest rate equation do not exist in the demand for money equation will show that the said demand for money equation is stable, and the money stock is endogenous; while both price and interest rate regressors in such demand for money equation are exogenous. This stable demand for money equation will not change (or is structurally invariant) with policy or regime change, and the model is not subject to the Lucas critique. See Lucas (1976) and McCallum (1989).

The ECM of the demand for money equation is inverted by making growth in price and income regressands conditioned on the growth in money stock as an exogenous variable. Results of endogeneity test of price and income conditioned on the money stock using the Cochrane-Orcutt estimation technique sourced from Table 3 of Ghartey (1998) are

$$\begin{aligned}\Delta\log \cdot p_t = {} & 0.192[2.384]-0.842[17.485]\Delta\log \cdot y_t \\ & + 0.172[2.517]\Delta\log \cdot M_t + 0.007[0.438]\Delta\log \cdot xr_t \\ & + 0.002[0.242]\mathrm{s}_2 + 0.032[2.023]\mathrm{s}_4 \\ & - 0.055[1.422]\log \cdot \mathrm{EC}_{t-1}\end{aligned} \tag{7.15}$$

$$N = 90,\ R^2 = 0.81,\ \mathrm{DW} = 1.843,\ \mathrm{F}(10, 76) = 38.411,\ \mathrm{SEE} = 0.043$$

and

$$\begin{aligned}\Delta\log \cdot y_t = {} & 0.139[1.732]-0.941[15.900]\Delta\log \cdot p_t \\ & + 0.107[1.407]\Delta\log \cdot M_t + 0.0001[0.004]\Delta\log \cdot xr_t \\ & - 0.005[0.607]\mathrm{s}_2 + 0.013[0.757]\mathrm{s}_4 \\ & - 0.031[0.811]\log \cdot \mathrm{EC}_{t-1}\end{aligned} \tag{7.16}$$

$$N = 90,\ R^2 = 0.74, \mathrm{DW} = 1.831,\ \mathrm{F}(10, 76) = 25.285,\ \mathrm{SEE} = 0.046$$

See Ghartey (1998), Hendry and Ericsson (1991), and Engle and Granger (1987).

Results of the inverted inflation and income growth functions conditioned on the growth of the money stock in both Eqs. (7.15) and (7.16) show that the error-correction terms of both inverted price and income Eqs. (7.15) and (7.16) have *t*-ratios of 1.422 and 0.811, respectively, and both are insignificant which means they are not cointegrated. Consequently, price and real income regressors in the demand for money in the country are not endogenous.

On the other hand, the error-correction model of the money demand function has a significant error-correction term. Thus, whereas the money demand equation is cointegrated, both inverted price and real income equations are not cointegrated. This means that only the money demand equation is endogenous, as price and income are both exogenous in the demand for money equation in Ghana.

7.7 Structural Stability of the Money Demand Model

The parameter and structural stability are tested by splitting the time span into pre- and post—1983.4 in Ghana. Reasons being as follows:

(i) 1983 served as a structural 'break' point period when military government of Ghana returned to the IMF and World Bank to adopt their structural adjustment policies.
(ii) It also marked the period of massive drop in agricultural production and food shortage in the country, and the mass expulsion of Ghanaian migrants from Nigeria.
(iii) This is not to mention the fact that the country's inflation jumped very sharply from 22.3% in 1982 to 122.8% in 1983.

The predictive failure test starting from 1982.1 to 1992.4 is $F(36, 48) = 0.996$ and a structural breakpoints over the same period has the $F(7, 77) = 1.271$ statistic. Both statistics are insignificant at 0.05 levels. The associated 1983 structural breakpoint has a root mean sum of squares predictive error of 0.068 which is robust.

In the annals of Ghanaian history, 1977 was also used as another structural breakpoint. It marked the first time the country's inflation rate surged to 78% using the consumer price index with 1995 as the base year. It was also the first time the country's inflation hit its highest level since it attained independence. In attempt to remedy the hyperinflation situation, the bank of Ghana embarked on several commercial bank policies by (i) requiring commercial banks to hold a mandatory currency reserve ratio to the tune of their immediate past twelve months average. However, because the reserve requirement ratio failed as a monetary tool, among other policies to curb inflation in the country, the government demonetized the cedi to mop up the excess liquidity in the system. The structural breakpoint obtained by using 1977.4 as a breakpoint resulted in predictive failure test of $F(60, 24) = 1.532$, and a structural stability test of $F(7, 77) = 1.113$, and both are insignificant.

Thus, although we have used 1977 and 1983 to assess the structural stability of the demand for money, we can argue further that other periods can be used also to determine the structural stability of the estimated money demand of the country. For instance, 1988 can equally serve as a possible structural breakpoint period. This is because 1988 can be justified as a possible structural breakpoint period, as it was the period when the Economic Recovery Program which was introduced in the country by the World Bank liberalized the financial market in the country.

There is therefore no unique structural breakpoint period, considering that 1977, 1983, and 1988 are possible structural breakpoints period in the country. It behooves that we adopt a structural stability test which requires several structural breakpoint periods. We have, therefore, employed cumulative sum (CUSUM) and CUSUM sum of squares (CUSUMSQ) tests which are recursive residuals which do not require specific dates as structural breakpoint dates to test the stability condition of the parameters.

The estimated error-correction demand for money Eq. (7.10) is used to test the structural stability condition of the model. The CUSUM and CUSUMSQ of recursive residuals of the coefficients of regressors Δp_t and Δy_t in the error-correction equation of the demand for money in Ghana are very stable. They are both within their respective 95% confidence intervals, which confirm that they are both stable, although they have not been reported in the text to conserve space. The recursive least squares estimation of coefficients of Δp_t and Δy_t in the error-correction demand for money Eq. (7.10) reported in Panels 7.1 and 7.2, respectively, are stable judging by the fact that they do not display sudden variations over the period of their estimation.

On the other hand, the inverted price and real income Eqs. (7.15) and (7.16) are unstable judging by their respective CUSUM and CUSUMSQ of recursive least squares of residuals violate the 95% confidence intervals. The figures were not reported in the text because of conservation of space. The least squares estimation of inverted price and real income equations, respectively, have recursive coefficient of regressor Δm_t which displays instability as more data are included in the recursive least squares estimation process as can be seen in Panels 7.3 and 7.4.

Thus, since both inverted price and real income Eqs. (7.15) and (7.16) are weak-form exogenous judging by the fact that their respective error-correction terms are insignificant, and their respective CUSUM and CUSUMSQ of recursive residuals of least squares of coefficients of

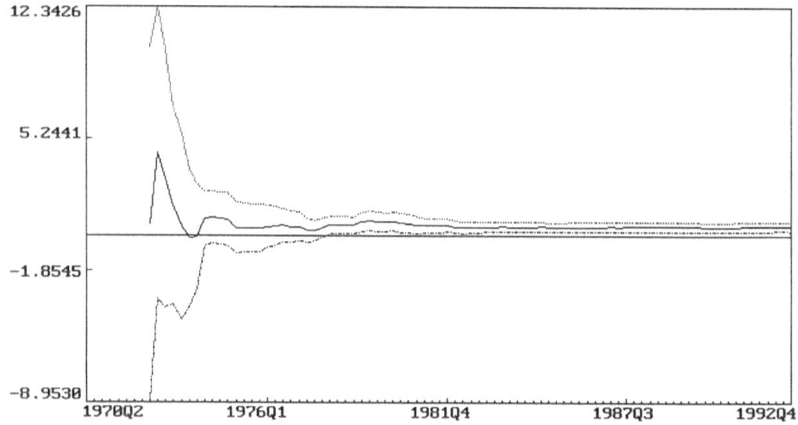

Panel 7.1 The coefficient of ΔP in Eq. 7.10 and its 2 S.E. bands based on recursive LS *source* Ghartey (1998), Journal of Development Economics

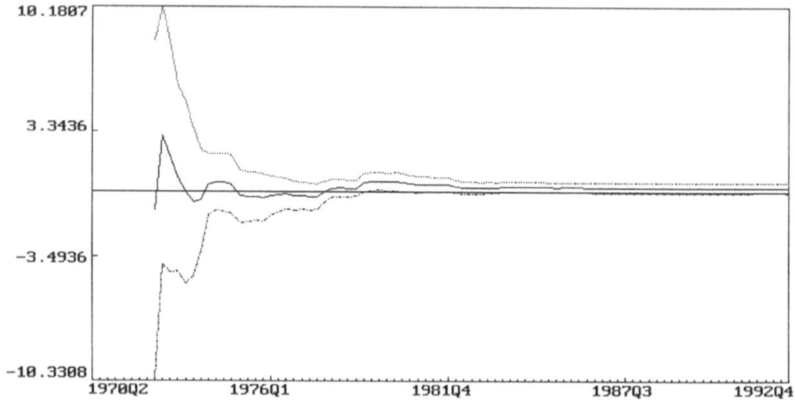

Panel 7.2 The coefficient of ΔY in Eq. 7.10 and its 2 S.E. bands based on recursive LS *source* Ghartey (1998), Journal of Development Economics

regressors Δp and Δy in the demand for money equation are stable. We infer that both price and real income are super exogenous while the fact that the error-correction term is significant in the demand for money equation, whereas the recursive coefficient of Δm in respective inverted price and real income Eqs. (7.15) and (7.16) are unstable as observed

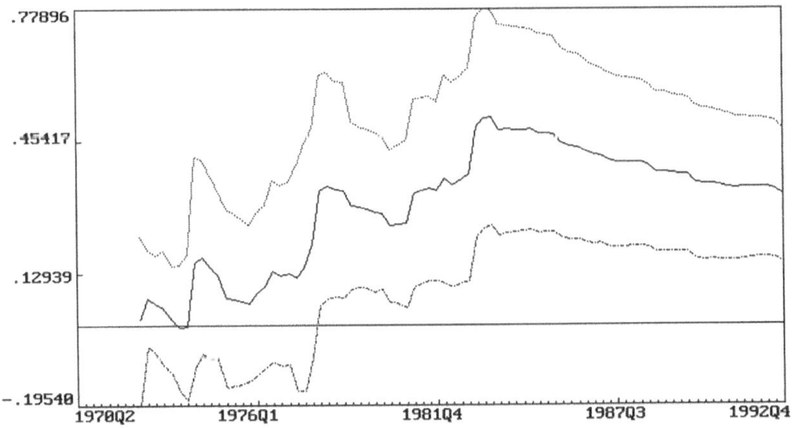

Panel 7.3 The coefficient of ΔM in Eq. 7.15 and its 2 S.E. bands based on recursive LS *source* Ghartey (1998), Journal of Development Economics

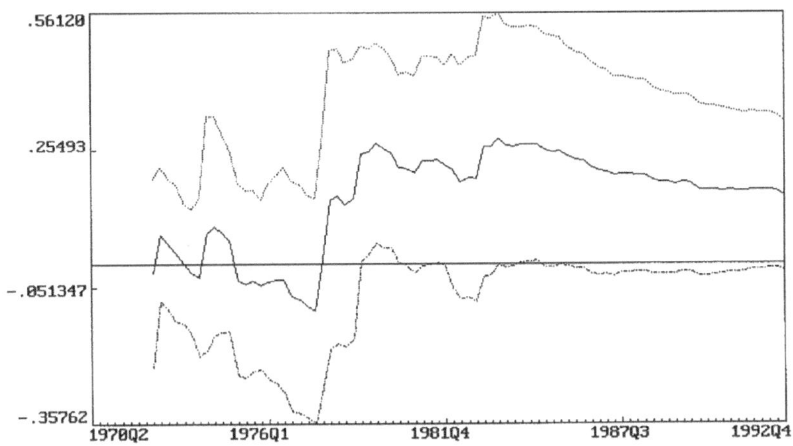

Panel 7.4 The coefficient of ΔM in Eq. 7.16 and its 2 S.E. bands based on recursive LS *source* Ghartey (1998), Journal of Development Economics

in CUSUMSQ Panels 7.3 and 7.4, respectively, suggests that the money stock in the demand for money is endogenous.

7.8 Summary

The traditional demand for money function is specified for empirical study of an open economy in developing countries by adding a variable which captures foreign sector to the standard demand for money. This has necessitated that we use Ghartey (1998) to discuss the empirical model used in developing countries. The long-run demand for money is cash balances expressed as a function of real income, prices, real effective exchange rate, and seasonal dummies which is sourced from Ghartey (1998). The error-correction model of demand for money is developed from a disequilibrium model. Estimates of error-correction model of the demand for money is used to identify and discuss the long-run demand for money and associated short-run dynamics. The estimated error-correction equation of the demand for money is inverted to obtain price and real income equations. The resulting inverted price and real income equations are used to test weak-form exogeneity or endogeneity of price and real income by testing the significance or insignificance of their respective error-correction terms.

Having established that price and real income are weak-form exogenous in the demand for money equation, we tested for the stability of price and real income in the demand for money equation. The error-correction model of the demand for money equation is used to test for price homogeneity and unit real income properties. The inverted price and real income error-correction equations are used to test for price homogeneity and unit elasticity of the real income properties of the demand for money, and the structural instability of the recursive residual of coefficient of the regressor of growth in money stock in inverted equations of price and real income. Furthermore, the structural stability of the coefficients of both price and real income in the demand for money equations show that both price and real income regressors in the demand for money in Ghana are super exogenous, and the money supply in the demand for money equation is endogenous.

7.9 Problems

(7.1) Partial adjustment of demand for money in an open economy is expressed by some researchers as follows:

$$\log M_t = \log M_{t-1} + \theta\left(\log M^*_{t-1} - \log M_{t-1}\right)$$

where $0 < \theta \leq 1$ is the speed of adjustment. The demand for desired money is given as $m_t^* = M_t^*/P_t$.

Describe the operational econometric procedure you will use to estimate the elasticity of the real income (y_t) or λ_1, the real interest rate (i_t) or λ_2, and the speed of adjustment θ by using time series data from the IMF's IFS data. Hint: $m_t^* = \lambda_0 + \lambda_1 y_t - \lambda_2 i_t$ and the parameters are the respective elasticities.

(7.2) The desired demand for money in an open economy is

$$\log M_t = \alpha_0 + \alpha_1 \log y_t + \alpha_2 \log p_t - \alpha_1 \log xr_t$$

where y_t is the real income or output, p_t is the price level, xr is the exchange rate, and M_t is the money supply with all parameters being nonnegative.

What is the elasticity of demand for money with respect to transactions or real income?

What is the elasticity of demand for money with respect to prices?

What is the elasticity of demand for money with respect to the real exchange rate?

(7.3) The estimated error-correction model is expressed as follows:

$$\begin{aligned}\Delta\log\cdot M_t = & -0.175[1.995] + 0.244[1.721]\Delta\log\cdot y_t \\ & + 0.453[3.496]\Delta\log\cdot p_t - 0.067[2.611]\Delta\log\cdot xr_t \\ & - 0.075[1.713]\log EC_{t-1} - 0.002[0.475]\Delta\log\cdot xr_{t-1} \\ & + 0.032[0.432]\Delta\log\cdot p_{t-1} + 0.051[2.913]s_2 \\ & + 0.209[11.725]s_4 \end{aligned} \tag{7.17}$$

$$\begin{aligned} & N = 90,\ R^2 = 0.65,\ F(8, 81) = 21.734, \\ & DW = 1.837,\ SEE = 0.065,\ \chi^2_{SC}(4) = 6.006, \\ & \chi^2_{FF}(1) = 1.074,\ \chi^2_{N}(2) = 2.273, \\ & \chi^2_{H}(1) = 0.008,\ \text{and } EC_{t-1} = m_{t-1} - p_{t-1} - y_{t-1}. \end{aligned}$$

What is the error-correction term?

What is the dynamic stability of the estimated error-correction model?

Write a general inverted price equation of the error-correction model of demand for money of the type expressed in Eq. 7.17 above.

(7.4) Define and/or explain the following terms and concepts:

(a) price homogeneity of the demand for money
(b) weak-form exogeneity of real income of the demand for money
(c) super exogeneity of price in the demand for money
(d) error-correction model

(7.5) Imagine yourself as an expert in international macroeconomics, describe the operation procedure you will employ to ensure that the demand for money in the country you are advising has a weak-form exogenous price and real income as explanatory variables in its estimated demand for money.

Selected References

Barro, Robert. J. (1987). *Macroeconomics,* (New York: Wiley and Sons Inc.).

Engle, R.F. and C.W.J. Granger (1987), "Cointegration and error-correction: representation, estimation and testing," *Econometrica*, 55: 251–769.

Ghartey, Edward E. (1998), "Monetary dynamics in Ghana: evidence from cointegration, error-correction modelling, and exogeneity," *Journal of Development Economics*, 57: 473–486.

Hausman, J.A. (1978), "Specification tests in econometrics," *Econometrica*, 46: 1251–1272.

Hendry, D.F. and Ericsson, N.R. (1991), "An econometric analysis of U.K. money demand in monetary trends in the United Kingdom by Milton Friedman and Anna J. Schwartz," *The American Economic Review*, 81 (1): 8–38.

Lucas, Robert E. (1976), Jr., "Econometric policy evaluations: a critique," in *The Phillips curve and labor markets*, Karl Brunner and Allan H. Meltzer, eds. (Amsterdam: North-Holland).

McCallum, Bennett T. (1989), *Monetary Economics: Theory and Policy*, (New York: Macmillan Publishing Company).

Wu, D.M. (1973), "Alternative tests of independence between stochastic regressors and disturbances," *Econometrica*, 41: 733–750.

CHAPTER 8

The IS and MP Curves, and Aggregate Demand Curve

Learning Outcomes

By the close of the chapter readers and students must gain mastery in the topic to do the following:

(1) Define and explain the following terms and concepts:

(i) transfer payments	(ii) net taxes	(iii) accelerator principle
(iv) financial friction	(v) animal spirit	(vi) Fisher's effect
(vii) Taylor's rule	(viii) monetary policy principle	(ix) IS curve
(x) aggregate demand	(xi) marginal propensity to consume	

(2) Explain factors which influence investments, the IS curve, and AD curve.
(3) List the factors which shift the IS curve, and AD curve.
(4) Compare Taylor's rule and the monetary policy principle.
(5) Derive the IS curve, MPC curve, and AD curve.
(6) Explain why the Hicks LM curve fails to serve as a reliable tool in explaining inflation dynamics for conducting macroeconomic policy analysis.

E. E. Ghartey, *International Macroeconomics and Finance*,
https://doi.org/10.1007/978-3-032-04145-6_8

8.1 Introduction

Keynesian General Theory, which pioneered the economic discipline of macroeconomics, was powered by Hick's IS-LM curves' gadget, to serve as the work horse of fiscal and monetary policy, to drive the world's economic recovery from the great depression, which the world economy experienced, after the World War II. However, it has become necessary to redress the deficiency which mars the IS-LM gadget, which is the LM curve. We have attempted to do so by relying on the monetary policy curve, which is a variant of Taylor's rule, to develop the aggregate demand in the Keynesian General Theory and Hicks' gadget. In this chapter, we have adopted the IS curve; and the LM curve which addresses the problem in the gadget, is discussed in the ensuing Chapter 9.

8.2 The IS Curve

The goods market consists of four sectors, namely: consumption sector, business sector, public sector, and foreign sector. The public sector includes government expenditure and taxes. In the tradition of Keynes (1936), the government expenditure is treated as an exogenous variable, while net taxes and the rest of the sectors are treated as behavioral equations.

8.3 Consumption Sector

The consumption sector is explained by the behavior of households. It is important to know that people who work with the government and public institutions are referred to as part of the government or public sector. However, the same people in their role as parents and decision makers as households are regarded as part of the private sector. In the General Theory, Keynes (1936) who pioneered the role of government activities in solving the massive unemployment which emerged during the Great Depression in the Second World War, and its aftermath, explained consumption as a function of autonomous consumption and the proportion of income consumed. Thus,

$$C = C_0 + C_1 \mathrm{YD}, 0 < C_1 < 1 \tag{8.1}$$

where, C_0 is autonomous consumption, which is independent of income, and C_1 is marginal propensity to consume (mpc), which is the fraction of disposable income consumed. YD = (Y – T) is disposable income which is real income (Y) after net taxes (T). Net taxes comprise of total direct taxes plus total indirect taxes minus transfer payments. Example of direct taxes are income taxes, while example of indirect taxes are sales taxes or general consumption taxes (GCT). Transfer payments are payments made to unemployed workers. Examples are welfare benefits, social security benefits to name two.

The disposable income can also be split up into consumption and saving. The saving function is expressed as

$$\begin{aligned} S &= \mathrm{YD} - C_0 - C_1 \cdot \mathrm{YD} \\ &= -C_0 + (1 - C_1) \cdot \mathrm{YD} \end{aligned} \tag{8.2}$$

where, the marginal propensity to save (mps) is (1 – mpc). The saving function relates to both income and interest rate. The square root formula of demand for money, which is also known as transaction demand for money, assumes that individual's monthly incomes are paid directly into their bank accounts. Thus, any income left in the depositor's banking account after withdrawing money from his/her banking account, which is saving account, earns interest. The saving function grows with income and is likely to increase with the expectation of increasing future consumption.

This means that both savings and consumptions are dependent on both income and interest rates. However, whereas increase in disposable income results in an increase in consumption and saving, increase in interest rate may not necessarily result in an increase in saving, and hence it causes a decrease in consumption. Furthermore, both consumption and saving are also likely to be non-linear, so in this respect, the consumption function and saving function can be generally expressed as

$$C = C(Y - T,\ i), 0 < C_1 < 1, \text{ and } C_2 < 0 \tag{8.3}$$

$$S = S(Y - T, i), 0 < S_1 < 1, \text{ and } S_2 < \text{ or } > 0 \tag{8.4}$$

where, $C_1 = \partial C(\ldots)/\partial \mathrm{YD}$ is the partial differential of C with respect to Y – T, and $C_2 = \partial C(\ldots)/\partial i$ is the partial differential of C with respect to i.

8.4 Business Investments Sector

Business firms are the principal group that engages in gross domestic private investments (I) in the economy. I consist of fixed investments (I^f) and changes in inventory stock (Δinv). Fixed investments comprise of planned investments spending in (a) buildings, (b) other construction works, (c) machinery and other equipment, (d) transportation, and (e) new residential buildings. In a static economy, a unit increase in capital stock (Δk) results in change in output (ΔY) which is known as the marginal productivity of capital (mpk). Thus, from the accelerator principle, an increase in real output results in increase in investment spending on capital.

Business firms compare the mpk or marginal efficiency of capital (mec) to the sum of real interest rate (i), which is the cost of borrowing and appropriate risk premium to decide whether to expand by borrowing from lenders. It is, therefore, reasonable that business firms increase their investment spending to grow their business by borrowing from lenders when i is low relative to the mpk. The behavioral equation of I is expressed as

$$I = I_0 - d_1 \cdot i_B + d_2 \cdot Y \tag{8.5}$$

where, I_0 is autonomous investment, i_B is interest rate of investments spending by business firms, d_1 is responsiveness of investments to interest rate of investments, and d_2 is marginal propensity to invest.

The interest rate of investments is a function of interest rates central banks pay on default free Treasury securities (i) and financial friction (ff). See Mishkin (2016). The ff is the cost of inefficiency in the financial market which stems from barriers to efficient functioning in the financial market due to asymmetric information, adverse selection, and moral hazard problems. It is expressed as

$$i_B = i + \text{ff} \tag{8.6}$$

Substituting Eq. (8.6) for i_B into Eq. (8.5) yields

$$I = I_0 - d_1 \cdot (i + \text{ff}) + d_2 \cdot Y = I_0 - d_1 \cdot \text{ff} - d_1 \cdot i + d_2 \cdot Y,\ d_1 > 0, 0 < d_2 < 1 \tag{8.7}$$

The non-linear form of Eq. (8.7) is as follows:

$$I = I(i, \text{ff}, Y, I_0), I_1 < 0, I_2 < 0, 0 < I_3 < 1 \text{ and } I_4 > 0 \tag{8.8}$$

Equation (8.7) which is generalized in non-linear form in Eq. (8.8) shows that increase in both the cost of borrowing and financial friction drags down investments, while increase in real income and optimistic business outlook of the market drive up investments.

It must be emphasized that the autonomous investment (I_0) is investment which is exogenous in the model. It is described by Keynes (1936) to be driven by emotional waves of optimism and pessimism which he termed as animal spirit. In Eq. (8.8) we have described it as emotional waves of optimism, hence it drives economic growth. In recent past, we can liken it to the role of computers in the economic growth of the 1990s.

8.5 Government Sector

The public (or government) sector is the sector controlled by the government. Following Keynes (1936) we have treated government spending as an autonomous policy variable (G_0) controlled by the government which is exogenous and independent of Y, i, and p. However, in the real business cycle, government purchase shocks change the quantity of goods available to the private economy for a given level of production, so like technological shocks, it is a real variable. The net tax is also assumed to be a function of autonomous taxes (T_0) and income in our analysis. They are specified as

$$G = G_0 \tag{8.9}$$

$$T = T_0 + T_1 Y, 0 < T_1 < 1 \tag{8.10}$$

Non-linear specification of net taxes is as follows:

$$T = T(y), 0 < T_1 < 1 \tag{8.11}$$

8.6 Foreign Sector

The foreign sector comprises of imports, exports, and current account balance. To simplify the analysis for the derivation of the IS curve, we have confined the model to the goods market. The net export (NX) is the difference between exports and imports of goods and services. Instead of specifying behavioral equations for imports and exports, we have specified net exports as a function of autonomous net export (NX_0), which is exogenous and is independent of interest rates, real income and prices, and a portion of net exports which is influenced by the real interest rates and real income.

Net export is therefore explained by autonomous net export (NX_0), real interest rate, and real income. Although increase in foreign real income results in increase in domestic exports whereas increase in real income results in increase in imports, in this analysis we have assumed that its effect is autonomous in the model. We have specified the behavioral equation of net exports[1] as

$$NX = NX_0 - e_1 \cdot i - e_2 \cdot Y, e_1 > 0, 0 < e_2 < 1 \tag{8.12}$$

where, e_1 is the responsiveness of NX with respect to interest rate, and e_2 is the marginal product of net export which is the fraction of income that originates from net exports. The NX_0 part decreases with a decrease in exports and increase in imports. Thus, if natural disaster like poor weather or bugs affect the domestic export products like sugar canes, cocoa, coffee, to name a few, exports earnings of the country decrease. Additionally, if imports increase because of improvement in taste for foreign wines, and manufactured products such as cars and computer gadgets, autonomous net exports decrease.

8.6.1 Derivation of the Keynesian multiplier and the IS curve

8.6.1.1 Geometric Perspective

The multiplier is derived both geometrically and algebraically. In the geometrical derivation we employ the diagram in Panel 8.1 by considering the right-angle triangles ABE and ABD. Angles EAB and BEA are

[1] See Ghartey (1987) for other specifications of exports and imports equations for Ghana.

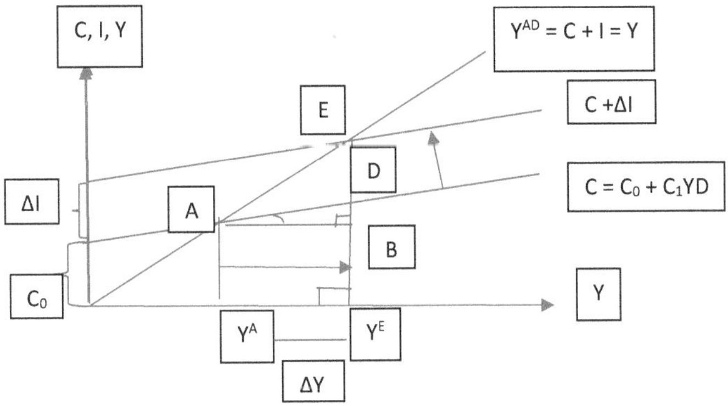

Panel 8.1 Deriving the multiplier with the aid of the Keynesian cross diagram

equal, and both are 45° which makes the right-angle triangle ABE an isosceles triangle. ||AB|| = ||BE|| and ||BE|| = ||BD|| + ||DE||.

Let angle DAB = α, so Tanα = ||DB||/||AB|| which is the slope of right angled ΔDAB. But ||AB|| = ΔY, ||DE|| = ΔI, and ||DB|| = |AB|| Tanα = $C_1\Delta Y$. So, ΔY = $\Delta I + C_1\Delta Y$ and ΔY = $\Delta I/(1 - C_1)$. The multiplier is ΔY/$\Delta I = 1/(1 - C_1)$.

8.6.1.2 *Algebraic Perspective*

Alternatively, the multiplier can be derived algebraically if businesses increase investment by an initial unit change (ΔI). Assuming C_1 as the marginal propensity to consume in the economy, the initial unit change in investment will result in a unit change in real output (ΔY). Thus, real output will change as follows:

$$\Delta Y = \Delta I + C_1\Delta I + C_1^2\Delta I + \ldots = \Delta I\left(1 + C_1 + C_1^2 + \ldots\right) = \Delta I/(1-C_1).$$

Thus, the multiplier which is always greater than unity is as follows:

$$\Delta Y/\Delta I = 1/(1-C_1)$$

where, the mpc denoted by C_1 which is a fraction of income that is consumed, lies between zero and unity, and ensure stability.

Real interest rates affect net exports through its effect on the value of the national currency or the exchange rate. See Chapter 3. For instance, increase in interest rates results in financial inflows which then cause appreciation of the domestic currency. This then causes price of foreign import to drop relative to domestic price of substitutes, which increases our demand for imports and net exports fall. Thus, appreciation makes foreign goods cheaper for domestic residents, so they demand more of foreign goods and net exports drop.

Additionally, a decrease in interest rates resulting from an expansionary monetary policy causes depreciation of the national currency, which makes domestic goods cheaper to foreigners. *All other things being equal*, demand for our exports increases while price of foreign import rises, which reduces local demand for imports, and this causes net exports to increase. Subsequently, real income rises.

Non-linear specification of net exports is as follows:

$$\mathrm{NX} = \mathrm{NX}(\mathrm{NX}_0, i, Y), \mathrm{NX}_1 > 0, \mathrm{NX}_2 < 0, 0 < \mathrm{NX}_3 < 1 \tag{8.13}$$

Using the definition of GDP from expenditure side in Eq. (1.5) and Keynes (1936), in real terms, aggregate output (Y) can be equated to planned expenditure when the economy is in equilibrium. This equilibrium is expressed as

$$Y = Y^{\mathrm{AD}} \tag{8.14}$$

So, given that planned aggregate expenditure of GDP (Y^{AD}) is from Eqs. (8.1), (8.7), (8.8), (8.10), and (8.12), we obtain the following:

$$\begin{aligned} Y^{\mathrm{AD}} &= C_0 + C_1(Y - T_0 - T_1 Y) + I_0 - d_1 \cdot \mathrm{ff} \\ &\quad - d_1 \cdot i + d_2 \cdot Y + G_0 + \mathrm{NX}_0 - e_1 \cdot i - e_2 \cdot Y \end{aligned} \tag{8.15}$$

At equilibrium in the goods market, we have

$$\begin{aligned} Y &= C_0 + C_1(Y - T_0 - T_1 Y) + I_0 - d_1 \cdot \mathrm{ff} \\ &\quad - d_1 \cdot i + d_2 \cdot Y + G_0 + \mathrm{NX}_0 - e_1 \cdot i - e_2 \cdot Y \end{aligned} \tag{8.16}$$

Solution of the above equation obtained by making Y the dependent variable is as follows:

$$\begin{aligned} &Y - C_1 Y + C_1 T_1 Y - d_2 Y + e_2 \cdot Y = \mathrm{C}_0 - C_1 T_0 + I_0 + G_0 \\ &+ \mathrm{NX}_0 - d_1 \cdot \mathrm{ff} - d_1 \cdot i - e_1 \cdot i[1 - C_1(1 - T_1) - d_2 + e_2] \cdot \end{aligned}$$

$$Y = (C_0 - C_1 T_0 + I_0 + G_0 + \mathrm{NX}_0 - d_1 \cdot \mathrm{ff}) - (d_1 + e_1) \cdot i$$
$$Y = (C_0 - C_1 T_0 + I_0 + G_0 + \mathrm{NX}_0 - d_1 \cdot \mathrm{ff})/[1 - C_1(1 - T_1) - d_2 + e_2]$$
$$-(d_1 + e_1) \cdot i/[1 - C_1(1 - T_1) - d_2 + e_2] \quad (8.17)$$

The solution of equation Y reported in Eq. (8.17) shows the denominator to be positive $[1 - C_1(1 - T_1) - d_2 + e_2] > 0$. Autonomous increase in consumption, investments, government spending, and net exports augments income, whereas increase in autonomous taxes and financial friction decreases income.

Equation (8.17) shows a negative slope relationship between real interest rate and real income. This negative relationship between real income and real interest rate occurs when the goods market is in equilibrium. The resulting curve is known as the IS curve. See John Hicks (1937).

The above relationship has been derived from simple linear functions, but the IS curve can be derived from non-linear functions. It is defined as the loci of points representing real interest rate and real output which occur when the goods market is in equilibrium or saving is equal to investment.

The movement from i_0 to i_1 which results in the real output increasing from Y_1 to Y_2 is what is described as the movement along the IS curve. See Panel 8.2. Note that anything which causes either i or Y moving is a factor that moves along the IS curve. This must be differentiated from factors which cause the IS curve to shift either upward or downward. See Panel 8.3.

8.7 Factors that Shift the IS Curve

All the autonomous factors and financial friction shift the IS curve. The causal direction resulting in increase in autonomous consumptions, investments, government spending, and net exports and a decrease in financial friction and autonomous taxes and improvement in taste and optimistic business outlook shift the IS curve outward, and the converse holds true. However, changes in interest rate and income result in movement along the IS curve, See Panels 8.2, 8.3, and 8.6.

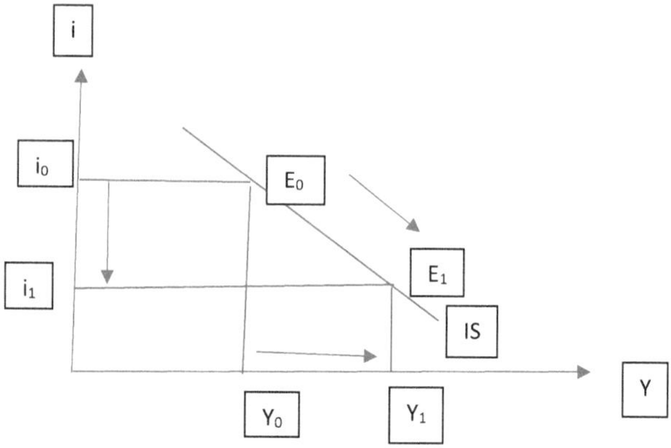

Panel 8.2 Movement along the IS curve

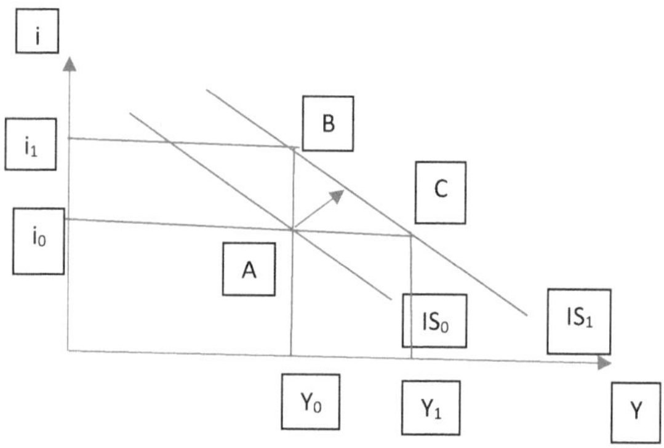

Panel 8.3 The effect of increase in C_0, I_0, G_0, and NX_0 on the IS curve

8.8 The Monetary Policy Curve (MPC)

The IS curve is normally combined with the LM curve to develop the aggregate demand curve, see John R. Hicks (1937) and John M. Keynes (1936). The LM curve is defined as the loci of points representing the real interest rate and the real output which occurs when the money market is at equilibrium. However, the LM curve has the limitations of assuming prices to be fixed in comparative static equilibrium policy analysis. It allows real output and real interest rates to change along the LM curve without affecting prices.

Consequently, because of this serious limitation, among others, in the LM curve analysis, we have found it necessary to revise the role of the LM curve in the derivation of the aggregate demand curve with the MPC as a substitute. This change corrects the afore-mentioned shortcomings of the LM curve in the derivation of the aggregate demand curve. The MPC is derived from the Fisher's effect and the Taylor's rule. The Fisher's effect is a relationship among real interest rate (i), the nominal interest rate (r), and expected inflation. See Irving Fisher (1930). It is expressed as[2]

$$r = i + \pi^e \tag{8.18}$$

Equation (8.18) is re-arranged as

$$i = r - \pi^e \tag{8.19}$$

where, i is real interest rate, r is nominal interest rate, and π^e is expected inflation.

In the short-term prices are sluggish downward and so is expected inflation. The central bank's control over the inter-bank rate or 91-day Treasury bill rate or federal fund rate, either of which is a nominal interest rate, has one-to-one effect on the real interest rate. Thus, contractionary monetary policy increases the inter-bank rate in the short-term as prices and expectation are sluggish downward.

The increase in the nominal interest rate also causes increase in the real interest rate which reduces real investments. The reduction in investments also reduces real output which also reduce prices and inflation. On the other hand, expansionary monetary policy reduces the cost of borrowing or the interest rate of short-term debt instruments. This encourages investments which promotes increase in real output and further increase in prices to fuel inflation. Thus, expansionary monetary policy tends to exacerbate inflation and deflation.

The Taylor's rule is a rule of the central bank's reaction to the state of economy. However, the Taylor principle, which we refer to as monetary

[2] Note that we have reversed the standard notations for interest rate because we want to maintain the fact that we have defined i as the real interest rate and r as the nominal interest rate in the Keynesian phase of the discussion presented in the earlier discussion of this chapter. Cf. Frederic S. Mishkin (2016).

policy principle, is a principle for setting interest rate to stabilize prices or inflation. It is consistent with the Keynesian liquidity preference model where market forces are dependent upon to correct the inflationary disturbance. Schematically, the stability of the Keynesian liquidity preference model and the monetary policy principle, respectively, are as follows:

$$\uparrow \pi \rightarrow \uparrow p \rightarrow \uparrow M^D \rightarrow \uparrow r \rightarrow \uparrow i \rightarrow \downarrow I \rightarrow \downarrow Y \rightarrow \downarrow p \rightarrow \downarrow \pi \text{ or}$$

$$\uparrow \pi \rightarrow \uparrow p \rightarrow \downarrow M^S \rightarrow \uparrow r \rightarrow \uparrow i \rightarrow \downarrow I \rightarrow \downarrow Y \rightarrow \downarrow p \rightarrow \downarrow \pi.$$

Thus, we can see that if the central bank follows the Taylor or monetary policy principle[3] by increasing the inter-bank interest rate or short-term debt instrument rate proportionately higher than the rate of the corresponding inflation, investment will fall, which will also reduce real output and cause prices and inflation to also fall. Thus, adherence to the said principle stabilizes the initial inflation.

In fact, we advocate that in developing countries, which tend to be (a) highly open economies, (b) price takers in the world economy, (c) producers of a few raw materials, and (d) have under-developed financial market, using the real interest rate as the operating target is likely to yield weaker effect on its economic goals. This is not to mention the fact that using exchange rate as operating policy instrument is not subject to the zero lower bound limitation of interest rate. In fact, we suggest that

[3] We have introduced the term monetary policy principle (MPP) as a substitute for Taylor's principle, because unlike the latter's principle which employs interest rate on short-term debt instruments such as federal fund rate or 91-Day Treasury bill rate (TBR) or policy rate as operating or policy instrument to influence intermediate policy instruments, the MPP is consistent with using either short-term debt instruments or exchange rate as operating or policy instruments. In most developing countries including the US, replacing the inter-bank interest rate or federal fund rate or policy rate or the 91-Day TBR with exchange rate often yielded more effective operating or policy instrument; because it is much easier to access the foreign exchange market, than the T-bills rate at the central bank's open market in the short-term money market. Additionally, the effect of exchange rate as an operating or policy instrument is more effective than using interest rates as operating or policy instrument as it can be observed from magnitude of estimated results in Table 8.1. This can be inferred from the effect of the size of the magnitude of estimated coefficients of exchange rates in bold letters (or interest rates) on inflation and deflation goals shown in Table 8.1, which was summarized from Ghartey (2018). The magnitude of coefficients of effect of exchange rate on economic goals such as inflation, stable prices and deflation are bigger than the effect of corresponding magnitude of real 91-Day T Bills rate effect on inflation and deflation in all five countries including the US. See Table 8.1 or Ghartey (2018).

policymakers can strengthen the stabilizing policy in the financial market by substituting exchange rate for real interest rate as the operating policy instrument in what I term as exchange rate principle. Schematically, the exchange rate principle is expressed as follows:

$$\uparrow \pi \rightarrow \uparrow p \rightarrow \downarrow M^S \rightarrow \uparrow r \text{ or } \downarrow \text{RXR (appreciation)}$$
$$\rightarrow \uparrow i \rightarrow \downarrow I \text{ or NX} \rightarrow \downarrow Y \rightarrow \downarrow p \rightarrow \downarrow \pi$$

Thus, the effect of the policy is a reversal or contraction of the inflation rate (or stabilization of the inflation rate).

On the contrary, the economy will be destabilized, if the central bank decides to embark on either an expansionary monetary policy to reduce the real cost of borrowing brought about by the inflation and prices increase or depreciate the real exchange rate. Schematically, such policy stance will yield the following destabilizing results:

$$\uparrow \pi \rightarrow \uparrow p \rightarrow \uparrow M^S \rightarrow \downarrow r \text{ or } \uparrow \text{RXR (depreciation)}$$
$$\rightarrow \downarrow i \rightarrow \uparrow I \text{ or NX} \rightarrow \uparrow Y \rightarrow \uparrow p \rightarrow \uparrow \pi.$$

8.9 Monetary Policy Response and Influence on Inflation

The reaction of monetary policy to inflation indicates the relationship between the real interest rate and inflation or price changes. This relationship is referred to as the monetary policy curve (MPC) and it is expressed as

$$i = r_0 + \mu\pi, \mu > 0 \tag{8.20}$$

where, r_0 is exogenous or autonomous component of the real interest. It is set by the central bank, and it is independent of any variable in the model, especially inflation rate. Thus, the real interest rate is responsive to inflation, and μ is its degree of responsiveness to inflation and it is nonnegative.

If we assume that $r_0 = 5$ and that μ is 0.5, the MPC becomes

$$i_0 = 5 + 0.5\pi \tag{8.21}$$

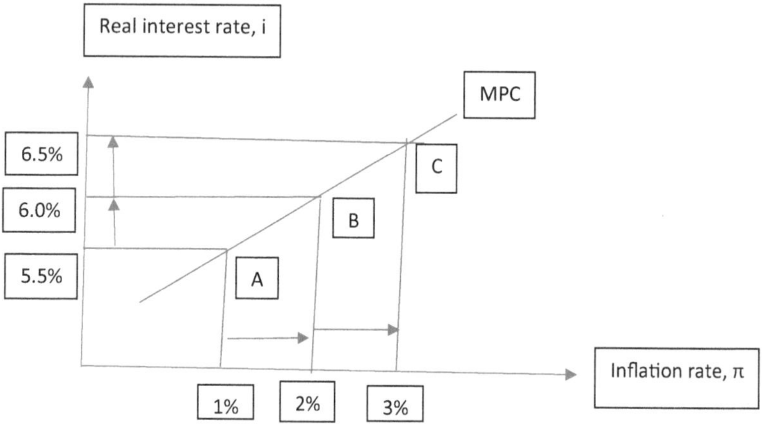

Panel 8.4 The MP curve

The MPC is upward slope. It shows that central banks react to inflation by raising the real interest rate when inflation increase by more than the initial increase in inflation. See Panel 8.4.

Panel 8.5 shows the effect of increase in inflation at point A on the initial MPC_0 curve at inflation rate of π_0 and corresponding real interest rate of i_0. A contractionary monetary policy causes the MPC curve to shift upward or leftward to MPC_1. On the initial MPC_0 curve, the increase in the inflation rate moves along the curve to π_1 which correspond to real interest rate of i_1 at point B. The loci of points at A and B are (π_0, i_0) and (π_1, i_1), respectively, and when traced in the interest rate and real output (y, i) space, it yields the IS curve, which is the equilibrium points A and B in the goods market depicted in Panel 8.6.

8.10 The Aggregate Demand Curve

The aggregate demand (AD) is a relationship between either price or inflation rates and real output which occurs when the goods market is in equilibrium. Point A has the locus of (i_0, Y_0) in Panel 8.6, and the locus of (i_0, π_0) in Panel 8.5. This gives us locus of (π_0, Y_0) at point A on the aggregate demand curve. Again, point B also has the locus of (i_1, Y_1) in Panel 8.6, and the locus of (i_1, π_1) in Panel 8.5. This also gives a locus (π_1, Y_1) at point B on the aggregate demand curve in Panel 8.7.

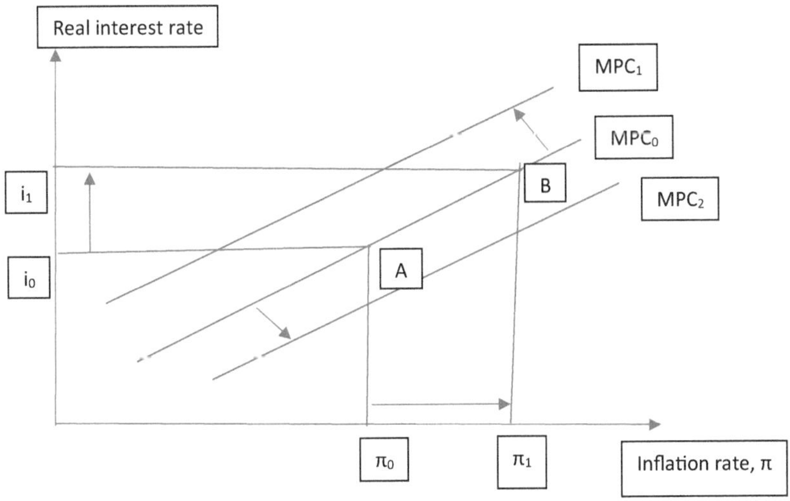

Panel 8.5 Shifts in the MPC

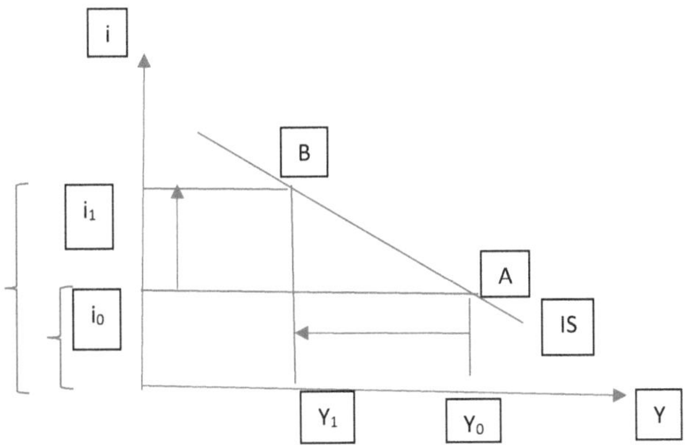

Panel 8.6 The IS curve traced from points A and B using the real interest rates

The loci of points A and B on the aggregate demand curve is plotted on the space of π and Y to obtain the aggregate demand curve shown in Panels 8.7, 8.8 and 8.9.

Algebraic derivation of the aggregate demand curve is obtained by substituting the real interest rate i in the MPC Eq. (8.20) into the IS

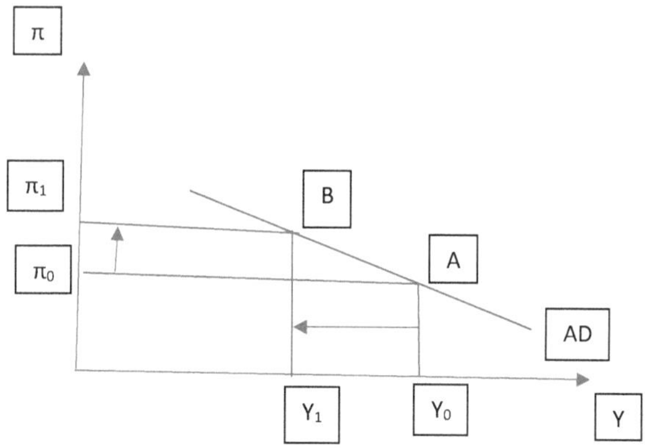

Panel 8.7 Derived Aggregate Demand Curve.in (π, Y) space

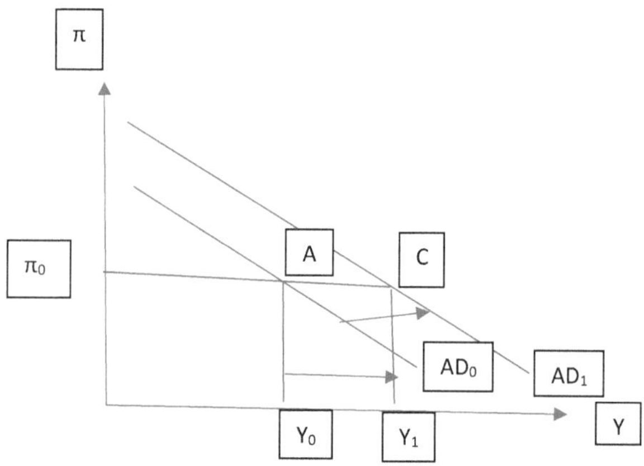

Panel 8.8 Increase in autonomous consumption C_0 shifts the AD curve rightward

curve Eq. (8.17). This yielded the following AD curve which is a negative relationship between Y and π:

$$\begin{aligned} Y = {} & (C_0 - C_1 T_0 + I_0 + G_0 + \mathrm{NX}_0 - d_1 \cdot \mathrm{ff})/[1 - C_1(1 - T_1) - d_2 + e_2] \\ & -(d_1 + e_1) \cdot (r_0 + \mu\pi)/[1 - C_1(1 - T_1) - d_2 + e_2] \end{aligned} \tag{8.22}$$

or

$$
\begin{aligned}
Y = & \left[C_0 - C_1 T_0 + I_0 + G_0 + \mathrm{NX}_0 - d_1 \cdot \mathrm{ff} \ - (d_1 + e_1) \cdot r_0\right] \\
& /[1 - C_1(1 - T_1) - d_2 + e_2] - [(d_1 + e_1) \cdot \mu]\pi \\
& /[1 - C_1(1 - T_1) - d_2 + e_2]
\end{aligned} \tag{8.23}
$$

8.10.1 *Effectiveness of Exchange Rate Targeting Policy Versus Interest Rate Targeting Policy*

In Table 8.1, we have presented non-linear asymmetric cointegration results on the effectiveness of interest rate as an operating or policy instrument, versus exchange rate as an operating or policy instrument to control economic goals such as inflation, deflation, price stability, stable exchange rate, stable interest rate, to name a few. Five countries, namely: The Bahamas, Belize, Ghana, Jamaica, which are emerging markets or developing countries, and US, a developed country are estimated to determine which of the two operating or policy instruments is effective in controlling economic goals, especially those mentioned above. See also Ghartey (2018).

We employed a non-linear autoregressive distributed lag model to estimate long-run (or reaction asymmetry) and short-term (or impact asymmetry) models[4] to determine the dynamic effect of exchange rate principle and Taylor's principle in four developing countries and the US, the leading developed country.

We employed secondary high frequency quarterly data spanning 1995Q1–2016Q2 in our study for The Bahamas, Belize, and Jamaica. The data is sourced from International Standard Organization Country Code Indicators, World Bank. Quarterly data is also used for the US spanning the same period, which is sourced from the website of FRED in St. Louis. However, in Ghana, we used monthly data spanning 1990M1–2016M9 which is sourced from the website of Bank of Ghana. Estimated results of Table 8.1 show that a unit increase in real 91-day TB rate in the US increases its rising prices by 0.6% and by 1.7% in Belize; whereas the same unit increase in TB rates reduces inflation by 4.5% in Ghana, 9.8% in Jamaica, and 0.5% in The Bahamas.

[4] See Borenstein et al. (1997), Apergis and Miller (2006), Shin et al. (2011), Schorderet (2001) and Granger and Yoon (2002).

Table 8.1 Effectiveness of interest rate versus exchange rate operating or policy instruments

	Regressors	*Inflation* (p^+)	*Deflation* (p^-)
The Bahamas:	$rtbr^+$	−0.005(0.01)	−0.005(0.02)
		$BG\chi^2_{SC}(1) = 0.000(1.00)$, $BPG\ \chi^2_H(2) = 1.028(0.60)$,	
		$WT_{SR}\chi^2(2) = 12.389(0.00)$	
	$reer^+$	**0.171(0.00)**	**−0.159(0.00)**
		$BG\chi^2_{SC}(1) = 0.000(1.00)$, $BPG\ \chi^2_H(2) = 3.648(0.16)$,	
		$WT_{SR}\chi^2(2) = 35.813(0.00)$	
Belize	$rtbr^+$	0.017(0.66)	−0.015(0.29)
		$BG\chi^2_{SC}(1) = 0.000(1.00)$, $BPG\ \chi^2_H(2) = 0.172(0.92)$,	
		$WT_{SR}\chi^2(2) = 0.609(0.43)$	
	$reer^+$	**0.597(0.00)**	**−0.162(0.06)**
		$BG\chi^2_{SC}(1) = 7.870(0.00)$, $BPG\chi^2_H(2) = 58.660(0.00)$,	
		$WT_{SR}\chi^2(2) = 46.247(0.00)$, FMOLS	
Ghana	$rtbr^+$	−0.045(0.04)	−0.275(0.02)
		$BG\chi^2_{SC}(1) = 88.155(0.00)$, $BPG\chi^2_H(2) = 40.871(0.00)$,	
		$WT_{SR}\chi^2(1) = 51.290(0.00)$, FMOLS	
	$reer^+$	**0.039(0.08)**	**−0.861(0.00)**
		$BG\chi^2_{SC}(1) = 24.607(0.00)$, $BPG\chi^2_H(2) = 174.687(0.00)$,	
		$WT_{SR}\chi^2(1) = 100.522(0.00)$, FMOLS	

	Regressors	*Inflation* (p^{+})	*Deflation* (p^{-})
Jamaica	$rtbr^{+}$	−0.098(0.01)	−0.074(0.00)
		$BG\chi^2_{SC}(1) = 0.000(1.00)$, BPG $\chi^2_H(2) = 5.121(0.08)$,	
		$WT_{SR}\chi^2(2) = 33.090(0.00)$, FMOLS	
	$reer^{+}$	**0.722(0.00)**	**− 0.373(0.07),**
		$BG\chi^2_{SC}(1) = 0.325(0.57)$, $BPG\chi^2_H(2) = 0.395(0.82)$,	
		$WT_{SR}\chi^2(2) = 40.435(0.00)$	
USA	$rtbr^{+}$	0.006(0.02)	−0.004(0.04)
		$BG\chi^2_{SC}(1) = 0.000(1.00)$, $BPG\chi^2_H(2) = 0.274(0.87)$,	
		$WT_{SR}\chi^2(2) = 10.232(0.00)$, VS	
	$reer^{+}$	**0.128(0.00)**	**−0.221(0.00)**
		$BG\chi^2_{SC}(1) = 0.000(1.00)$, $BPG\chi^2_H(2) = 3.959(0.14)$,	
		$WT_{SR}\chi^2(2) = 29.849(0.00)$.	

Note Where p_t^{+} ($rtbr_t^{+}$ and rxr_t^{+}) is a partial sum of processes of positive changes (inflation), and p_t^{-} ($rtbr_t^{-}$ and rxr_t^{-}) is a partial sum of processes of negative changes (deflation). See Schorderet (2001), Granger and Yoon (2002), and Shin et al. (2011), and Ghartey (2019); tbr and rxr are logarithmic form of real 91 Day Treasury Bills rate and real effective exchange rate, respectively. $WT_{SR}\ \chi^2(1)$ is the χ^2 of short-term Wald Test, probability-values are reported in parentheses, although for χ^2 tests, degrees of freedom have been reported in parentheses. BG $\chi^2_{SC}(1)$ is Breusch-Godfrey's serial correlation LM test, BPG $\chi^2_H(2)^a$ Breusch-Pagan-Godfrey's heteroscedasticity test, FMOLS is fully modified Phillips and Hansen maximum likelihood estimator.

Source Presidential address at ASSA organized AFEA and AEA Meeting in Philadelphia, 2018

The Fisher's effect, which is an important tenet of the Taylor's principle, is a long-run phenomenon.[5]

It is therefore important that in modeling it, we maintain the long-run feature. Furthermore, since prices tend to be sluggish downward and/or remain the same in the short-term, but rise rather quickly, we have adopted a model that addresses such important feature to conduct the research. We also note that the response of inflation to the real interest rate and exchange rate tends to be different when prices are rising faster than when they are falling, while the effect of rising or declining inflation tends to either affect or be affected by rising and falling real interest rate and exchange rate differently.

Consequently, we have adopted a non-linear asymmetric cointegration model which addresses these important features discussed above to conduct the research. See Ghartey (2018) and summary of some results presented in Table 8.1.

Rising prices or inflation is significantly driven by depreciation in The Bahamas, Belize, Jamaica, Ghana, and the US. One percent depreciation drives inflation by 0.13% in the US, 0.72% in Jamaica, 0.60% in Belize, 0.17% in The Bahamas, and about 0.04% in Ghana. One percent appreciation reduces inflation significantly by 0.22% in the US, 0.86% in Ghana, 0.37% in Jamaica, and about 0.16% in both Belize and The Bahamas. Furthermore, 1% decline in the real 91-day TBR results in inflation declining by about 0.27% in Ghana, 0.07% in Jamaica, 0.01% in Belize which is insignificant, but has almost no effect in The Bahamas and the US. See Ghartey (2018).

Thus, the effectiveness of the use of appreciation in reducing inflation in all five countries with diverse level of development cannot be gainsaid. Considering that reducing inflation or maintaining stable prices is the chief among six monetary policy goals of central banks, adopting the real exchange rate as an operating or policy instrument, as proposed in the exchange rate principle, will effectively reduce inflation to achieve the goal of price stability, without encountering the problem of zero-bound limitation on interest rate which is associated with the practice of the Taylor's principle.

Exchange rate appreciation is the most effective means for reducing inflation in all five developing countries, and the US, as their empirical

[5] Studies that have modeled Fisher's effect as a short-term phenomenon have failed to yield significant results. See Mishkin (2016) and Fisher (1930).

results are significant, and have larger magnitudes relative to results from the real short-term interest rates in all the countries in the study. See the bold coefficients displayed in Table 8.1. We therefore propose that the exchange rate principle, where the real effective exchange rate is used as the operating or policy instrument, instead of short-term interest rates like the real 91-day TB rates, be used as operating or policy instrument to control and stabilize inflation in especially developing countries.

Additionally, developing countries do not have long-term bonds to serve as an intermediate target. Consequently, their central banks do not have long-term bonds to engineer short-term interest rates operating or policy instruments to effectively influence to achieve their realized monetary policy goal of reducing or stabilizing inflation. Exchange rate principle which employs exchange rate as operating or policy instrument does not suffer from the problems associated with zero nominal lower bound limitation on interest rate, which the Federal Reserve System was blamed for by critics, for relying too much on the Taylor principle.

8.11 Factors that Shift the AD Curve

The relationship between π and Y is the aggregate demand curve presented above in Eqs. (8.22 or 8.23). Factors that shift the AD curve upward or rightward are increase in autonomous C_0, I_0, G, NX_0, improvement in taste, optimistic business outlook, and a decrease in autonomous T_0, r_0, and ff; and the converse holds true. The fiscal policy instruments among the variables are G and T_0, and monetary policy instruments are r_0, and regulations relating to changes in ff.

Effect of an Increase in C_0 on the IS Curve.

The shift in the IS curve from IS_0 to IS_1 which can result from an increase in autonomous consumption, investment, government spending, net exports, and a decrease in autonomous taxes, also increases equilibrium output from Y_0 to Y_1. Their respective effect on aggregate demand is shown in Panel 8.7b. In both situations, at the same inflation rate, π_0, equilibrium output increases from Y_0 to Y_1.

8.12 Summary

The IS curve is developed both graphically and mathematically from the Keynesian model using the open economy. All factors which shift it are discussed with their directions of impact.

The monetary policy curve is derived from Fisher's effect and Taylor's rule.

Using the monetary policy principle, we demonstrated schematically to show that raising the real interest rate higher than the inflation rate stabilizes the latter.

We use the IS curve and the MP curve to derive the AD curve which shows a relationship between inflation and real output. We then split factors which shift the AD curve into fiscal policy and monetary policy, and their directional impact.

Appendix

Derivation of the LM Curve

Summary of Hicks (1937) rudimentary interpretation of Mr. Keynes and the "CLASSICS":

A. Classical Theory:

(i) Money demand: $M(y) = ky$, $M_1 > 0$ where $M_1 = \partial M(y)/\partial y$
Transaction demand

(ii) Investment: Inducement to invest in consumption or propensity to consume
$I = C(i)$
$I = S(i, y)$, $S_1 < 0$, $0 < S_2 < 1$ where $S_1 = \partial S(i, y)/\partial I$ and $S_2 = \partial S(\ldots)/\partial y$

(iii) Consumption: Income earned by trading in consumption
$I = C(i)$

(iv) Income (Y): Total income
$y = C(i) + S(i, y)$

B. Keynesian General Theory:

(v) Liquidity preference: $M(i) = L(i)$, $L_i < 0$ where $L_1 = \partial L(i)/\partial i$
Speculative demand

(vi) Investment
$I = C(i)$

(vii) Investment = Saving
$I = S(y)$, $0 < S_1 < 1$ where $S_1 = \partial S(y)/\partial y$

C. Hicks' Generalized General Theory:

Hicks considered two models, namely: the Classical model, and the Keynesian model. He revised them to obtain his Generalized General theory. Note that Hicks expressed his equations in a non-linear form.

Money demand: $M(i, y) = L(i, y)$, $L_1 < 0$, $0 < L_2 < 1$ where $L_1 = \partial L(i, y)/\partial i$ and $L_2 = \partial L(\ldots)/\partial y$

(viii) $I = C(i, y)$, and $I = S(i, y)$

(ix) Investment and Saving

(x) Income: $y = C(i, y) + S(i, y)$

In Hicks interpretation of Keynes' General Theory, he summarized the Classical Theory by using equations (i)–(iv). Equation (i) is the classical economists' emphasis that the motive for holding money is for transaction, which is expenditure mainly spent on transaction purpose. He captured it by an increase in real output, and as an inducement to invest or the effect of real income on the marginal efficiency of capital (mec) which is captured by interest rate. He accepted the classical notion that money is used mainly for transaction purpose which is driven by real income. However, he also included Keynes' revision in the General Theory in the tradition of Marshall which considered the quantity of money or the money demand to be influenced by speculative motive which is predominantly driven by interest rate, and transaction purpose motive. Consequently, he also included interest rate in the saving function in his invention of the gadget. We have set up Hicks' gadget by considering two markets, namely: the money market and the goods market which resulted in the invention of his gadget which included the LM curve and the IS curve derived below in C1 and C2.

C1 Money Market

Demand for money: $M(i, y) = L(i, y)$, $L_1 < 0$, $0 < L_2 < 1$

$$\text{Liquidity Preference}: M/P = \lambda_0 + \lambda_1 y - \lambda_2 i \tag{8.24}$$

$$\text{Money supply}: M^S \tag{8.25}$$

$$\text{At equilibrium}: M^D = M^S = M \tag{8.26}$$

Fixing price by setting $P = 1$, Eq. (8.24) becomes as follows:

$$M = \lambda_0 + \lambda_1 y - \lambda_2 i$$

The LM curve is:

$$y = (M - \lambda_0 + \lambda_2 i)(1/\lambda_1) \tag{8.27}$$

The above equation is the LM curve derived from using Hicks' gadget. It has a positive slope real interest rate.

C2 Goods Market

$$C(i, y), C_1 < 0, C_2 > 0 \tag{8.28}$$

$$C = c(i, y) = \alpha_0 + \alpha_1 y - \alpha_2 i \tag{8.29}$$

$$S(i, y), S_1 < 0, S_2 > 0$$
$$S = s(i, y) = \beta_0 + \beta_1 y - \beta_2 \cdot i \tag{8.30}$$

where,

$$Y = C + S \text{ or } y = c + s \tag{8.31}$$

From Eq. (8.31) we obtain

$$y = \alpha_0 + \alpha_1 y - \alpha_2 i + \beta_0 + \beta_1 y - \beta_2 i \tag{8.32}$$

$$y - (\alpha_1 + \beta_1)y = \alpha_0 + \beta_0 - (\beta_2 + \alpha_2)i$$
$$y = (\alpha_0 + \beta_0)/[1 - (\alpha_1 + \beta_1)] - (\alpha_1 + \beta_1) \cdot i/[1 - (\alpha_1 + \beta_1)] \tag{8.33}$$

where, $1 - (\alpha_1 + \beta_1) > 0$

The above Eq. (8.33) is Hicks' IS curve in a closed economy. It has a negative slope real interest rate, which means an increase in real interest rate results in a decrease in real output. See C2 and Panel 8.6 for derivation of the IS curve.

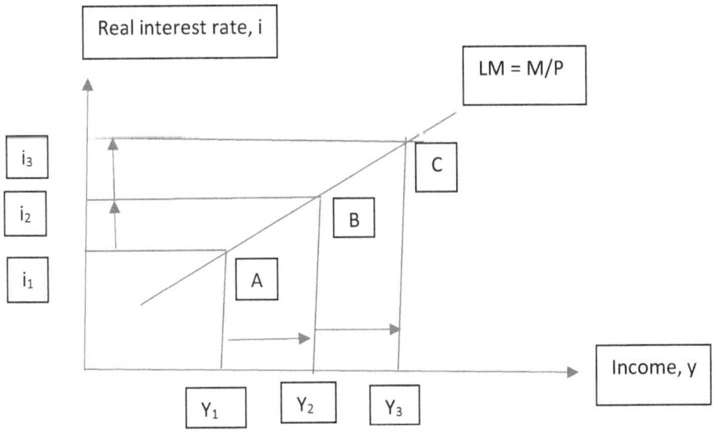

Panel 8.9 Graphic derivation of the LM curve from Eq. (8.27) of C1: Money Market

Limitations of the LM curve

An increase in government spending which causes the IS curve to shift from IS_0 to IS_1 results in the real interest rate rising from i_0 to i_1, and the real output increases from y_0 to y_1 while the price level remains the same at p_0. as it is shown in Panel 8.10. The fixed price level which remains the same when government spending changes is a major flaw of the LM curve. This major flaw means that the LM curve cannot be used to effect fiscal policy in the economy to address counterfactual policy analysis and scenarios to reflect inflation dynamics in the real world.

An increase in monetary policy which causes the LM curve to shift from $LM_0 = (M_0/p_0)$ to $LM_1 = (M_1/p_0)$ as the money supply increases from M_0 to M_1, results in the real interest rate falling from i_0 to i_1 and real output rising from y_0 to y_1 while prices remain at the same price before the increase in the money supply.[6] See Panel 8.11. This also is a major flaw in using the LM curve in Hicks' gadget to implement monetary policy in the economy.

[6] Prices remain the same in the analysis because during the period of Hicks' writing, the world's economy was in a deep depression, a period of mass unemployment where market prices were dictated by producers and employers, and consumers were mere price takers.

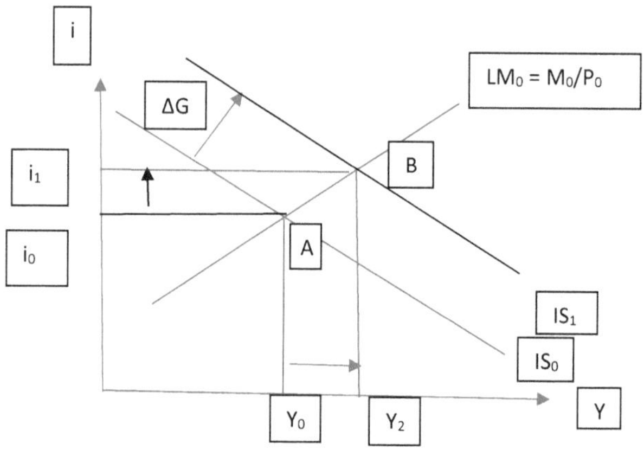

Panel 8.10 Effect of an increase in government spending from G_0 to G_1 in the IS-LM economy

Thus, the IS and LM curves apparatus developed by Hicks from his interpretation of Keynes' *General Theory of Employment, Interest and Money* has a serious shortcoming which he acknowledged in his 1937 interpretation of Keynes' (1936) General Theory, which he referred to as Generalized General Theory.

Problems

(8.1) Using the MP curve and the IS curve derive the AD curve.

(8.2) Assuming that planned expenditure is expressed as

$$E = C(Y-T) + I\left(i-\pi^{e}\right) + G$$

i. Does balance budget, which means an equal increase in G and T, affect the position of the IS curve?
ii. What is the specific effect of the balance budget on Y for a given interest rate i?
iii. Does the balance budget affect the position of the AD curve?
iv. Specifically, explain the effect on Y for a given price level P?

(8.3) The MP curve is given by $i = 5 + \mu\pi$, and the IS curve is given by Y = 50 – 5i when $\mu = 1$.

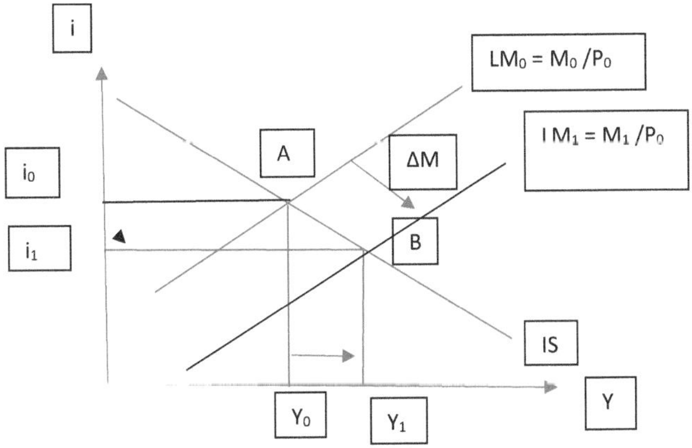

Panel 8.11 An effect of an increase in monetary policy from M_0 to M_1 in the IS-LM economy

(a) Derive the AD curve and draw a graph for it by labeling points at $\pi = 0$, $\pi = 3$, and $\pi = 5$.
(b) Assume that μ increases to $\mu = 3$. Derive an equation for the new AD curve, and draw the new AD curve using the graph from part (a).
(c) What does the answer to part (b) imply about the relationship between the slope of the AD curve and why central banks eschew inflation?

(8.4) If the governor of the central bank of an emerging market's public stance is summarized by his desire to create employment. Consequently, his desire to use monetary policy to fight inflation is placed on top of the shelf of his priority list by easing monetary policy. How do you expect his attitude to affect the monetary policy curve?

(8.5) "The monetary authorities of a small island economy decreased the inter-bank interest rate during the financial meltdown in 2007-2008, although inflation was on ascension. This action violated the Taylor's principle." Is this statement True, or False, or Uncertain? Explain your answer,

(8.6) "Autonomous monetary policy is more effective in changing real output when the responsiveness of real interest rate to inflation, μ, is higher." Is the above statement True, False, or uncertain? Explain your answer.

(8.7) Assume that the Minister of Finance and Economic Planning increase government spending on goods and services but decrease net taxes (NTX) by an equal amount. Thus, the Minister of Finance and Economic Planning has undertaken a change in fiscal policy such that $\Delta G = -\Delta NTX$.

(a) Do you think the fiscal policy change will cause the equilibrium income to rise or fall or uncertain? Explain your answer.

Use the following example to support your answer. Assume that initially mpc $= 0.6$, $t = 0.30$, and $Y_0 = 800$. If $\Delta G = 30$ and $\Delta NTX = -30$.

(b) Calculate the change in equilibrium income ΔY_0.

(c) What is the change in the budget surplus ΔBS? Why has the budget surplus (BS) changed?

(8.8) Consider an economy which is described by the following:

C = J\$3.25 billion
I = J\$1.7 billion
G = J\$4 billion
T = J\$5 billion
NX = –J\$2 billion
$f = 1$
mpc $= 0.7$
$d_1 = 0.4$
$\mu = 2$
$e_1 = 0.2$

where, d_1 is responsiveness of investments to interest rate of investment spending, f is financial friction, mpc is marginal propensity to consume, e_1 = responsiveness of NX with respect to interest rate, and μ is interest rate degree of responsiveness to inflation.

(i) Derive an expression for the consumption function, and net export function.

(ii) Derive an expression of the IS curve.

(iii) Let the real interest $i = 3$, what is the equilibrium output? If it is $i = 5$, what is the equilibrium output?
(iv) Draw a graph of the IS curve by using the information from (iii).
(v) If government spending increases to J$6 billion, what will be the output by using information from (iii)?

Selected References

Apergis, N. and Miller, S. (2006), "Consumption asymmetry and the stock market: Empirical Evidence." *Economics Letters*, 93 (3), 337–342.

Borenstein, S., Cameron, C. and Gilbert, R. (1997), "Do gasoline prices respond asymmetrically to crude oil price changes?" *The Quarterly Journal of Economics*, 112 (1), 305–339.

Dornbusch, Rudiger, Fischer, Stanley, and Sparks, Gordon, R. (1982), *Macroeconomics*, New York: McGraw-Hill Ryerson Limited.

Fisher, Irving (1930), *The Theory of Interest*, New York: Macmillan.

Ghartey, Edward E. (1987), "Devaluation as a balance of payments corrective measure in developing country: a study relating to Ghana." *Applied Economics*, 19 (7): 937–947.

Ghartey, Edward E. (2018), "Exchange Rate Principles in Especially Developing Countries," Presidential Address, AFEA/ASSA/AEA Annual Meeting, Philadelphia, January 5.

Ghartey, Edward E. (2019), "Asymmetries in exchange rate pass-through and monetary policy principle: Some Caribbean empirical evidence," North American Journal of Economics and Finance, 47, 325–335.

Granger, C.W,J. and Yoon, G. (2002), "Hidden Cointegration," unpublished manuscript, San Diego: University of California.

Hicks, John R. (1937), "Mr. Keynes and the 'CLASSICS' a suggested interpretation," *Econometrica*, 5 (2), April: 147–159.

Keynes, John M. (1936), *The General Theory of Employment, Interest, and Money*, London: Macmillan Press.

McCallum, Bennett T. (1989), *Monetary Economics: Theory and Policy*, New York: Macmillan Publishing Company.

Mishkin, Frederic S. (2016), *The Economics of Money, Banking, and Financial Markets*, New York: Pearson.

Schorderet, Y. (2001). "Revisiting Okun's law: An hysteretic perspective," unpublished manuscript, University of California, San Diego.

Shin, Y., Yu, B., and Greenwood-Nimmo, M. (2011). "Modelling asymmetric cointegration and dynamic multipliers in a nonlinear ARDL framework." SSRN Electronic Journal.

CHAPTER 9

The Aggregate Supply (AS) Curve

In this chapter, we employed the Phillips curve and Okun's law to develop the aggregate supply curve, by substituting real wages for the nominal wage rate used in the original Phillips curve, and translating unemployment in the Okun's law into real output by substituting output gap for unemployment gap. Furthermore, we have replaced the adaptive expectation in the original Phillips curve with rational expectation to avert systematic errors which carry in their trail autocorrelation problem which plagued early studies because of their reliance on adaptive expectations. Thus, the aggregate supply curve is a positive slope in the (p, y) space. Factors that shift the aggregate supply curve are: (i) expected inflation, (ii) output gap which measures slackness or tightness in the labor market, (iii) inflation shock, (iv) supply shock, (v) wage push, (v) changes in cost of production independent of labor or supply cost, and (vi) changes in exchange rate. Dynamics of the AD and especially the AS curves allow us to analyze the effect of fiscal and monetary policies, and the effect of temporary and permanent shocks in the economy. Equilibrium in the market are determined by free interplay of AD and AS curves. Tightness

This model was developed from a paper which was presented during the author's Presidential address at the AFEA session of the ASSA and AEA Meeting in Pennsylvania, USA, January 5, 2018.

E. E. Ghartey, *International Macroeconomics and Finance*,
https://doi.org/10.1007/978-3-032-04145-6_9

in the labor market results in prices rising as the AS curve shifts leftward till the AD and the AS curves intersect each other on the potential output of the long-run aggregate supply (LRAS) curve, where the market clears at a permanent equilibrium. The Chapter is closed with a discussion of real business cycle which is fluctuation of natural rate of real output, and hysteresis.

9.1 Topics Covered

Phillips curve	Okun's law
aggregate supply curve	dynamics of the AS and AD curves
business cycle and real business cycle	self-correction mechanism

9.2 Learning Outcomes

Readers of this chapter should be able to have acquired clear knowledge and understanding of the materials, among others, to do the following:

(1) Define the following terms and concepts:

(a) Phillips curve	(b) hysteresis
(c) Okun's law	(d) expectation-augmented Phillips curve
(e) unemployment gap	(f) tightness in labor market
(g) natural rate of unemployment	

2. Derive the AS curve with the aid of the Phillips curve by using the output gap to capture the unemployment rate and the inflation rate to capture the wage rate.
3. Illustrate market determination of equilibrium when output is below potential output (Y^P)
4. List and discuss factors which shift the AS curve.
5. Explain and discuss dynamics of short-run, medium-term, and long-run AS and AD curves.

9.3 Introduction

The AS curve is developed from the Phillips curve, and the Okun's law after adjusting for wages and expectations. Alban W. H. Phillips modeled and estimated a relationship between wages and unemployment for the UK, which he published in 1958, the year he became a Professor at London School of Economics, his alma mater. His finding indicated that at a low unemployment rate, which can be used to capture tightness in the labor market, wages rose faster, whereas at a high unemployment rate, when the labor market is slack, wages tended to either drop or remain the same.

It is believed that his idea originated from Irving Fisher, one of his favorite economists. Thus, the original Phillips curve illustrated a pattern of inverse relationship between wage rate and unemployment rate. It is asymmetrical as wages tend to rise faster at a low unemployment rate, while they stabilize or fall gradually at a high unemployment rate.

9.4 The Phillips Curve

The Phillips curve is expressed as

$$\Delta w_t = f(U_{t-1}),\ f' < 0 \tag{9.1}$$

where, w_t is logarithmic form of nominal wage rate, and $U_{t\text{-}1}$ is the unemployment rate of the previous year with subscript t denoting time.

The Phillips curve (PC) was modified following Friedman (1968) and Phelps (1967) criticism, that people are more interested in expected real wage rates when they are negotiating their remuneration, than the nominal wage rate which was used in the original Phillips curve. This caused equation (9.1) to be re-specified as follows:

$$\Delta w_t - \Delta p_t^e = f(U_{t-1}),\ f' < 0 \tag{9.2}$$

Equation (9.2) is re-expressed as expectation-augmented PC as

$$\Delta w_t = f(U_{t-1}) + \Delta p_t^e,\ f' < 0 \tag{9.3}$$

Considering that the wage rate strongly correlates with inflation,[1] the Phillips curve can be re-expressed as

$$\Delta p = f(U) + \sigma \Delta p^e, \ f' < 0, (0 < \sigma \leq 1) \tag{9.4}$$

According to empirical studies $\sigma = 1$, which means Eq. (9.4) becomes

$$\Delta p = f(U) + \Delta p^e = \Delta p^e - \kappa\left(U - U^n\right) \tag{9.5}$$

where, p_t is logarithmic form of prices in the form of consumer price index, Δp is actual inflation, Δp^e is expected inflation, $U - U^n$ measures tightness in the labor market $f(U)$, with κ as the measure of responsiveness of inflation to the tightness in the labor market. U is the unemployment rate, U^n is the natural rate of unemployment, Y is the real output, and Y^n is the natural rate of real output.

9.5 Okun's Law

We then invoke the Okun's law which states that for every 2% (or say 3%) increase in aggregate demand for real output or economic growth above trend, in an environment of involuntary unemployment, unemployment rate declines by 1%. According to Cornwall (1983) about 67% of the 3% increase in output emanates from induced increase in labor input, as their participation rates increase with the declining unemployment rate, and the remaining 33% can be explained by the productivity of existing labor force in the market.

Thus, the law relates unemployment gap $(U - U^n)$ to output gap $(Y - Y^n)$, so by substituting $U = -\beta Y$ and $U^n = -\beta Y^n$ into equation (9.5), we can then re-specify the result as follows:

$$\Delta p = \Delta p^e + \kappa\beta\left(Y - Y^n\right) + \xi \tag{9.6}$$

[1] The wage rate is equal to the inflation rate, if the real wage is equated to productivity, and the latter is constant.

Equation (9.6) is then made estimable by using a backward-looking expectation which sets $\Delta p^e = \Delta p_{t-1}$.[2] The resulting aggregate supply equation is then re-specified as

$$\Delta \dot{p}_t = \Delta p_t - \Delta p_{t-1} = \kappa\beta(Y_t - Y^n) + \xi_t \tag{9.7}$$

where, $\Delta \dot{p}_t$ $(= \Delta p_t - \Delta p_{t-1})$ is the rate of change in inflation, and ξ is inflation shock which originates from supply shock. Thus, the Philips curve shows the conflict between the economic goal of reducing inflation and unemployment simultaneously, which policymakers encounter when they apply monetary policy to achieve either of the goals.

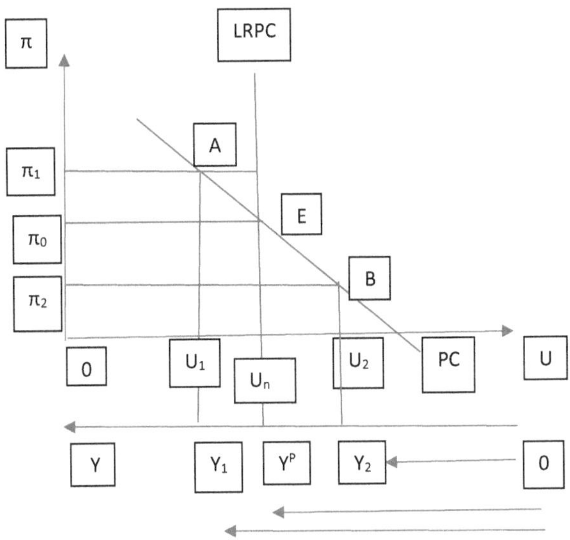

Panel 9.1 The Phillips curve (PC)

[2] The problem with the adaptive expectation is that predictive errors tend to be consistent. A more realistic view will be to employ a rational expectation, $\Delta p_t^e = E(\Delta p_t/\Omega_{t-1}) = E_{t-1}\Delta p_t$, where Ω is all available information. Modern Keynesians set $\Delta p^c = \Delta p_t^e$ and refer to Δp^c as the core or underlying inflation, which is dependent on the environment, but insensitive to transitory inflation resulting from say food and energy prices. Modern Keynesians who found the core inflation to be inconsistent when prices are either high or low for prolonged periods, substitute weighted average of the past and future inflation for it.

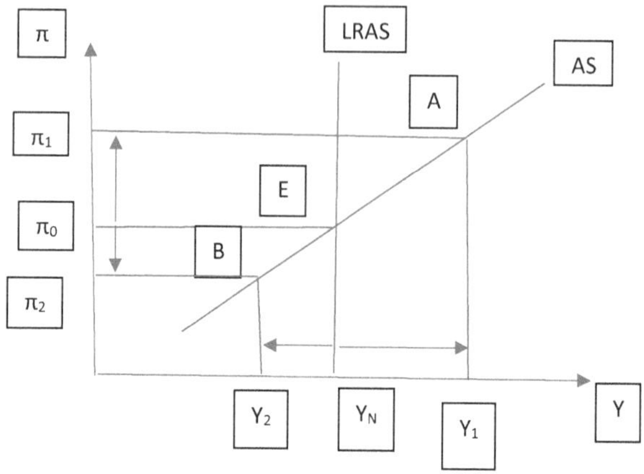

Panel 9.2 Graphic derivation of the aggregate supply curve

9.6 Aggregate Supply

Equations (9.6 and 9.7) are different specifications of the aggregate supply (AS) curve. Equation (9.6) says that the current inflation can be explained by expected inflation, output gap, and inflation shock. The sensitivity of inflation to the output gap is kβ. Factors that shift the AS curve are inflation, output gap, and inflation shock. The graph of the AS curve is presented in Panels 9.2 and 9.3. It is upward slope. We see that when inflation is at π_0, the real output is at the natural rate or full employment level or potential output level at Y^P and the economy and the labor market is at equilibrium. The AS curve is derived from both the Phillips curve and Okun's law. The latter allowed us to translate the unemployment in the original Phillips' curve into real output through the output gap as explained through equations (9.1–9.7) and shown in Panels 9.1 and 9.2.

Panel 9.3 illustrates the state of the labor market, and the response of the AS curve to market dynamics which returns it to market equilibrium.

9.7 Dynamics of AD and AS Curves

The long-run AS curve is vertical at Y^P and is parallel to the inflation line shown in Figrue 9.4. At $Y_0 > Y^P$, the market equilibrium is beyond the full employment output level at E_0. The labor market is tight, and that

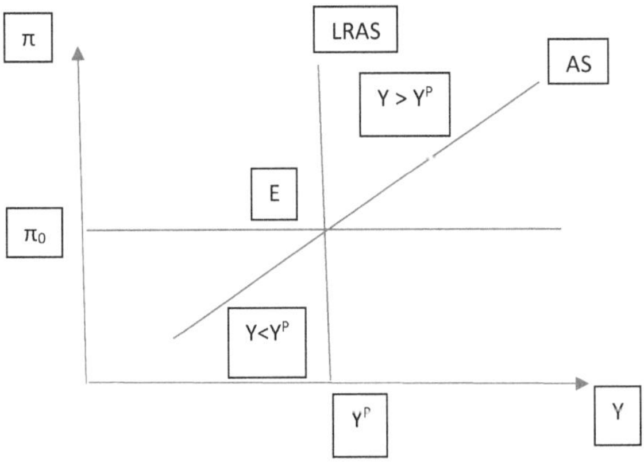

Panel 9.3 Dynamics of the aggregate supply curve

tightness results in employers and producers haggling for limited available labor and intermediate output by offering higher prices and wages for the limited available resources. The higher prices and wages cause increase in inflation expectation which feeds into further increase in prices and wages to cause the AS curve to shift leftward. The process continues as shown in Panel 9.4 till equilibrium is reached at E_2 where inflation is π_2 and real output is at the long-run potential real output level Y^P.

At $Y < Y^P$ the labor market is slack, and that slackness causes inflation to fall because wages drop due to mass unemployment. This results also in fall in inflation expectation which drives down prices and wages. The cost of production also drops which encourages producers to increase production and the AS curve to shift downward. The process continues repeating itself till equilibrium is reached at E_2 on the long-run real output (Y^P) in Panel 9.5.

On the long-run AS curve the market is in equilibrium as there is neither slackness nor tightness in the labor market. See Panel 9.7.

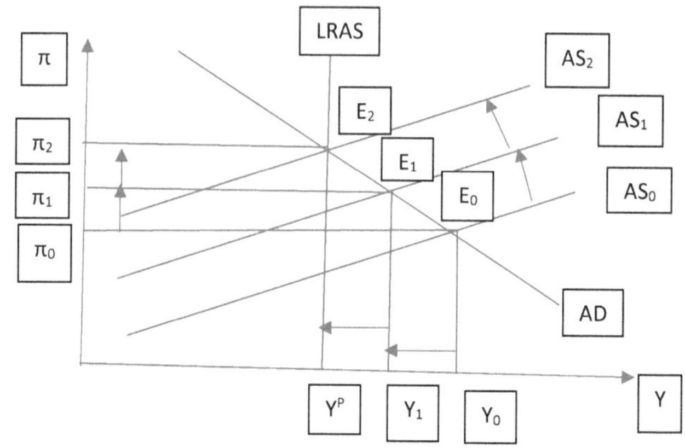

Panel 9.4 Market determination of equilibrium when initial output is beyond Y^P

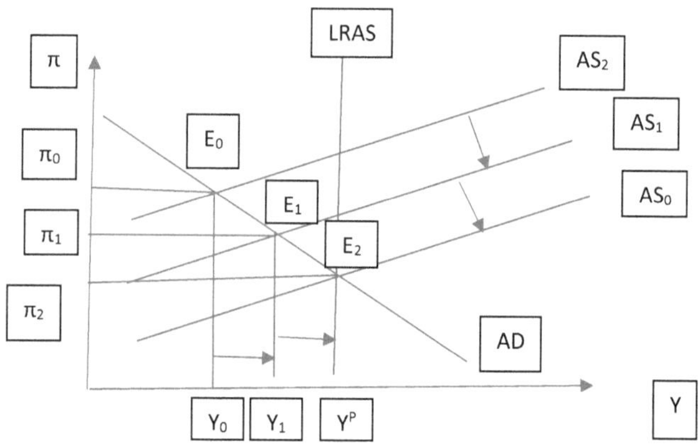

Panel 9.5 Market determination of equilibrium when real output is below Y^P

9.8 Factors which Shift the AS Curve in the Short Run

Factors which shift the AS curve are (i) expected inflation, (ii) output gap which results in either tightness or slackness of the labor market, (iii) inflation shock such as (iv) wage push (v) changes in the cost of production unrelated to labor and supply cost, and (vi) changes in exchange rate or appreciation or depreciation of the exchange rate. This latter factor is discussed further in Chapter 12.

Related to the output gap are increase and decrease in productivity, and related to inflation shock are wage push and supply shock. The supply shock emanates from changes in the cost of production which are not related to labor cost. It can either be a negative supply shock or a positive supply shock. A negative supply shock, which originates from either increase in price of raw materials or natural disasters like an earthquake or hurricanes or Vulcanic eruptions, causes an increase in the cost of production which decreases profits of firms.[3]

This negative supply shock causes the AS curve to shift leftwards in the short run, driving upward the inflation rate and reducing the real output. On the other hand, a positive supply shock originating from a fall in prices of raw materials due to an unusually good weather resulting from a bumper harvest or new innovations in technology, shifts the AS curve rightward. This causes inflation rate to fall and real output to increase.

In Panel 9.4, the output Y_0 is in initial temporary equilibrium at E_0 and the inflation rate is π_0. However, because $Y_0 > Y^P$, the labor market is tight. This means employers compete among themselves for the existing workers in the labor market by wooing them with higher wages. Increase in wages in the labor market is passed on to consumers by hiking up prices. This continuous increase in prices results in inflation rising to π_1 and output drops from Y_0 to Y_1 at a new equilibrium E_1. Again, because $Y_1 > Y^P$, the labor market continues to tighten, and this causes producers to haggle among themselves to hire the existing labor by out bidding each other.

This results in further increase in wages, and the resulting increase in the cost of production forces producers to shed production to reduce the real output from Y_1 to Y^P. However, at Y^P because the market is in long-run equilibrium at the natural rate or full employment level, inflation

[3] La Soufriere, the St. Vincent island's tallest stratovolcano which erupted from 9 April 2021 throughout April 2021 causing the citizens to flee the island, is an example of a negative supply shock, and so is the effect of coronavirus disease in 2019 known as covid-19, which was alleged to have originated from 'wet market' in Wuhan, China in November 2019. Note that China disputed the origin of covid-19. Most countries in the world resorted to lockdown at various periods, which resulted in the world's economic growth falling by 4.3% from the economic growth which prevailed in the late November 2019. Example of positive shock is the introduction of computers in mid 1990s, and the fiscal and social policies introduced by the Clinton administration during that period.

becomes stable and both the long-run and short-run AS curves intersect the AD curve at a permanent equilibrium E_2. The market forces discussed above which unite the short-run and long-run equilibrium at E_2 is termed as the self-correcting mechanism.

The economy is in temporary equilibrium at E_0 where output is Y_0 which is less than the potential output Y^P as it is shown in Panel 9.5. There is slackness in the labor market as there is high unemployment in the economy. Producers and employers bid down wages as the labor unions or workers bargaining power are weaken by the high unemployment of labor and resources.

Consequently, the cost of production falls, so producers reduce the price of their goods and services to expand their production and market shares. The continuous reduction in prices drags down inflation so producers expand production further and hire more workers. The economy improves and moves to another temporary equilibrium at E_1, and real output increases to Y_1.

However, there is still slackness in the labor market because $Y_1 < Y^P$. Producers and employers reduce wages further because of the high employment, and this also causes further reduction in the cost of production which allows employers to hire more workers and expand their production to the full employment or natural rate of unemployment at a final equilibrium output where $Y = Y^P$.

At this equilibrium E_2 there is no more imbalance in the labor market and inflation ceases as expected inflation vanishes in the market. Both employers, producers, and workers are satisfied. The dynamics which return the economy back to equilibrium when it is displaced from there as shown in Panels 9.4 and 9.5 is known as the self-correction mechanism of the free market competitive system.

The AD and AS analysis is combined to establish equilibrium in the market economy in the short run as depicted above in Panel 9.6. However, it is important to note that in the short-run and even medium-term, the equilibrium is determined outside of the long-run equilibrium at the intersection of the AD curve and short-run or medium-term AS curve as discussed above. The slope of the short-run or medium-term AS curve is less than 90° while the slope of the LRAS is 90°.

Additionally, factors in the economy which shift the short-run AS curve and the long-run AS curves are different. It should be abundantly clear thus far, that factors that shift the LRAS curve are factors that shifts

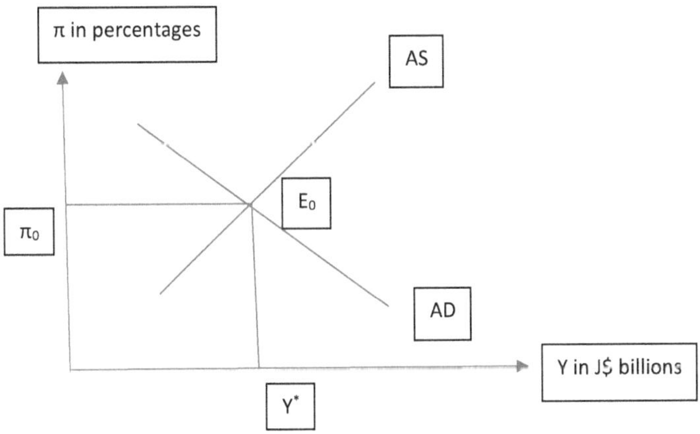

Panel 9.6 Equilibrium in the short run

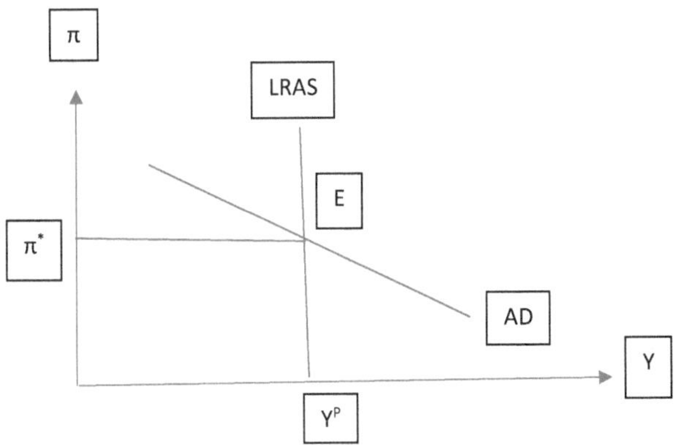

Panel 9.7 Long-run equilibrium

the potential or natural rate output or the natural rate of unemployment (U_N). See Panels 9.5, 9.8, and Sect. 9.9.

The long-run equilibrium occurs when the LRAS and AD curves intersect at the real potential output Y^P level. There is no excess demand or supply of inputs like labor, capital, and raw materials in the market, so there is no rising or falling prices of inputs and output. Laborers are satisfied with their wages, producers are satisfied with prices of inputs and final

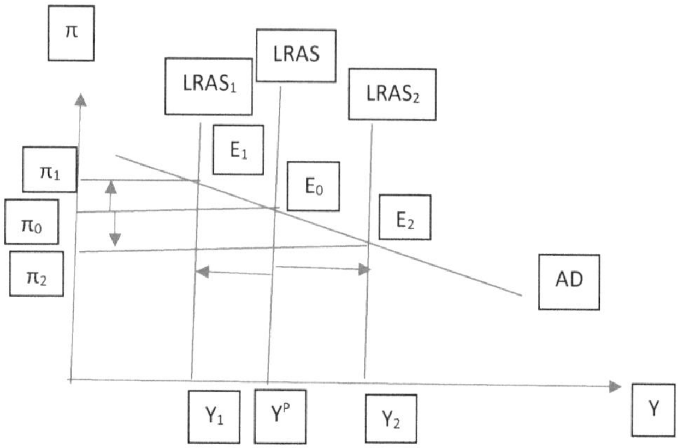

Panel 9.8 Factors which shift the LRAS

products, and there is no unexpected inflation in the economy as is shown in Panel 9.7.

9.9 Factors Which Shift the LRAS Curve

Temporary shocks or fluctuations of real output Y around the potential or normal or natural rate output Y^P is referred to as a business cycle. However, permanent shocks or fluctuations of potential output Y^P is known as the real business cycle (RBC). Y^P is fixed so temporary shifts in AD or AS curves do not have any effect on it. Factors that permanently shift the real business cycle Y^P are mainly shocks to taste, which are the willingness to work, and technology which originate from productivity.

Contrary to traditional Keynesian models where output growth is largely caused by monetary and other aggregate demand disturbances in an environment of sluggish adjustment of nominal prices and wages, the RBC theory rather observes that monetary policy has no effect on real output and unemployment. Instead, it is real output and unemployment that cause monetary shocks.

Monetary authorities do not directly control monetary policy to achieve desired target of predetermined money stock. They influence monetary policy indirectly through short-term interest rates and bank reserve operating targets instruments.

Consequently, they take actions to stabilize or smoothen fluctuations in interest rates. It is for this reason that the money supply expands during periods when positive productivity shocks result in above-normal output levels. Conclusion of the RBC theory are very much akin to the classical economic model, and the super-neutrality property of money observed in the Lucas' (1972) monetary misperception theory.

The RBC theory also finds fiscal policy to be effective in driving business cycle as shocks due to government purchase are effective in changing the quantity of goods available to the private economy for a given level of production. The RBC theory is said to have earned its name from the fact that shocks relating to technology that drive the theory are all real. Main proponents of the RBC theory are Prescott, Kydland, Plosser, and King, although it is said that Plosser and Long dubbed the fluctuations of Y^P the term RBC. See Kydland, Finn E., and Edward C. Prescott (1982); King, Robert G., and Charles I. Plosser (1984).

The second permanent factor which is used to explain the shift in Y^P is hysteresis, which is the deviation from potential output Y^P due to past level of high unemployment. A reduction in aggregate demand which shifts the AD curve leftward as shown in Panel 9.9 changes the equilibrium from the long-run equilibrium at E_0 and natural rate unemployment of U_N to a lower equilibrium E_1 and higher unemployment rate of U_1 above the full employment at Y^P.

The new natural rate of unemployment associated with Y_1 is seen to be higher at U_1 above the U_N which is associated with Y^P. This rising unemployment occurs because of the following reasons:

(1) The unemployed become discouraged and therefore either look less for jobs or become reluctant to look for job because they become used to leisure by depending on unemployment benefits.
(2) Employers may become reluctant to hire workers who have been unemployed for a long time because they assume that the long spell of not working has made the worker undesirable.

It is due to these reasons that the unemployment which emerges because of the reduction in the AD curve cannot be corrected by the self-correction mechanism inherent in the economy to move the equilibrium E_1 from the new natural rate of unemployment back to the full employment equilibrium A on the LRAS curve as shown in Panel 9.9.

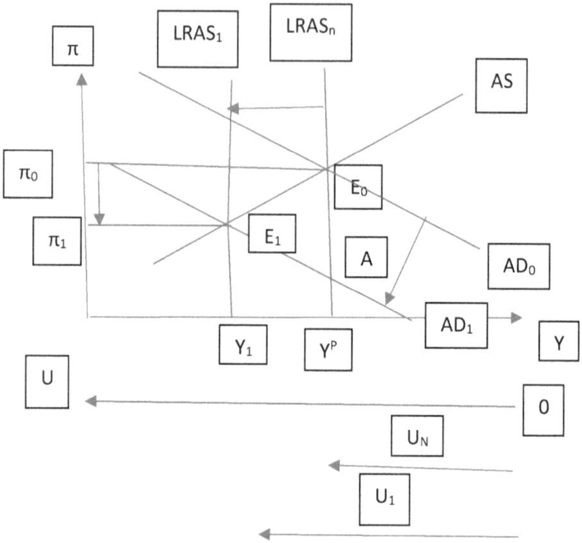

Panel 9.9 Hysteresis

It, therefore, becomes necessary to employ expansionary AD policies to restore the economy to the full employment at E_0. Proponents of hysteresis tend to be Activists who believe in the effectiveness of demand management policies. See Blanchard, Olivier J. and Lawrence H. Summers (1987).

9.10 Summary

The aggregate supply curve is derived both graphically and mathematically from the Phillips curve, by substituting real wages for nominal wages, and inflation for nominal wages in the original Phillips model. Output gap was substituted for unemployment rate in the Okun's law to translate unemployment rate in the Phillips curve to real output in the AS curve.

We discussed factors which shift the AS curve when there is slackness in the labor market, and tightness in the labor market. We also related how the tightness and slackness in the labor market influence real wages to cause inflation, and how the resulting prices increase cost of production to cause the AS curve to shift in both the short run and the long run.

We differentiated supply shock from demand shock and explained how a policy such as an increase in government spending during periods of high unemployment influence both aggregate demand and aggregate supply curves and affect both output and inflation in short-term, medium-term, and long run. We also discussed factors which shift the full employment or the long-run aggregate supply curves.

9.11 Problems

9.1. The government has just increased autonomous taxes, what is its effect on the economy?

9.2. Explain the effect of increase in taxes and government spending on equilibrium output and real interest rate.

9.3. There is increase in the general consumption tax. Discuss the effect on the multiplier with the aid of the Keynesian cross.

9.4. The central bank of Belize has decreased the money supply. Will this policy result in the monetary neutrality property? Explain your answer by considering the money market, the IS curves, AD-AS curves, and the foreign exchange market schedules.

9.5. The economy has an aggregate demand and supply expressed as follows:

$$y_t = \alpha + \lambda(m_t - p_t) + u_t(\text{AD})$$
$$y_t = y^P + \phi(p_t - E_{t-1}p_t)\ (\text{AS})$$

The random demand disturbance u_t is first-order serially correlated as

$$u_t = \rho u_{t-1} + \xi$$

where ξ is white noise unrelated to the u_t process, and y^P is potential output.

Assuming the central bank conducts monetary policy according to

$$m_t = \pi_0 + \pi_1 u_{t-1} + \varepsilon_t,$$

where ε_t is white noise unrelated to the u_t process.

Solve for p_t. Then use it to obtain an expression for $(p_t - E_{t-1}p_t)$ and substitute it into equation (AS) to obtain a solution for y_t.

9.6. (a) Explain succinctly why the expected rate of inflation influences the position of the aggregate supply curve.

(b) Explain succinctly the mechanism whereby the nominal interest rate adjusts to inflation in the long run?

9.7. Given that a country's growth rate of money changes unexpectedly and that the country experiences a backward-looking expectation such that its expected inflation is based on its previous period's money growth which is expressed as $\pi^e = \Delta m_{t-1}$. Analyze the short-run and long-run effects of the changed in money growth on output, inflation, and the real and nominal interest rates.

9.8. Explain the following terms and concepts:

(i) Okun's law, (ii) Phillips curve, (iii) natural rate of unemployment, (iv) non-accelerator inflation rate and unemployment (NAIRU), (v) tightness in labor market, (vi) output gap, (vii) self-correcting mechanism, (vii) core inflation (Δp^c), and (vii) real business cycle.

9.9. (a) Differentiate unemployment gap from output gap

(b) Using the Okun's law and the Phillips curve derive the aggregate supply curve.

(9.10) (i) Explain negative supply shock and positive supply shock.

(ii) Suppose the potential or natural rate of output is below aggregate output, explain the effect of this on inflation rate over time. Hint: assume that the aggregate demand curve remains the same.

9.11. The ruling government has legislated to raise the general consumption tax, predict (i) the effect of such a tax on the aggregate supply and demand curves and (ii) depict the effect on output and inflation.

9.12. Which of the following factors can you classify as a supply shock or demand shock:

(a) Financial frictions increase, (b) public outbreak of covid-19 pandemic in 2019, (c) Advent of internet of things and computer technology in the mid-1990s, (d) eruption of stratovolcano in April 2021 in St, Vincent Island (e) Households and businesses' pessimistic view of the future of the economy's future of a war-torn economy.

Selected References

Blanchard, Olivier J. and Lawrence H. Summers (1987), "Hysteresis in unemployment," *European Economic Review*, 31, 288-295.

Dornbusch, Rudiger, Fischer, Stanley, and Sparks, Gordon, R. (1982), *Macro Economics*, (New York: McGraw-Hill Ryerson Limited).

Fisher, Irving (1930), *The Theory of Interest*, New York: Macmillan.

Friedman, Milton (1968), "The role of monetary policy," *American Economic Review*, 58, March, 1–17.

King, Robert G. and Charles I. Plosser (1984), "Money, credit, and prices in a real business cycle," *American Economic Review*, 74, June, 363–80.

Kydland, Finn E. and Edward C. Prescott (1982), "Time to build and aggregate fluctuations," *Econometrica*, 50, November, 1345–70.

Long, John B. and Charles I. Plosser (1983), "Real business cycles," *Journal of Political Economy*, February, 1345–1370.

Lucas, Robert E., Jr., (1972), "Expectations and the neutrality of money," *Journal of Economic Theory*, 4, April, 103–24.

McCallum, Bennett T. (1989), *Monetary Economics: Theory and Policy*, New York: Macmillan Publishing Company.

Mishkin, Frederic S. (2016), *The Economics of Money, Banking, and Financial Markets*, New York: Pearson.

Nelson, Charles R. and Charles I. Plosser (1982), "Trends and random walks in macroeconomic time series: some evidence and implications," *Journal of Monetary Economics*, 10, September, 139–167.

Okun, M. Arthur (1962). "Potential GNP: Its Measurement and Significance." Proceedings of the Business and Economic Statistics Section, American Statistical Society.

Phelps, Edmund S. (1967). "Phillips Curves, Expectations of Inflation, and Optimal Unemployment over Time." *Economica*, 34, 254-81.

Phillips, Alban W. H. (1958). "The Relation between Unemployment and the Rate of Change of Money Wage Rates in the United Kingdom, 1861-1957." *Economica*, 25, 283-300.

Romer, David, (2001), *Advanced Macroeconomics*, New York: McGraw Hill.

CHAPTER 10

Effect of Easy Money in an Open Economy

In this chapter, easy money is implemented to illustrate its dynamic effects in both developed and developing open market economies. This expansionary monetary policy embarked on by central banks through the purchase of Treasury Bills from nonbanking public in open market operation, increase prices which cause interest rates to fall. Exchange rates depreciate causing the cost of production to rise and profits of firms to fall and the aggregate supply curve to shift inward. Equilibrium prices rise to clear at a new equilibrium on the long-run aggregate supply (LRAS) curve at the full employment or potential real output. The exchange rate experiences overshooting, as the short-run effect of the initial increase in the money supply caused the fall in real interest rate results in a sharp jump in depreciation of the exchange. It then reversed, causing the exchange rate to appreciate and settle around midway between the initial depreciation level at the full employment or potential output. Results are traced on phase diagrams. All nominal variables increased following the monetary expansion policy, whereas all real variables except interest rates remained constant. Thus, a once-and-over increase in money supply results in all nominal variables such as money supply, prices, income, wages, and exchange rate increasing, whereas all real variables such as real money, real income, real wages, real exchange rate, and labor remain the same. The separation of real variables in response to a once-and-over increase in monetary expansion from the response of nominal variables to

E. E. Ghartey, *International Macroeconomics and Finance*,
https://doi.org/10.1007/978-3-032-04145-6_10

similar once-and-over increase in monetary expansion policy is referred to as the classical dichotomy

10.1 Topics Covered

Central Bank's Implementation of Easy Money Policy
Effect of Easy Money on the Market
Effect of Easy Money in the Open Market
Phase Diagrams Summary
Macroeconomic Policy Issues

10.2 Learning Outcomes

Readers and students of this chapter will be expected to have acquired knowledge and clear understanding to among others do the following:

1. Explain the self-correction mechanism of the labor, and goods and services markets.
2. Define the super-neutrality property of money. explain it in the context of exchange rate overshooting by using phase diagrams.
3. List the effect of expansionary monetary policy on real output, labor, real wages, real interest 'rate, nominal money, inflation, and nominal exchange rate.

10.3 Introduction

The effect of easy money on interest rate by the central bank is discussed and shown in Panel 10.1. It is followed with a discussion of the effect of interest rate on inflation rate when the central bank seeks to stabilize inflation in the country. This task is achieved by the central bank when it follows monetary policy principle (MPP) which is otherwise referred to as Taylor's principle. The principle is captured by the monetary policy curve (MPC). See also Chapter 8. The reverse of the monetary policy principle (MPP) is an expansionary monetary policy which requires the central bank to expand the money supply in the economy to contract the interest rate proportionately more than the existing interest rate from i_0 to i_1. Thus, in pursuance of an easy monetary policy, the central bank

Panel 10.1 Effect of permanent easy monetary policy in the open economy

increases the money supply to shift the MPC rightward from MPC_0 to MPC_1, which is a lower interest rate from i_0 to i_1, as is shown in Panel 10.3.

We have discussed the response of the market to the effects of easy monetary policy on inflation and real output, which is depicted in Fig. 10.4. It is followed by discussing the effect of easy money on inflation, exchange rate, and the real interest rate, which is also depicted in Fig. 10.5. The effect of easy money on labor and real output is captured by the production function, which is discussed and illustrated in Fig. 10.6. The effect of the easy money on wages and labor is also discussed and shown in Panel 10.7.

10.4 Central Bank's Implementation of Easy Money or Expansionary Monetary Policy

In the money market, a permanent increase in the money supply effected at time t_0 by the Central Bank through the open market purchasing of Treasury bills, results in the money supply curve shifting to right from M_0 to M_1 where $M_0 < M_1$ as shown in the first diagram of Fig. 10.2. Consequently, the money market equilibrium which occurs at the intersection of the money supply and liquidity preference curves at the original equilibrium E_0, shifts along the liquidity preference curves to a new equilibrium at E_1, and the real interest rate drops immediately from i_0 to i_1.

The monetary policy curve shifts rightward from its initial position at interest rate i_0 on MPC_0 curve to the MPC_1 curve in response to the easy monetary policy. At interest rate of i_0 and inflation rate π_0 on the MPC_0

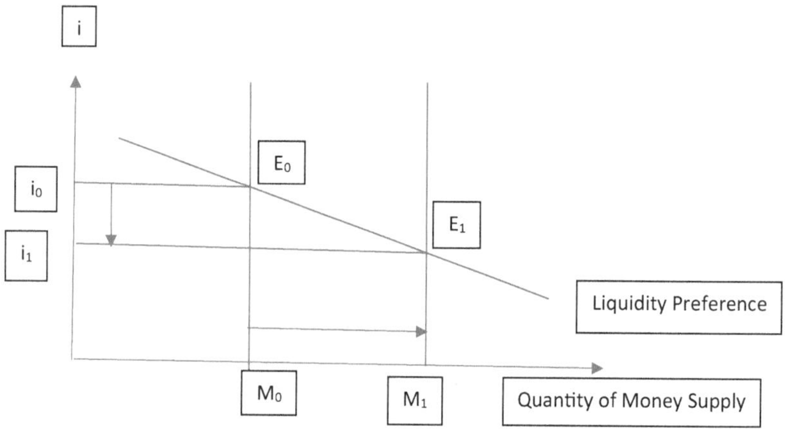

Panel 10.2 Effect of easy monetary policy on real interest rates

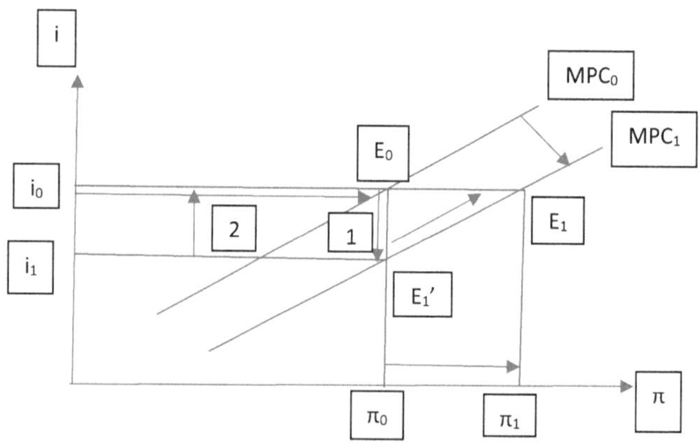

Panel 10.3 Effect of easy monetary policy on MPC (MPC_0 < MPC_1)

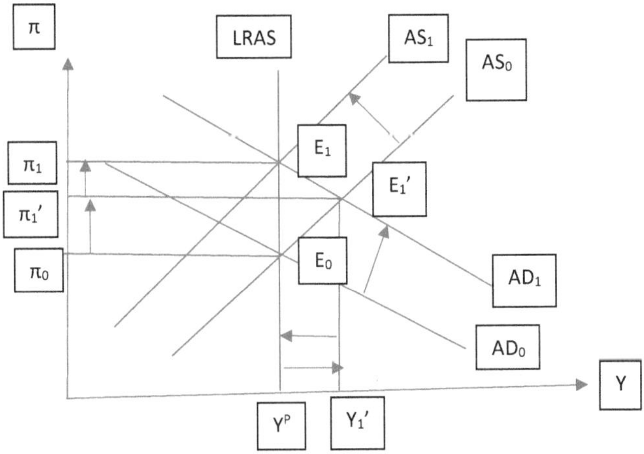

Panel 10.4 Effect of easy monetary policy on the real output and inflation

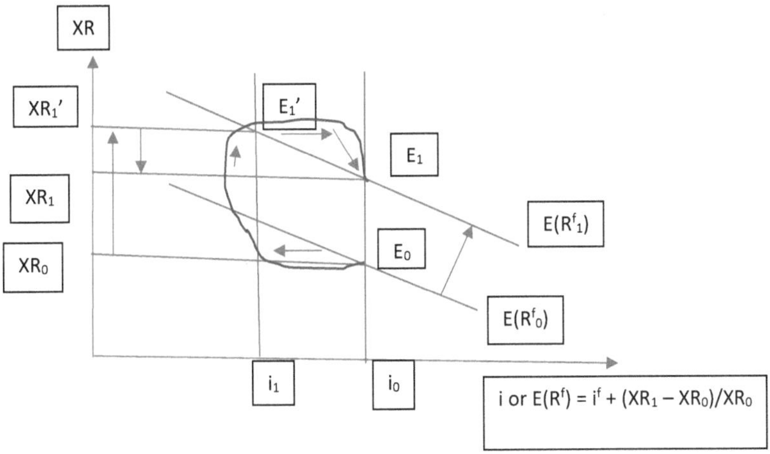

Panel 10.5 Effect of easy monetary policy on the exchange rate

curve, the interest drops instantly from i_0 to i_1 on the initial inflation rate π_1 on the MPC_1 curve at a temporary equilibrium E_i'. However, on the MPC_1 curve, demand for labor increases, and the resulting tightness in the labor market and competition for raw materials and labor causes the

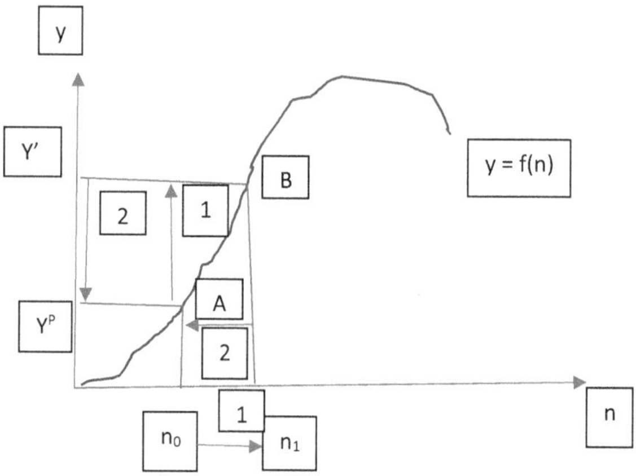

Panel 10.6 Effect of easy monetary policy on labor and real output

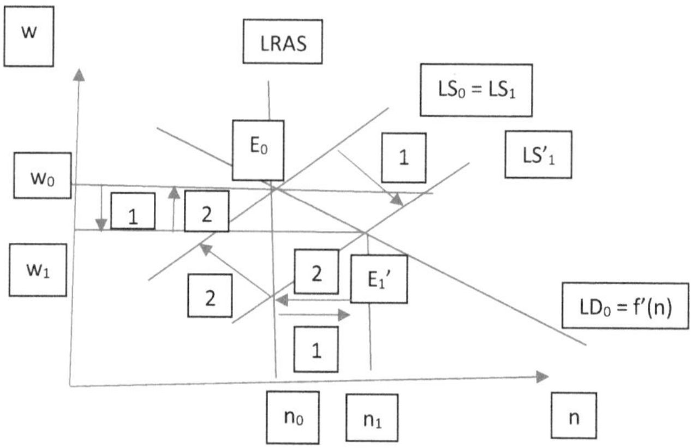

Panel 10.7 Effect of easy monetary policy on labor and real wage rate

inflation rate to rise from the low inflation π_0 at interest rate i_1 and move along the MPC1 curve back to its original high interest rate i_0 to settle at a high inflation π_1 at a final equilibrium E_1. See the second diagram on Panel 10.3.

10.5 Effect of Easy Money in the Market

Real output and inflation rate are determined by the point of intersection of the AS, AD, and the vertical LRAS curves at the full employment and natural output level Y^P. Inflation ceases to accelerate in the absence of any further expansion of money supply through monetary engineering by the monetary authorities (MAs). The initial equilibrium E_0 occurs at the intersection of AS_0 and AD_0 where the inflation rate is π_0 and the real output is Y^P, before the initiation of the easy monetary policy.

However, when the money supply is increased at time t_0, the aggregate demand curve shifts from AD_0 to AD_1. This moves the market equilibrium from E_0 to E_1' at the intersection of AD_1 and AS_0. The real output shifts from Y^P to Y_1' which causes excess demand, and results in inflation rate rising from π_0 to π_1' as shown in Panel 10.4.

At E_1', where $Y_1' > Y^P$ the labor market becomes tight, so even though inflation increases to π_1', the continuous competition for workers and raw materials among producers and employers causes further increase in the cost of production which reduces profits further, and forces producers to reduce their production cost by hiring less workers and resources as inputs. As a result, inflation continues to rise, and the aggregate supply curve shifts leftward until the AS_1 curve intersects AD_1 curve on the LRAS curve at a long-run equilibrium E_1, where inflation is π_1 and full employment and natural output is Y^P. See the third diagram in Panel 10.4. At E_1, the inflation rate π_1 ceases to accelerate, and the LRAS curve is referred to as a non-accelerating inflation rate and unemployment (NAIRU) as both inflation rate and unemployment cease to accelerate.

10.6 Effect of Easy Money in the Open Market under Flexible Exchange Rate

The effect of the easy monetary policy on the exchange rate is illustrated in diagram 4 of Panel 10.5. The increase in the money supply at time t_0, first results in the real interest rate falling from i_0 to i_1. The resulting increase in inflation also causes depreciation of home currency and the expected return of foreign currency demand schedule shifts sharply upward or rightward from $E(R^f_0)$ to $E(R^f_1)$ as shown in Panel (10.5). The combined effect of fall in domestic real interest rate and rise in the foreign expected return in domestic economy causes the exchange rate to overshoot from XR_0 to XR_1' in response to an upward shift of the foreign expected return curve from $E(R^f{}_0)$ to $E(R^f{}_1)$ as shown in Panel 10.5. See also Dornbusch (1976).

In response to increase in money supply, following the exchange rate overshooting to XR_1', the labor market contracts due to competition among employers and producers. This causes wages and prices to rise, forcing the domestic real interest rate to rise to its initial level i_0 before the easy monetary policy was implemented. The rise in domestic interest rate causes partial appreciation of the domestic currency from XR'_1 to XR_1 on the original level of the domestic real interest rate i_0. The exchange rate is said to be volatile because it overshoots as it moves from XR_0 to XR'_1 before finally settling at XR_1. Additionally, the easy monetary policy causes the economy to experience a phenomenon known as the super-neutrality property of money. Super-neutrality property of money means arbitrary variations in the entire path of money supply affect only the path of nominal variables without affecting (or are invariant with) real variables.

The effect of easy monetary policy on real output, labor, and wages is illustrated in diagrams five and six of Panels 10.6 and 10.7, respectively. In the fifth diagram the production function is presented for labor and real output for a fixed value of capital. As a result of the increase in the money supply, assuming that the economy was initially operating at full employment and the real output was at its potential level, the increase in the money supply which resulted in increase in aggregate demand causes the real output to expand beyond the potential output level to Y_1'.

Consequently, there is tightness in labor market as $Y_1' > Y^P$ and $n_1 > n_0$. This results in increase in demand for goods and services, and employers and producers in competing for the tight resources of both raw materials and labor ends up bidding higher prices for the available resources. Wages and prices of both factors of production, final goods, and services increase. The increase in the cost of production causes a decrease in the profit of employers and suppliers which necessitate the need to cut down production, which ends up reducing real output from Y_1' till it reaches Y^P. The reduction in real output drags down factors of production including labor from n_1 back to n_0. See Panels 10.4–10.6.

The labor market which is captured by labor supply and demand for real wages is shown in diagram six of Panel 10.7. The effect of the increase in the money supply causes the labor supply (LS) curve to shift rightward or downward from LS_0 to LS'_1. This shifts the real wage rate w_0 from its initial equilibrium E_0 to w_1 at lower equilibrium E'_1.

However, because of tightness in the labor market at the new equilibrium E'_1 the self-correction mechanism of the free market system compels employers and suppliers to hike up wages and prices of labor and productive resources by reducing those inputs and intermediate resources. This causes the labor supply curve to shift backward from LS_1' to LS_0. Thus, wages increase from w_1 to w_0 at its original equilibrium E_0, and the labor supply also drops from the new equilibrium n_1 to its original position n_0 as output returns from Y'_1 to Y^P as shown in Panel 10.6.

10.7 Phase Diagrams Summary

The path of the money supply, real interest rate, real output, inflation rate, the labor employed, and exchange rate from the beginning of the expansionary monetary policy to infinity is shown in phase diagrams inPanel 10.8. It is observed that at time t_0 when the increase in the money supply commenced, the money supply jumped from its horizontal M_0 path to its M_1 path and continued thereon to infinity as is shown in diagram 1 of Panel 10.9. Thus, there is a permanent increase in the money supply following the implementation of the policy.

In diagram 2 of Panel 10.10, the increase in the money supply triggered the real interest rate to fall immediately from its normal i_0 path to

Panel 10.8 Phase diagrams of time path of economic variables' response to easy monetary policy

Panel 10.9 Money supply

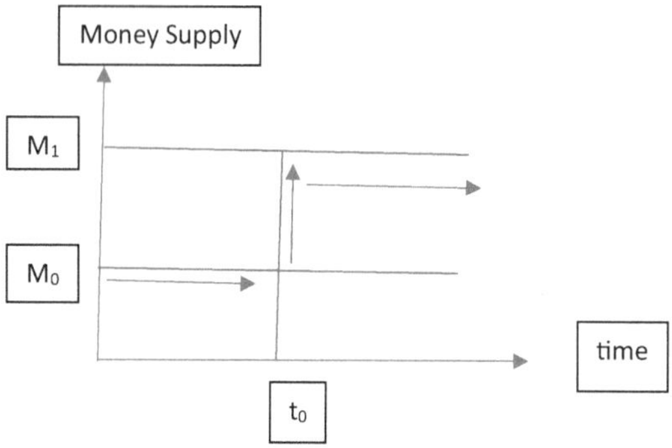

i_1 path. It thereon started immediately to rise asymptotically toward its original i_0 path and continued thereon. Thus, its final path following the implementation of the easy monetary policy remained on the original i_0 path before the policy.

The effect of an increase in money supply at time t_0 resulted also in inflation rate rising immediately from its original π_0 path, by moving gradually and asymptotically upward toward the higher path of inflation rate π_1 where it continues thereon on the parallel path of the original inflation path. See diagram 3 of Panel 10.11.

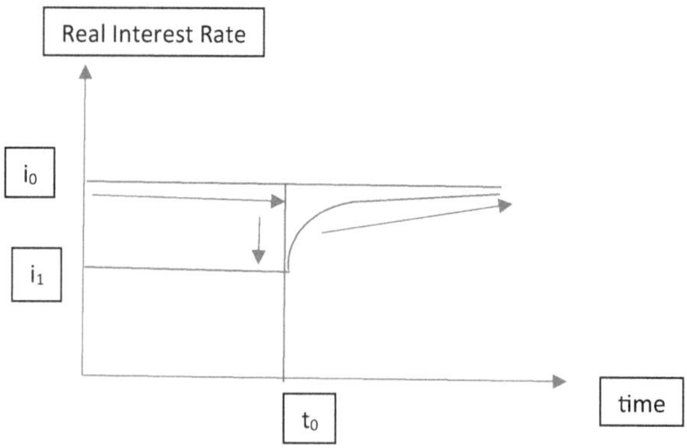

Panel 10.10 Real interest rate

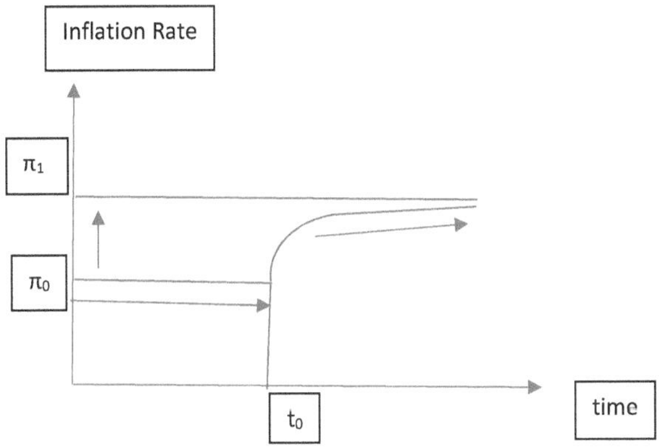

Panel 10.11 Inflation rate

The central issue here is the effect of the increase in money supply on the path of the exchange rate. At time t_0 when the expansionary monetary policy is implemented, the exchange rate jumped immediately to its highest depreciating point to reach the exchange rate of XR'$_1$ which is designated as B on the phase diagram numbered Panel 10.12. Two factors which contributed to the highest increase in depreciation from XR_0 to XR'$_1$ is the following: (a) the contraction in the domestic real interest rate from i_0 to i_1 and (b) the upward shift of foreign expected return from $E(R^f{}_0)$ to $E(R^f{}_1)$.

However, at E'_1 because $Y_1 > Y^P$ the tightness in the labor market results in prices increasing as competition among producers and suppliers for intermediate inputs increases the cost of production and the general price of goods and services in the country. This results in interest rate rising and the exchange rate appreciating until the interest rate reaches its original level i_0 before the expansionary monetary policy at exchange rate of XR_1 on E_1 equilibrium level with real output Y^P. Thereafter, the exchange rate reversed its course by partially appreciating gradually and moving asymptotically toward the exchange rate XR_1 which is between the original point A and the highest depreciating point B. Thus, the response of the exchange rate to monetary expansion is highly volatile. See also diagram 4 of Panel 10.5.

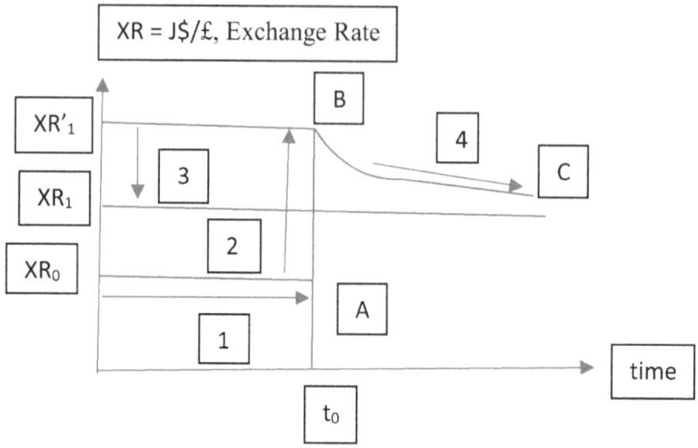

Panel 10.12 Exchange rate

10.8 Macroeconomic Policy Lessons

In the long run following an easy monetary policy, the economy experiences the classical dichotomy, monetary neutrality property and in the case of international finance, exchange rate overshooting.

The nominal variables in the model discussed are money supply, inflation, and exchange rate, and the real variables are real interest rate, real wages, real output, and labor.

The classical dichotomy is the fact that in the long run an increase in the money supply separates its effect on nominal variables from its effect on real variables. In the context of the economy, an expansionary monetary policy has a long-run effect on increasing the money supply, inflation rate and exchange rate because prices are completely flexible over that period. However, expansionary monetary policy has no long-run effect on real output, real interest rate, real wages, and labor.

Neutrality of money property is the phenomenon where, in the long run, a once-and-for-all expansionary monetary policy causes all nominal variables to increase, while all real variables remain the same, as observed from response of variables in the study. If, however, arbitrary changes in the path of the money supply does not affect all real variables including interest rates, then money is said to be super-neutral. The Phase diagrams in Panels 10.9–10.12 illustrate the cases of an expansionary monetary policy effect on the three nominal variables and four real variables.

Exchange rate overshooting is the situation where in response to a permanent or long-run increase in the money supply the initial fluctuation of the exchange rate to the monetary shock is greater than its long-run response. The movement of the exchange rate from XR_0 to XR_1' is much higher than the final level of exchange rate XR_1. This phenomenon is what is described as exchange rate overshooting as it is observed in the fourth diagrams of Panels 10.5 and 10.12, respectively.

10.9 Appendix

The system of equations in a closed economy employed in the analysis for the above discussion are as follows:

The AD curve

$$Y = (C_0 - C_1 T_0 + I_0 + G_0 + NX_0 - d_1.\text{ff})/[1 - C_1(1 - T_1) - d_2 + e_2]$$
$$-(d_1 + e_1).(r_0 + \mu\pi)/[1 - C_1(1 - T_1) - d_2 + e_2]$$

The AS curve

$$\Delta\dot{p}_t = \Delta p_t - \Delta p_{t-1} = \kappa\beta(Y_t - Y^n) + \xi_t$$

Production Function[1]

$$y = f(n)$$

Labor Market

$$w = \Delta W/W - \pi = \text{mpl}$$

Demand for Labor

$$f'(n) = w,\ f' \geq 0,\ f'' \leq 0.$$

Supply of labor

$$n = h(w), h \geq 0, \text{ or } h' \geq 0 \text{ and } h = f'^{-1}$$

Money Market

$$M/P = L(y,\ i),\ L_y > 0 \text{ and } L_i < 0$$

Exchange Rate

$$\text{XR} = P/P^f$$

Open Economy Market

$$\text{BOP} = \text{CA}(i,\ i^F,\ y,\ y^F,\ \text{xr}) + K(i - i^F)$$

where,

[1] The general production function can be expressed as follows:
$\Upsilon = F(N, K)$,
where Υ is output, N is labor or population, and K is the capital stock.
Thus, for a fixed capital stock, the production function can be expressed as.
$Y/K = F(N/K,\ 1)$ and $y = F(n,\ 1) = f(n)$ or $Y/N = F(K/N,\ 1) = f(k)$ where $y = f(n)$ is output per person or labor or population for a fixed capital stock.

$f(n) \equiv F(n, k)$ for a fixed value of capital, $f' \geq 0$, $f'(n)$ is marginal product of labor (mpl), w is the real wage rate; W is nominal wage rate, $\dot{p}_t = \Delta p_t = \pi_t$ is inflation rate, and y is real output as a function of labor with fixed capital stock. BOP is balance of payments, CA is current account, and $K(i - i^F)$ is the capital account. The rest of the notations maintain their earlier definitions. The capital account is balanced when domestic interest rate (i) is equal to foreign interest rate (i^F), and BOP = CA((i, i^F, y, y^F, xr).

10.10 Summary

The effect of the money supply on interest rate is discussed from the money market by increasing the money supply in the central bank. The easy monetary policy implemented by the central bank is illustrated in the money market.

Its effect on inflation and real interest rate are used to derive the monetary policy principles curve. The effect of the easy monetary policy is also used in goods and service market through aggregate demand and supply curves to determine real output and inflation.

The effect of the easy money on exchange rate and real interest rate are discussed and supported with graphs and phase diagrams in the foreign exchange market. Here we examined the volatility of the exchange rate through what is known as the exchange rate overshooting.

10.11 Problems

10.1 (a) Is exchange rate pass-through generally complete? What reason(s) will you use to support your answer?

(b) Define the following terms and concepts:

(i) neutrality property of money
(ii) exchange rate overshooting
(iii) classical dichotomy
(iv) self-correction mechanism
(v) bullion
(vi) price-specie flow model

10.2 The central bank of a mythical country has implemented a contractionary monetary policy (MP) by reducing its money supply. Will this policy result in the 'neutrality' property of money and the classical dichotomy? Explain your answer with the aid of the MPC, AD, and AS curves, and the foreign exchange market schedules. Use phase diagrams to support your answers.

10.3 When a central bank adopts a fixed exchange rate it may forego its autonomy to set domestic monetary policy. This is presented in the following argument:

"Assuming that workers demand higher wages which employers give their consent, but they in turn raise prices of output to recover their higher production costs. Consequently, the price level is higher and real cash balances are temporarily lower. However, to avoid interest rate from rising and triggering appreciation of the currency, the central bank decided to buy foreign exchange to cause expansion in the money supply. This response accommodates the initial wage demands. Thus, causing the economy to move permanently to a higher level of wages and prices. Under a fixed exchange rate regime, wages and prices cannot be prevented from falling."

Is the above argument true or false? Explain.

10.4 The central bank of an island economy is faced with a rise in the world interest rate, i^F. Does this affect the country's foreign reserve holdings? How does it affect the country's money supply? Can it offset either of these effects through the country's open market operations?

Selected References

Dornbusch, Rudiger (1976). Expectations and Exchange Rate Dynamics, *Journal of Political Economy*, 86 (6), December, 1161–1176.

Fleming, J. M. (1962), "Domestic Financial Policies under Fixed and under Floating Exchange Rates," *IMF Staff Papers*, November 1962.

Krugman, Paul R., Maurice Obstfeld, and Marc J Melitz (2000). *International Economics: Theory and Policy*, New York: Pearson.

Lucas, Robert E., Jr., (1972), "Expectations and the neutrality of money," *Journal of Economic Theory*, 4, April, 103–24.

Magee, Stephen P. (1973), "Currency constraint, pass-through, and devaluation," *Brookings Papers on Economic Activity*, 1, 303-325.

McCallum, Bennett T. (1989), *Monetary Economics: Theory and Policy*, New York: Macmillan Publishing Company.

Mishkin, Frederic S. (2016), *The Economics of Money, Banking, and Financial Markets*, New York: Pearson.

Mundell, Robert (1963), "Capital Mobility and Stabilization Policy under Fixed and Flexible Exchange Rates," *Canadian Journal of Economics and Political Science*, November.

Nelson, Charles R. and Charles I. Plosser (1982), "Trends and random walks in macroeconomic time series: some evidence and implications," *Journal of Monetary Economics*, 10, September, 139–167.

Okun, M. Arthur (1962). "Potential GNP: Its Measurement and Significance." Proceedings of the Business and Economic Statistics Section, American Statistical Society.

Phelps, Edmund S. (1967). "Phillips Curves, Expectations of Inflation, and Optimal Unemployment over Time." *Economica*, 34: 254-81.

Phillips, Alban W. H. (1958). "The Relation between Unemployment and the Rate of Change of Money Wage Rates in the United Kingdom, 1861-1957." *Economica*, 25: 283–300.

Romer, David, (2001), *Advanced Macroeconomics*, New York: McGraw Hill.

CHAPTER 11

External Imbalance Models

Learning Outcomes

Readers of this chapter will be expected to have acquired knowledge and clear understanding to do the following, among others:

(a) Derive the elasticities approach to the BOPs; the absorption approach to the BOPs; the exchange market pressure model; the monetary policy approach to the BOPs under a fixed exchange rate; and the monetary approach to the exchange rate.
(b) Define or explain absorption, beachhead effect, exchange rate pass-through, J-curve effect, and price-specie flow mechanism.
(c) Calculate the Marshall-Lerner condition; short-run elasticities and long-run elasticities.

11.1 Introduction

The main economic developments that have been proposed to deal with external imbalances of countries can be traced from the 'elasticities' approach to balance of payments, which was pioneered by Robinson (1937) for conditions of deep depression and mass unemployment

E. E. Ghartey, *International Macroeconomics and Finance*,
https://doi.org/10.1007/978-3-032-04145-6_11

in the 1930s. It was followed by the Keynesian multiplier approach by Harberger (1950), which was later modified into the 'absorption approach' by Alexander (1952).

The 'economic policy' approach was independently developed by Meade (1951) and Tinbergen (1952) to extend the existing model to deal with the twin policy objectives of internal and external balances. Unfortunately, it failed to treat the role of domestic monetary policy in correcting external imbalances.

In this chapter we shall discuss important aspects of models that are relevant in dealing with balance of payments deficit problems. We shall also present empirical papers that have been used to resolve disequilibrium in the BOPs. We shall discuss the elasticities approach, the absorption approach, monetary approach, the exchange market pressure (EMP) model, and the monetary approach to the BOPs under fixed and floating exchange rate for dealing with the BOPs problem.

11.2 Price-Specie Flow Mechanism

David Hume developed the price-specie flow mechanism to depict how disequilibrium in the balance of trade is self-corrected under the gold standard. Balance of trade deficit in a country under the gold standard leads to automatic outflow of gold from the country, whereas a balance of trade surplus results in automatic inflow of gold to the country. The analysis of Hume's price-specie flow mechanism is very similar to the monetary approach to the balance of payments and prices.

The gold inflow which is triggered by balance of trade (or payments) surplus during the gold standard, where the central bank does not have to use monetary policy to counter the effect of an increase in the money supply, will experience an increase in prices in the country. The increase in price of the gold recipient country will cause its prices of all goods and services including exports to increase. The increase in exports price will cause the country's exports to decrease, while encouraging its imports to increase, to the point where the country's balance of trade (or payments) surplus dries out.

Thus, the price-specie flow mechanism serves as a self-correction mechanism. It considered only bullion, which is the bulky bars of gold often held as reserves by central banks, and no involvement of a fiat money in its analysis. Thus, it operated very much like the role of the IMF fixed exchange rate regime, during the first thirty years of the Bretton Woods

System, where gold was fixed to be exchanged at the rate of $35 for an ounce of gold, although it was adjustable within a 1 percent band to the dollar.

The Bretton Woods System came to an end in 1971, when the US dollar experienced crisis because of stagflation, which originated from oil and agricultural shortfall in the world market. This resulted in a dual occurrence of inflation and unemployment which is termed as stagflation in the US and the rest of the world in general. The US ended the conversion of dollars into gold in August of that year. The dollar was devalued by $38 to an ounce of gold which was equivalent to $120 per ounce of gold under the free market system.

Thus, the fixed exchange rate regime which was adopted by the institutions of the IMF and International Building of Reconstruction and Development (IBRD), also known as the World Bank, which were established in Bretton Woods on 27 December 1945, was dismantled. The IMF and IBRD adopted a flexible exchange rate for the currencies of other developed countries in March 1973, while most developing countries remained under the slightly modified arrangement (or managed float) of the Bretton Woods era.

11.3 Monetary Approach to the Balance of Payments and Exchange Rate

The monetary approach to the balance of payments (BOPs) was developed by several economists to treat the role of domestic monetary policy in the determination of exchange rate and the BOPs [see Polak (1957), Johnson (1977), Frenkel and Johnson (1976), Mundell (1971), and Dornbusch (1973), to name a few]. The monetary approach views the balance of payments as a monetary phenomenon. It maintains that payment imbalances reflect stock disequilibria between the supply of and demand for money, and the latter is assumed to be a function of national income. Balance of payments are assumed to operate as safety-valve which opens-up automatically either to remove excess supply of money which results from balance of payments deficits or to admit additional national money supply in the form of balance of payments surplus in response to excess demand for money. Thus the 'monetary approach' is very similar to Hume's (1963) price-specie flow mechanism, as both views deal with a self-correcting mechanism of monetary flows associated with balance of payments deficits and surpluses. But, unlike the 'monetary approach' which operates through both demand for and supply of money, Hume's price-specie flow discussed earlier operated through commodity prices.

Thus, the import-demand elasticities which are important lubricant for the smooth functioning of the price-specie flow mechanism, are not crucial for the 'monetary approach.' The 'monetary approach' assumes that the best way of analyzing macroeconomic phenomena is by using both demand for and supply of money. It also assumes that the world does not consist of separable national economies but instead, it is an integrated closed economy. As a result, there is a perfect commodity arbitrage which ensures that the law of one price holds in integrated world commodity market [see also Johnson (1977) and von Whitman's (1975) survey].

11.4 The Exchange Market Pressure (EMP) Model

The EMP model was developed by Girton and Roper (1977) for Canada, as a synthesis of monetary approach to balance of payments and monetary approach to exchange rate determination for a small open economy, which takes the world prices as given. The EMP model is defined as the mechanism by which a dependent variable consisting of changes in exchange rates and foreign reserves absorbs the 'pressure' exerted by external imbalance when there is excess (or diminish) growth in the money supply of a country relative to money demand under a dirty float regime [see Girton and Roper (1977, p.537) and Connolly and da Silveira (1979, p.448)].

Weymark (1997, p.59) defines the EMP as a measure of "the total excess demand for a currency in international markets as the exchange rate change that would have been required to remove this excess demand in the absence of exchange market intervention, given the expectations generated by the exchange rate policy actually implemented." She argues that her definition removes the basic problems inherent in the Girton-Roper model, namely: (i) the latter's model is derived from restrictive monetary model as a result it is not malleable to be applied to other models, and (ii) the latter's methodology is based on a model dependent definition which makes it arbitrary as it fails to identify a unique formula for measuring intervention activity.

Upon a careful review of both studies, we decided to use the Girton-Roper model because their methodology is simpler, and easy to derive without sacrificing substance and intent of the model. Additionally, unlike

Weymark's intervention index, it does not rely on definition of forward-looking expectation, the calculation of which is arbitrary at best, and the use of intervention index. This means that different researchers may use different variables to define the conditioned all available information, so the resulting Weymark's computed intervention index will at best be arbitrary.[1]

In theory, the EMP model is a two-country single equation which basically shows that exchange market pressures are absorbed either through loss of (gain in) foreign reserves or depreciation/devaluation (appreciation/revaluation) of the exchange rate. It is therefore a useful means to empirically test the exchange rate regime practiced by a country and measure the degree of its monetary autonomy. Note that under a flexible exchange rate regime, exchange market pressures are absorbed by depreciation, whereas under a fixed exchange rate regime such pressures are absorbed by loss of foreign reserves. The EMP model has also been applied to study the economic situation of Brazil by Connolly and da Silveira (1979), Argentina by Modeste (1981), Korea by Kim (1985), Costa Rica by Thornton (1995), G7 by Bahmani-Oskooee and Bernstein (1999), and Jamaica by Ghartey (2002).

11.5 Derivation of the EMP Model

Literature clearly is replete with several exchange market pressure research studies for many countries. We have used the model used by Ghartey (2009) for Mexico in the study. To derive the EMP model, we first specify a stable money demand for Mexico in the classical tradition as a function of real income (Y) and national price (P) as

$$L = k.P.Y \tag{11.1}$$

where, k is the Cambridge constant. This specification allows us to eliminate interest rates to avoid introducing simultaneous equation bias problem in the analysis, since capital flows affect domestic interest rates which are likely to be endogenous in the EMP model [see Obstfeld (1982), Connolly and da Silveira (1979), and Girton and Roper (1977)].

[1] Note that any model that employs rational expectation is in theory not arbitrary because of the conditioned all available information; however, in empirical studies the conditioned all available information depends on the researcher's specific model.

The money supply is specified as a function of domestic credit (DC) and international reserves (IR) which are consolidated from the banking system. In the context of Hume's price-specie flow mechanism the IR represents gold bullion. The liabilities of the banking system consolidated from the central and private banks are denoted by the money stock (M). The domestic component of the monetary base is referred to as domestic credit, and the foreign component of the monetary base is known as international reserves. The resulting identity for the money supply is expressed as

$$M = mm.(IR + DC) \tag{11.2}$$

where, mm is a constant money multiplier, and (IR + DC) is the resulting base money. The exchange rate is defined as

$$XR = P/P^F \tag{11.3}$$

where, XR is the nominal exchange rate which describes the foreign country's denominated value of the US dollar, and P^F is the price of international or US with the latter representing reserve country. The domestic country is assumed to be a small open country that faces a fixed price. Thus, it is assumed that in case of any need for official settlement adjustment, the domestic country will be forced to bear the burden of adjustment. By invoking the Walras Law, the monetary inter reaction when money supply is equal to demand from Eqs. (11.2) and (11.3), respectively, yields the following:

$$mm.(IR + DC) = k.P.Y \left(= k.XR.P^F.Y\right) \tag{11.4}$$

The left-hand side of Eq. (11.4) is expressed in percentages as

$$(\Delta M/M) = \Delta IR/(IR + DC) + \Delta DC/(IR + DC) \tag{11.5a}$$

The right-hand side of Eq. (11.5a) is also expressed in percentages as

$$\left(\Delta XR.k.P^F Y\right)/\left(k.XR.P^F.Y\right) + \left(\Delta P^F.k.XR.Y\right)/\left(k.XR.P^F.Y\right) + \left(\Delta Y.k.XR.P^F\right)/\left(\right.$$
$$= (\Delta XR)/(XR) + \left(\Delta P^F\right)/\left(P^F\right) + (\Delta Y)/(Y) \tag{11.5b}$$

Equation (11.4) is therefore expressed in terms of percentage changes by using Eqs. (11.5a-5b) as follows:

$$\Delta IR/(IR + DC) + \Delta DC/(IR + DC) = \Delta lnXR + \Delta lnP^F + \Delta lnY \quad (11.6)$$

It is further expressed as an EMP model as follows:

$$\Delta IR/(IR + DC) - \Delta lnXR = -\Delta DC/(IR + DC) + \Delta lnP^F + \Delta lnY \quad (11.7a)$$

where, EMP = $\Delta IR/(IR + DC) - \Delta lnXR$

But lnY = lny – lnP; where, y = nominal GDP or GNP. Substituting the real income in terms of the nominal income minus prices above into Eq. (11.7a) we obtain the following equation:

$$\Delta IR/(IR + DC) - \Delta lnXR = -\Delta DC/(IR + DC) + \Delta lnP^F + \Delta lny - \Delta lnP \quad (11.7b)$$

Since Eq. (11.7b) is an identity, we have further expressed it in a general behavioral form as follows:

$$\Delta IR/(IR + DC) - \Delta lnXR = -\beta_1 \Delta DC/(IR + DC) + \beta_2 \Delta lnP^F + \beta_3 \Delta lny - \beta_4 \Delta lnP + \nu \quad (11.8)$$

where, all the parameters are nonnegative.

Note that the left-hand side dependent variables, ($\Delta IR/(IR + DC) - \Delta lnXR$), of Eq. (11.8) constitute the EMP model. Its coefficients are constrained to unity. This means that an increase in domestic credit, which is the offset coefficient variable, will result in either an outflow of foreign reserves or depreciation or both. By substituting lower case letters for the logarithmic variables, the EMP model which is finally estimated is expressed as follows:

$$\Delta IR/(IR + DC) - \Delta xr = -\lambda \Delta DC/(IR + DC) + \alpha_1 \Delta p^F + \alpha_2 \Delta y - \alpha_3 \Delta p + \varepsilon' \quad (11.9)$$

where, all the parameters are nonnegative, ε' is the error term, and the offset coefficient λ is unity and measures the extent of monetary policy independence in the country. A significant negative unit coefficient of λ, with the rest of the explanatory variables being insignificant or a stable demand for money, means if monetary authorities increase money growth, they will face either depreciation or lose foreign reserves, or face both.

However, if the monetary authorities (MA) increase the base money by buying domestic assets through open market operations, then they can fix the exchange rate only if they raise the foreign reserves to the same extent as the initial increase in the base money. Thus, under a pegged rate, the central bank's scope to pursue an independent monetary policy will be restricted by its available foreign reserves.

Equation (11.9) also shows that an increase in income and foreign inflation rates, and a fall in national inflation rates, all other things being equal, will either cause the exchange rate to appreciate or an inflow of foreign reserves or both. The converse holds true. The sensitivity of the EMP to its composition allows us to measure and test the policy reaction of the MA. It is estimated by adding EF which is defined as the ratio of exchange rates to foreign reserves as a regressor to the expression in Eq. (11.9).

If the coefficient of EF is negative and significant, then all other things being equal, the EMP is sensitive to its composition, so the central bank absorbs exchange market pressure by losing foreign reserves. This policy reaction is consistent with an optimal pegged exchange rate regime. If the coefficient of EF is positive and significant, then the monetary authorities absorb exchange market pressures by depreciation, so a floating rate regime is optimal. An insignificant coefficient of EF means that exchange market pressures are absorbed by both depreciation/devaluation and loss of foreign reserves so the optimal exchange rate regime for the country is a 'dirty' float. See Edward Ghartey (2009).

11.6 Monetary Approach to the Balance of Payments Under a Fixed Exchange Rate

The monetary approach model to the balance of payments under a fixed exchange rate, which is commonly referred to as the Mundell-Fleming model, was derived by using the IS-LM-BP model.[2] However, because of the shortcoming of the LM curve component, we have used the EMP model specified in Eq. (11.9). Under a fixed exchange rate regime, the

[2] See Mundell (1963) and Fleming (1962).

change in exchange rate is zero. The resulting model by setting $\Delta xr = 0$ in Eq. (11.9) becomes as follows:

$$\Delta IR/(IR + DC) = -\lambda \Delta DC/(IR + DC) + \alpha_1 \Delta p^f + \alpha_2 \Delta y - \alpha_3 \Delta p + \varepsilon'' \tag{11.10}$$

Equation (11.10) is the monetary model to the balance of payments under a fixed exchange rate. Consequently, the monetary authorities cannot control the exchange rate. Increase in the money supply or domestic credit translates into loss of international reserves or balance of payment deficit. Increase in money demand brought about by increase in real income or excess demand for money results in increase in domestic credit which is the money supply. If the monetary authorities desist from increasing the money supply, there will be an increase in financial inflow which is international reserves or balance of payments surplus. Thus, the BOPs turn into surplus when the IR is rising, and the converse holds.

On the other hand, an increase in DC and hence the money supply when money demand remains the same, flows out of the country by causing either a fall in IR or BOPs deficit. A surplus in the BOPs results from an excess in the stock of money demand that is not satisfied by an increase in the DC, while a deficit in the BOPs resulting from an excess in the money stock of the country which has not been eliminated by monetary authorities, leads to outflows of international reserves for correction.

Thus, excess demand for money results in balance of payments surplus which is an inflow of international reserves, and the money supply increases by the same amount. Similarly, an excess in the stock of money supply leads to outflow of international reserves which causes balance of payments deficit to eliminate the excess supply of money of equal magnitude in the nation.

Therefore, under a fixed exchange rate regime, the country does not have any control over the money supply in the long run. The country's balance of payments surplus or deficit is temporary, they are self-corrected in the long run under a fixed exchange rate regime. The BOPs equilibrium occurs when the money demand is equal to the money supply so that there are no outflow or inflow of international reserves into the country.

11.7 Monetary Approach to Exchange Rate

The monetary approach under a flexible exchange rate is what is known as the monetary approach to exchange rate (MAER). Under a flexible exchange rate regime, the BOPs deficits are corrected immediately by automatic changes in exchanges rates without any need for international flow of reserves or money. The nation's monetary authorities have a complete control over its money supply and monetary policy. The EMP model is therefore used to carry the adjustment of imbalance in the BOPs by assuming that the net international reserves are zero. This means that the flexible exchange rate or the monetary approach to the exchange rate model which is derived by setting IR to zero in the EMP model in Eq. (11.9) is as follows:

$$\Delta xr = \lambda \Delta DC/(IR + DC) - \alpha_1 \Delta P^f - \alpha_2 \Delta y + \alpha_3 \Delta P + \varepsilon''' \quad (11.11)$$

The above equation shows that under a flexible exchange rate adjustments to external imbalance take place through changes in domestic prices in response to changes in the exchange rate. For instance, a BOPs deficit (which originates from excess money supply) causes automatic depreciation of the domestic currency, which causes prices to increase and the demand for money to increase large enough to absorb the excess supply of money, to automatically eliminate the BOPs deficit.

On the other hand, a BOPs surplus which emanates from an excess demand for money automatically results in appreciation of the national currency. This then reduces the domestic prices which then eliminates the excess demand for money and the resulting BOPs surplus.

Thus, under a fixed exchange rate, a BOPs disequilibrium occurs due to international flow of money or reserves, so the nation has no control over its money supply. In fact, money flows between countries to adjust to external imbalance. External equilibrium occurs when international flow of money reaches equilibrium, and that situation occurs when export flows are equal to import flows.

On the contrary, under flexible exchange rates, the BOPs disequilibrium is immediately corrected by an automatic change in exchange rate without any international flow of money or reserves. In fact, market forces interplay of supply of and demand for currencies between countries establish the exchange rate. Thus, the nation retains a complete control of money supply and monetary policy.

11.8 Elasticities Approach to the Balance of Payments (BOPs)

The elasticities approach to the balance of payments or trade was developed independently by Alfred Marshall and Abba P. Lerner.

In deriving the elasticities approach to the BOPs, we assume that (i) there is equilibrium in the BOPs, (ii) there are mass unemployment and under-utilization of resources, and (iii) net factor income and transfers, and the net capital account ($K(i - i^F)$) are balanced at zero. This means X = XR.IM.

So,

$$\begin{aligned} BOT &= CA \\ &= X - IM.XR \end{aligned} \quad (11.12)$$

where, exports of goods and services (X), and imports of goods and services (IM) are denominated in domestic currency by using the prevailing exchange rate (XR). Balance of trade (BOT) is defined as current account (CA).

Differentiating Eq. (11.12) with respect to XR we obtain

$$\partial BOT/\partial XR = \partial X/\partial XR - [IM + XR \partial IM/\partial XR] \quad (11.13)$$

But for balance of trade (BOT), IM = X/XR, $\partial X/\partial XR > 0$, and $\partial IM/\partial XR < 0$ in the long run.

So, Eq. (11.13) can be re-expressed as

$$\begin{aligned} (1/IM).\,\partial BOT/\partial XR &= (1/IM).\partial X/\partial XR - 1 - (XR/IM).\partial IM/\partial XR \\ &= (XR/X).\,\partial X/\partial XR - 1 - (XR/IM).\partial IM/\partial XR \end{aligned}$$

Again, using $\eta_X = (XR/X).\ \partial X/\partial XR$, and $\eta_{IM} = -\ (XR/IM).\ \partial IM/\partial XR$ we obtain

$$\begin{aligned} (1/IM).\,\partial BOT/\partial XR &= \eta_X - 1 + \eta_{IM} \\ \partial BOT/\partial XR &= [\eta_X - 1 + \eta_{IM}].IM \end{aligned} \quad (11.14)$$

But since IM > 0 or IM $\neq$ 0, then $\partial BOT/\partial XR > 0$ iff. $\eta_X - 1 + \eta_{IM} > 0$.

Therefore,

$$|\eta_X| + |\eta_{IM}| > 1, \text{(A necessary condition) for } BOT > 0 \quad (11.15)$$

The above equation is the Marshall-Lerner condition, and

$$|\eta_X| + |\eta_{IM}| > 1 + \text{ mpim}, \text{ (A necessary and sufficient condition)} \tag{11.16}$$

where, mpim is the marginal propensity to import, and $(\partial IM/\partial Y)$ is the change in imports resulting from a unit change in income of the country. The rest of the notations maintain their earlier definitions.

The Marshall-Lerner condition states that for devaluation or depreciation to succeed in improving the BOPs or the balance of trade of a country, the sum of the magnitudes of its price elasticities of imports and exports of its demand equations must exceed unity, which is Eq. (11.15). This is a necessary condition for devaluation or depreciation policy to improve the balance of trade.

The necessary and sufficient condition of the Marshall-Lerner condition states that for devaluation or depreciation to improve the BOPs or BOT of a country, the sum of the magnitudes of its price elasticities of imports and exports of its demand equations must exceed the sum of unity plus its marginal propensity to import, which is Eq. (11.16).

11.9 Illustrative Example

Practical insights for the elasticities approach to the balance of payments is provided from the model below which was developed and estimated for Ghana by Edward E. Ghartey and was published in *Applied Economics* journal in 1987.

Equilibrium case of the import function

$$im_t^d = a_0 + a_1(pim/p)_t + a_2 y_t + u_t \tag{11.17}$$

$$im_t^s = A_0 + A_1 pim_t + A_2 y_t^w + U_t \tag{11.18}$$

$$im_t^d = im_t^s \tag{11.19}$$

Equilibrium case of the export function

$$x_t^d = b_0 + b_1(px/p^w)_t + b_2 y_t^w + v_t \tag{11.20}$$

$$x_t^s = B_0 + B_1 px_t + B_2 p_t + y_t + V_t \tag{11.21}$$

$$x_t^d = x_t^s \tag{11.22}$$

Dynamic case of the import function

$$im_t^d = c_0 + c_1(pim/p)_t + c_2 y_t + c_3 im_{t-1} + w_t \tag{11.23}$$

$$im_t^s = C_0 + C_1 p_t^w + C_2 pim_t + C_3 y_t^w + C_4 pim_{t-1} + W_t \tag{11.24}$$

$$im_t^d = im_t^s \tag{11.25}$$

Dynamic case of the export function

$$x_t^d = d_0 + d_1(px/p^w)_t + d_2 y_t^w + d_3 x_{t-1} + \varepsilon_t \tag{11.26}$$

$$x_t^s = D_0 + D_1 p_t + D_2 y_t + D_3 px_t + D_4 x_{t-1} + \zeta_t \tag{11.27}$$

$$x_t^d = x_t^s \tag{11.28}$$

where, im is quantity of imports, x is quantity of exports, px is price of exports, pim is price of imports, p is domestic prices or consumer price index, p^w is world prices, y^w is world income. The variables in small case letters are specified in their logarithmic form, with subscript t denoting time. The error terms u_t, U_t, v_t, V_t, w_t, W_t, ε_t, and ζ_t are white noise innovations.

All the behavioral equations can be estimated by using the ordinary least squares (OLS) estimator. Equations of significance are the import and exports demand equations. However, in the equilibrium case model, because Eqs. (11.17) and (11.20) are over-identified, we have used the two-stage least squares (2SLS) with p, y, p^w, and y^w as instruments. Furthermore, for similar over-identification reason, we have estimated Eqs. (11.23) and (11.26) in the dynamic case model with the same 2SLS using p_t, y_t, $p^w{}_t$, $y^w{}_t$, and x_{t-1} as instrumental variables. See Ghartey, *op. cit.* for detail discussion.

11.10 Application in a Developing Economy

Assuming that the estimated import demand for the equilibrium case of Ghana is (Tables 11.1 and 11.2)

$$\ln IM_t = 2.21 + 1.68 \ln Y_t - 1.01 \ln P_t \tag{11.29}$$

The dynamic imports demand equation of Ghana is

$$\ln IM_t = 2.26 + 1.73 \ln Y_t - 1.04 \ln P_t - 0.02 \ln IM_{t-1} \tag{11.30}$$

The marginal propensity to import (mpim) is $\partial IM/\partial Y$.
Differentiating Eq. (11.29) w.r.t. IM yields

$$(1/IM).(\partial IM/\partial Y) = 1.68.(1/Y)$$

So, mpim = $(\partial IM/\partial Y) = 1.68(IM/Y)$.
In 2019, IM = 46,424.13 and Y = 164,560 in real or constant prices.
In 2018, IM = 46,661.97 and Y = 154,548.
Data source is the International Financial Statistics, IMF.

Table 11.1 Impact estimates of the magnitudes of price and income elasticities of imports and exports

Elasticities	ηX	ηIM
Income	4.78	1.68
Price	–0.58	–1.01

Table 11.2 Long-run estimates of the magnitudes of price and income elasticities of imports and exports

Elasticities	ηX	ηIM
Income	4.96	1.89
Price	–0.04	–1.03

Source Edward E. Ghartey (1987), "Devaluation as a balance of payments corrective measure in developing countries: a study relating to Ghana," *Applied Economics*, 19, 937–947. See Tables 3 and 4

Thus in 2019,

$$\text{mpim} = (\partial \text{IM}/\partial \text{Y}) = 1.68(\text{IM}/\text{Y}) = 1.68(46,424/164,560) = 0.282.$$

The Marshall-Lerner condition in Ghana using the information from the source above is

$$\eta_{\text{X}} = -0.58,\ \eta_{\text{M}} = -1.01 \text{ and mpim } = 0.282$$

The necessary Marshall-Lerner condition is

$$|\eta_{\text{X}}| + |\eta_{\text{IM}}| = 0.58 + 1.01 = 1.59 > 1$$

The necessary and sufficient Marshall-Lerner condition is

$$|\eta_{\text{X}}| + |\eta_{\text{IM}}| = 0.58 + 1.01 = 1.59 > 1 + \text{ mpim } = 1.282$$

Therefore, both the necessary and sufficient conditions for the Marshall-Lerner conditions are satisfied, so devaluation will improve either the BOT or BOPs of Ghana based on the structure of the country in the empirical source above.

11.11 Response Policy Lag

Devaluation or depreciation is sensitive to response lag of the country which is employing the devaluation policy. This is achieved by using the dynamic model. The adjustment lag of the devaluation policy can be calculated by using the disequilibrium or dynamic model reported in Eq. (11.30). The adjustment coefficient which is the lagged coefficient of the imports demand equation is - 0.02.

In this context, the relevant dynamic import demand is Eq. (11.23) or (11.30). The speed of adjustment is $[1/(1 - C_3)] = [1/(1 + 0.02)] = 0.98$. Thus, the speed of adjustment in case of any displacement associated with the devaluation is very fast in the country during the period of study.

11.12 Other Lags

11.12.1 Median Lag

The median lag = (log0.5)/(logC_3) using Eq. (11.23), where C_3 is the coefficient of the lagged dependent variable. From Eq. (11.30), C_3 = - 0.02, so the median lag = log0.5/log(1 + 0.02) = - 0.693147/0.0198 = - 35.007.

11.12.2 Mean Lags

The mean lag is the weighted average lags. The mean lag = - 0.02/(1 + 0.02) = - 0.0196.

11.12.3 Income and Price Elasticities

Short-run effect of income = 1.73, short-run effect of price = 1.04.

Long-run effect of income = (1.73)/(1.02) = 1.696, long-run effect of price = (1.04)/(1.02) = 1.0196.

11.12.4 Impact Effect

Impact effect is obtained from the equilibrium case of import-demand Eq. (11.29). The impact effect of price is -1.01 and the impact effect of income is 1.68.

11.13 The J-Curve Effect

The BOT schedules we derived suggest that a real depreciation of the home currency immediately improves the current account, while a real appreciation immediately worsens the current account. In real life situations, this is not so as the behavior underlying trade flows are complex than what have been previously discussed. The dynamic elements of supply and demand required for tradable to cause the current account adjustment in response to exchange rate changes are gradual. In fact, important dynamic factors explain the actual pattern of current account adjustment in response to depreciation and it is termed as the J-curve effect.

The J-curve effect is the tendency of a nation's trade balance to first deteriorate before improving during devaluation or depreciation of the nation's currency.

The current account which is measured in domestic currency prices or output units deteriorates sharply from A to B after the currency depreciation, because most import and export orders are placed several months in advance before the depreciation or devaluation.

In the first few months after the depreciation, export and import volumes may reflect buying decisions that were made during the old real exchange rate before the depreciation, so they do not change much. The primary effect of the depreciation is to raise the value of the precontracted level of imports in terms of domestic products.

The national exports which are measured in terms of domestic prices or output do not change, while imports measured in domestic output or prices rise shortly after the depreciation or devaluation, with quantities of exports remaining the same initially. Even after the old export and import contracts have been fulfilled, new shipments still take time to adjust fully to the relative price changes.

On the production side, producers of exports may have to build new or additional plants and equipment and hire new workers to meet the increase demand. Imported inputs also adjust gradually as intermediate materials which are imported to produce domestic goods take some time for domestic producers to find replacements for those imported intermediate materials.

There are also lags on the consumption side because consumption of domestic exports will require building new retail outlets abroad to market the expansion of domestic exports. These reasons explain why improvement in current account after devaluation or depreciation is gradual and takes some time.

Consequently, although the path of the CA balance in response to the implementation of the expansionary monetary policy at time t_0 drops immediately into a deficit from A to B, it then starts to recover from B to C, and completes recovering at C. The CA then begins to record surplus which it maintains till it attained its maximum surplus at period D. It then maintains the CA balance it attained at its maximum surplus level which is equal to the original speed before the policy was implemented.

Figure 11.1 shows the J-curve effect of depreciation or devaluation on the current account. The current account deteriorates immediately after depreciation from A to B. It then rises gradually over time to C and continues thereafter rising till it reaches some height and maintains it thereon over the long run. Note that after point C, the current account rises above the pre-depreciation level, and eventually the rise tapers off as the recovery adjustment to the real depreciation is completed.

The J-curve effect takes at least six months but not more than a year to complete in most advance developed countries (ADCs), although in most developing countries it may even take longer. The J-curve effect suggests that monetary expansion may not capture the full effect of its impact as we have discussed in Chapter 10. This is because increase in the money supply depresses output in the short run, which means interest rate will have to fall farther for the domestic market to clear. Consequently, the exchange rate will overshoot more sharply, and will require much larger expected domestic currency appreciation to clear the foreign exchange market in the final foreign exchange equilibrium. The J-curve effect means exchange rate volatility is more amplified than what we discussed under the exchange rate overshooting in Chapter 10.

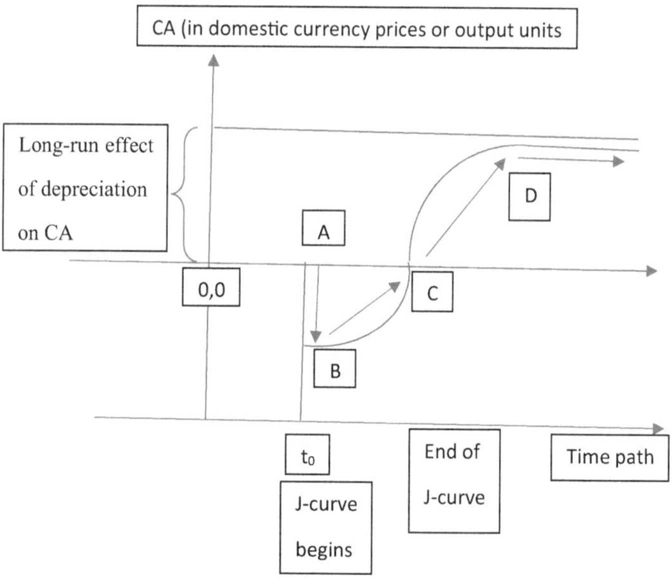

Fig. 11.1 The effect of depreciation or devaluation on current account (CA)

11.14 Exchange Rate or Currency Pass-Through and Inflation

It is assumed in the analysis used thus far that changes in nominal exchange rates cause proportional changes in real exchange rate in the short run. Thus, since the real exchange rate, $q = XR.P^F/P$, the nominal output prices (GDP deflators), P and P^F cannot suddenly jump when there is a change in XR, so a change in XR is assumed to result in a proportional change in q with P and P^F remaining the same over the short run. However, this is not so in the real world, because the effect of changes in XR and q is less than perfect although they move closely to each other.

The effect of XR on the current account can be understood better by examining the link between the nominal exchange rate on prices of exports and imports. The domestic currency price of foreign output is $XR.P^F$, which is the product of the exchange rate (XR) and foreign prices (P^F). The assumption made in previous analysis is that as the XR changes because P and P^F are fixed in the short run, the domestic currency price of imported goods, $XR.P^F$, rises proportionally.

Exchange rate pass-through is the degree by which a one percent change in exchange rate (depreciation) of domestic currency causes import prices to rise. This means from our analysis, that the degree of exchange rate pass-through is 1 (or 100%). Thus, the exchange rate change completely passes through to import prices.

However, the above assumption and conclusion are generally not true in real world. Exchange rate pass-through is not complete. Among the reasons for the incompleteness are the following:

International market segmentation causes imperfectly competitive firms to charge different prices for similar or even the same good in different countries. Thus, if the US dollar depreciates by say 10%, because of fear of losing market, a foreign large firm supplying cars in the US may not pass on the 10% increase in the exchange rate on prices of cars they supply to the US market. Rather, the foreign firm may only pass 40% of the 10% depreciation to its prices in the US and absorb 60% of the depreciation. Thus, it reduces its profits to maintain its share in the US market.

This means that a permanent change in the exchange rate may not fully reflect in the price of imports in the US, especially in the short run. Thus, the exchange rate pass-through is incomplete in the short run, although in the long run the permanent change in nominal exchange rate may be fully reflected in import prices.

The pass-through is higher in the long run than in the short run. It is also higher for industrial goods than for other goods. It is smaller for primary raw materials and unprocessed goods—like bauxite, banana, cocoa, etc. It also tends to be low in a low-inflationary environment, a common feature in most fiscal discipline economies.

11.15 Beachhead Effect

Beachhead effect is the situation when exporters or producers of exports to the depreciating country are reluctant to increase prices by the full amount of the dollar depreciation. This may occur if they are suspicious that the depreciation of the dollar will be temporary and can be reversed in the future. Considering that it is very expensive to plan and build or dismantle production plants and enter or leave new markets, firms avert the risk of losing their existing market by raising their export prices by a lesser amount than what is dictated by the size of the dollar depreciation.

A case in point is that from 1985 to 1988, Japanese automakers did not raise prices of their cars exported to the US by the full effect of the depreciation when the US depreciated its dollars. Rather, the Japanese automakers passed only 42% of the dollar depreciation on their cars exported to the US consumers and bore the remaining 58% in losses to their profit. The US accused them of dumping when their profit was realized to be dropping. At the same period, US automakers rather raised their car prices to rebuild their profit instead of maintaining their car prices to recapture their waning market share from the Japanese. Thus, the depreciation during the said period resulted in incomplete exchange rate pass-through in the US.

Incomplete pass-through have complicated effect on the timing and adjustment of the current account during exchange rate depreciation. On the one hand, the short run J-curve effect of a nominal change in currency is dampened by a low responsiveness of import prices to the change in the exchange rate. On the other hand, incomplete pass-through shows that currency movements have less-than-proportional effect on the relative prices determining trade volumes. The fact that relative prices fail to adjust quickly also shows that trade volumes adjust slowly.

It should be noted again that the connection between nominal and real exchange rates, may be weakened further by domestic price responses.

Countries with high inflation cannot easily change the real exchange rate ($q = XR.P^F/P$) by simply changing the nominal exchange rate (XR). This is because the increase in aggregate demand which follows from the change in XR also causes an increase in domestic prices or inflation which directly influence the prices of exports. The fact that currency depreciation causes export prices to rise removes any favorable effect the country gains on its competitive position in the world markets. Thus, the increase in domestic prices or export prices, like partial pass-through, weakens or dampens the J-curve effect.

Note that the J-curve existence shows that currency depreciation has contractionary effect on output initially, and this amplifies exchange rate overshooting. Furthermore, incomplete exchange rate pass-through, and the fact that domestic prices increase following depreciation, reduces the effect of a change in nominal exchange rate on the real exchange rate. Consequently, any favorable effect gained from the depreciation improving the country's competitive position in the world market vanishes.

There are two crucial periods that devaluation policy experience. These are the currency contract period and the pass-through period. The period which covers the implementation of the devaluation policy is referred to as the currency contract period, and the pass-through period is the period both domestic and foreign prices and wages adjust to the devaluation policy over the short term. Both currency period and pass-through period cover the period from A to C in Fig. 11.1.

11.16 Absorption Approach and Balance of Trade

The elasticities approach to the balance of trade or payments depends on the price elasticities of imports and exports. However, it assumes that the economy has unemployed resources which allows it to respond to the devaluation by allowing the economy to supply resources required to be used to provide for increase production in the country to meet foreigners increase in demand for domestic exports. The devaluation operates by increasing exports and reducing imports, with the net effect of yielding balance of trade or payments surplus.

The question then is, what will be the impact of devaluation or depreciation in a country that is operating at or near full employment? The absorption approach attempts to resolve the above question.

The rudimentary derivation of the absorption approach to the balance of trade or payments expresses the balance of trade as a relation between real output of goods and services, which is real income (Y) net of absorption (A), with the latter comprising of total real spending on consumption, gross investments, and role of government. Thus, if the GDP is expressed as

$$Y = C + I + G + X - IM \tag{11.31}$$

with $A = C + I + G$

Then

$$X - IM = Y - A \tag{11.32}$$

The elasticities approach to the balance of trade assumes that $Y > A$, so there are unemployed resources which can be employed to increase spending to produce more domestic real output, when the country devalues or depreciates the national currency. Thus, if the Marshall-Lerner condition is met, spending on exports increases and spending on imports decreases.

As Eq. (11.31) shows, there are no capital flows in the absorption approach, and under the condition of the presence of unemployed resources, spending on domestic goods and services are not inflationary. However, if the pre-depreciation or pre-devaluation economy is already operating at the full employment level, then devaluation/depreciation becomes inflationary, as the resulting increase in spending from domestic residents and foreigners through net exports will lead to increase in prices and inflation. For detail discussion on the absorption approach to the balance of trade or payments, we recommend readers to refer to Sidney S. Alexander (1952).

11.17 Summary

External imbalance models are developed, and different models are used to illustrate how they respond to external imbalance. The price-specie flow mechanism of David Hume is discussed. The exchange market pressure model is developed. It is then modified to develop the monetary approach to the balance of payment under a fixed exchange rate by setting the exchange rate to zero. We also developed the monetary approach to determine the exchange rate under a flexible exchange rate by setting the international reserves in the exchange market pressure model to zero.

The elasticities approach shows that price elasticities of exports and imports can be used to prove whether the Marshall-Lerner condition is met. The path of the J-curve effect which shows that devaluation or depreciation effect on improving the balance of trade experience some deterioration before it improves is discussed.

We explained that the deterioration stemming from the J-curve effect occurs because contracts on traded goods and services respond to devaluation/depreciation with a lag. Exchange rate effect on prices of exports which is also known as exchange rate pass-through is measured, and its effect on prices and inflation rate is determined. The absorption approach to the balance of payment which deals with the effect of income on the balance of trade is used to measure the effect of devaluation or depreciation on inflation is also discussed. It must be pointed out that, the elasticities approach to the balance of payments relies on availability of unemployed resources for devaluation or depreciation to improve the balance of trade or payments. However, in a situation of full employment, where there is a threat of inflation, employing easy monetary policy by expanding money supply is likely to result in inflation so the elasticity approach to the balance of payment cannot be used. It is during such times when the economy is operating near full employment that the absorption approach is recommended.

11.18 Problems

1. (11.1) Is the statement: "under a fixed exchange rate regime the monetary authorities always have complete control over the money supply" true or false? Use an appropriate model to demonstrate a support for your answer.
2. (11.2) Define the following terms and concepts: (i) Marshall-Lerner condition, (ii) exchange rate overshooting, (iii) bullion, (iv) beachhead effect, and (v) exchange market pressure.
3. (11.3) Prices in Jamaica have decreased because of decrease in prices of petroleum products. Discuss what will happen to the Balance of Payments accounts under a fixed exchange rate? Will the outcome be different under a flexible exchange rate regime? Explain. (Hint: you may use monetary approach to the BOPs and exchange rate determination).

4. (11.4) The Minister of Finance of Suriname has hired you to advise the country on a policy event that would cause its nominal interest rate to increase and its currency to appreciate simultaneously in a world of perfectly flexible prices. Provide a model to discuss your policy advice. Use phase diagrams to highlight your discussion.
5. (11.5) Imagine yourself to be an expert in international finance. Develop a model that can be estimated and employed to evaluate that devaluation policy will improve the Balance of Trade position of a country.

11.6 With the aid of Hume's price-specie flow mechanism gold standard, analyze how balance of payments equilibrium between two countries, X and Y would be restored after a transfer of income from country X to Y.

11.7 A country's exports and imports demand are expressed as the following disequilibrium equations:

$\ln X_t{}^D = 70 - 0.59\ln P_t{}^X + 1.68\ln Y_t{}^W + 0.42\ln X_{t-1}{}^D$

$\ln M_t{}^D = 120 + 0.79\ln P_t{}^M + 2.45\ln Y_t{}^H + 0.25\ln M_{t-1}{}^D$

If the country's import multiplier is 0.03, will such a country improve its Balance of Payments accounts over the long run by devaluing its currency? Calculate the short run and long-run elasticities, and median lags of both exports and imports, and explain their significance.

11.8 Using a model discuss what will happen if there is a decrease in demand for money in a country under the Bretton Woods system of fixed exchange rates.

(i) With the aid of the monetary approach model, explain the effect of the following events on the value of the foreign exchange rate of the domestic country:

(a) The foreign inflation rate increases.

(b) Hurricane destroys a large portion of domestic factories and roads which are productive capacity of the country.

(c) The home central bank reduces the growth rate of the domestic credit component of the monetary base in its attempt to reduce the domestic inflation rate.

(d) A foreign oil cartel doubles the market price of oil which the domestic economy heavily depends on in its imported oil.

(ii) Assuming that the interest rate is i = 12% in Kingston and i^F = 5% in New York. If the spot rate is SXR = J\$120/\$1 today and is expected to be J\$125/\$1 in three months.

(a) Show why the uncovered interest parity condition is met?

(b) What do you say will happen if there was a change in expectations so that the spot rate in three months became J\$130/\$1 and the interest rate differential stayed the same?

11.9 Explain similarities and dissimilarities between the specie flow mechanism and monetary approach to the balance of payments.

Selected References

Alexander, S. S. (1952). Effects of Devaluation: A Simplified Synthesis of Elasticities and Absorption Approach. *American Economic Review*, 49, 22-42.

Bahmani-Oskooee, M. and D. Bernstein (1999). Exchange Market Pressure during the Current Managed Float. *Applied Economic Letters*, 6, 585- 588.

Dornbusch, R. (1973). Devaluation, Money, and Non-traded Goods. *American Economic Review*, 63, 871-880.

Dornbusch, R. (1976). Expectations and Exchange Rate Dynamics, *Journal of Political Economy*, 86 (6), December, 1161–1176.

Connolly, M. and J. D. da Silveira (1979). Exchange Market Pressure in Postwar Brazil: an Application of the Girton-Roper Monetary Model. *American Economic Review*, 69 (3), 448-454.

Fleming, J.M. (1962). "Domestic Financial Policies under Fixed and under Floating Exchange Rates," *IMF Staff Papers*, November.

Frenkel, J. A. and H. G. Johnson, eds., (1976). *The Monetary Approach to the Balance of Payments*, (University of Toronto Press, Toronto).

Ghartey, Edward E. (2009). "The Mid 1990s Peso Crisis in Mexico: An Application of the Girton-Roper Model," *Frontiers in Finance and Economics*, 6 (1), 73–92.

Ghartey, Edward E. (2002). Exchange Market Pressure and Optimal Foreign Exchange Regime in Jamaica. *Social and Economic Studies*, 51 (2), 49-62.

Ghartey, Edward E. (1987). "Devaluation as a balance of payments corrective measure in developing countries: a study relating to Ghana," *Applied Economics*, 19, 937-947.

Girton, L. and D. Roper (1977). A Monetary Model of Exchange Market Pressure Applied to the Postwar Canadian Experience. *American Economic Review*, 67 (4), 537 - 548.

Harberger, A. C. (1950). Currency Depreciation, Income, and the Balance of Trade. *Journal of Political Economy*, 58, 47-60.
Hume, D. (1963). *Essays: moral, political, and literary*, (Oxford University Press, London).
Husted, Steven and Michael Melvin (1993). *International Economics*, (New York: Harper Collins College Publishers).
Johnson, H.G. (1977). "The Monetary Approach to the Balance of Payments: A Non-technical Guide." *Journal of International Economics*, 7, 251-68.
Kim, I. (1985). Exchange Market Pressure in Korea: An Application of the Girton-Roper Monetary Model. *Journal of Money, Credit, and Banking*, 17(2), 258-263.
Krugman, Paul R., Maurice Obstfeld, and Marc J Melitz (2015*). International Economics: Theory and Policy*, (New York: Pearson).
Meade, J. (1951). *The Theory of International Economic Policy. In The Balance of Payments, I* (London: Oxford University Press).
Magee, Stephen P. (1973). "Currency contracts, pass-through, and devaluation," *Brookings Papers on Economic Activity*, 1, 303-325.
Modeste, N. C. (1981). "Exchange Market Pressure during the 1970s in Argentina: An Application of the Girton-Roper Monetary Model). *Journal of Money Credit and Banking*, 13 (2), 234-240.
Mundell, R. (1971). *Monetary Theory*, (Pacific Palisades: Goodyear).
Mundell, R. (1963). "Capital Mobility and Stabilization Policy under Fixed and Flexible Exchange Rates," *Canadian Journal of Economics and Political Science*, November.
Obstfeld, M. (1982). Macroeconomic Policy in the Open Economy: Can We Sterilize? Theory and Evidence. American Economic Review, 72 (2), 45-50.
Polak, J.J. (1957). Monetary Analysis of Income Formation and Payments Problems. *International Monetary Fund Staff Papers*, 8, 212-226.
Robinson, J. (1937). *The Foreign Exchanges. In J. Robinson, Essays in the Theory of Employment*. (Macmillan, London).
Salvatore, Dominick (2010). *International Economics*, (New York: John Wiley & Sons Inc.).
Thornton, J. (1995). Exchange Market Pressure in Costa Rica, 1986-92: An Application of the Girton-Roper Model. *International Economic Journal*, 9, 67-72.
Tinbergen, J. (1952). *On the Theory of Economic Policy*, (North-Holland).
von Whitman, M. (1975). Global Monetarism and the Monetary Approach to the Balance of Payments. *Brookings Papers on Economic Activity*, 3, 491-555.
Weymark, D.N. (1997). Measuring the Degree of Exchange Market Intervention in a Small Open Economy. *Journal of International Money and Finance*, 16 (1), 55-79.

CHAPTER 12

Exchange Rate Regimes, Interventions, and the Money Supply

Learning Outcomes

This Chapter readers will be expected to have acquired knowledge and clear understanding to do the following, among others:

(1) Define the following terms and concepts:

(i) unsterilized foreign exchange intervention (iv) anchor currency
(ii) sterilized foreign exchange intervention (v) over-valued exchange rate
(iii) speculative attacks

(2) (2) Illustrate the foreign exchange intervention which is independent of the money supply with the aid of foreign exchange graphs and bookkeeping T-account table(s).
(3) Explain why under a completely flexible exchange rate system, the foreign exchange market has no effect on monetary policy.
(4) Demonstrate to show if the foreign exchange market under the regime of completely floating exchange rate system has effect on monetary policy or not?
(5) Explain sterilized foreign exchange intervention and how to correct over-valued and under-valued foreign exchange rate when the

E. E. Ghartey, *International Macroeconomics and Finance*,
https://doi.org/10.1007/978-3-032-04145-6_12

central bank is operating under the IMF's fixed exchange rate regime.

12.1 Introduction

Central banks intervene in the foreign exchange market to control it because of daily fluctuations in the exchange rate. Thus, central banks of domestic countries buy and sell foreign assets or assets denominated in foreign currencies to correct imbalance in the foreign exchange market to maintain desirable exchange rate.

12.2 The Foreign Exchange Market Intervention Physiology and the Money Supply

12.2.1 *The Case of Unsterilized Foreign Exchange Intervention*

What is the physiology of the monetary base and the money supply when the central bank sells foreign denominated assets to influence the economy?

We shall use two different methods to answer the above question. In the first method, we shall use the bookkeeping T-account table for the banking system discussed and used in Chapter 5. In the second method, we shall use graphs of the relationship between current GH¢/$ exchange rate (XR_t) and expected GH¢ return on $ deposits developed, discussed, and used in Chapter 4 to answer the question.

If the central bank sells foreign denominated assets (net international reserves, NIR) which is worth say GH¢10 m to the public who pays for it with cash, the resulting T-account will be as shown in

$$MB = C + R$$

where C is currency in circulation, MB is monetary base, and R is reserves in the banking system.

$$\Delta MB = \Delta C + \Delta R$$

so

$$\Delta MB = \Delta C$$

= – GH10m

Graphic illustration of the central bank's sale of foreign assets which relate current GH¢/$ exchange rate (XR_t), expected return of GH¢ deposit return, and expected GH¢ return on $ deposits is presented in Fig. 12.1.

Both results of the central bank's sale of foreign assets presented in the T-account in Table 12.1 and the graphic illustration reported in Fig. 12.1 show that the monetary base and currency in circulation fall by—GH¢10 m. As a result, the money supply also falls by the same—GH¢10 m. The reduction in the money supply causes the domestic interest rate or expected return to rise. This explains the rightward shift of the interest rate or expected return schedule of the domestic country from $i_0^{GH¢}$ to $i_1^{GH¢}$, and the country's exchange rate appreciates from XR_t^0 to XR_t^1. See Fig. 12.1.

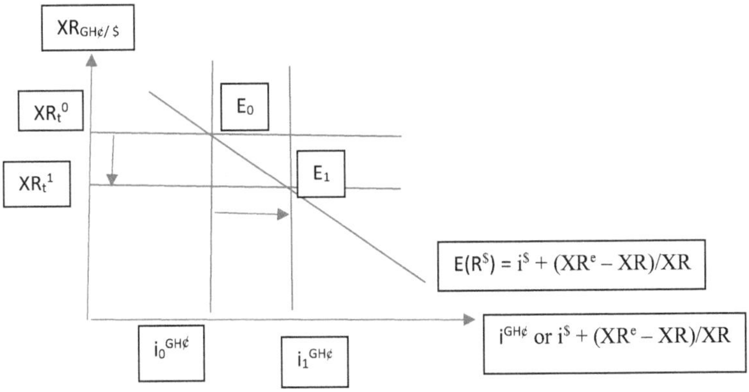

Fig. 12.1 Unsterilized intervention through the central bank's sale of foreign assets

Table 12.1 T-account of the central bank's sale of foreign assets (Unsterilized Intervention)

Assets	*Liabilities & Net Worth*
Foreign assets (NIR)—GH¢10 m	Currency in circulation (C)—GH¢10 m

The intervention described above is known as unsterilized intervention or (foreign exchange intervention). It results from the central bank's purposeful pursuit of foreign exchange intervention by either selling (or buying) foreign assets to reduce (or increase) the monetary base. Note that this type of foreign exchange intervention causes (a) the money supply to reduce (or increase), (b) interest rate to rise (or fall), and (c) the current exchange rate to appreciate (or depreciate). The outcome of this intervention activity on the monetary base is the same even if the members of the public use checks to pay for the central bank's sale of the foreign assets instead of using currency in circulation.

The unsterilized intervention in the form of the central bank's sale of foreign assets which is worth -GH¢10 m results in international reserves or monetary base falling or decreasing by the same amount, and the converse holds true.

12.3 The Case of Sterilized Foreign Exchange Intervention

Is there a foreign exchange intervention that does not cause any change in the economy in the sense that the money supply, interest rate, and current exchange rate remain unaffected by the intervention?

The response is in affirmative. The foreign exchange sale by the central bank which is offset with open market purchase of bonds results in the monetary base, money supply, interest rate, and the exchange rate remaining the same.

Let us assume that the central bank sells GH¢10 m worth of foreign assets and uses the receipt from that transaction to buy GH¢10 m worth of bonds to offset the initial transaction through the open market with the intention of leaving the monetary base unchanged (Table 12.2).

$$MB = C + R$$

Table 12.2 T-account of Central bank's sale of foreign assets and purchase of bonds (Sterilized Intervention)

Assets	*Liabilities & Net Worth*
Foreign assets (NIR)—GH¢15 m	Reserve—GH¢15 m
Bonds GH¢15 m	Reserve GH¢15 m

$$\begin{aligned}\Delta MB &= \Delta C + \Delta R \\ &= \text{GH } 15\text{m} - \text{GH}15\text{m} \\ &= 0\end{aligned}$$

Following the same format of the response to the first question, we have answered the above question by using both T-account method and graphic illustration method.

In the above situation we are looking at two actions of the central bank. In the first instance, the central bank's sale of GH¢10 m foreign assets will remove the same GH¢10 m amount of cedis from the public, whether the foreign asset is bought by the public residing in the country or by foreigners. However, using the proceeds to buy bonds from the domestic public or foreigners will increase the money supply in the country by GH¢10 m.

Thus,

$$MB = C + R$$

So

$$\begin{aligned}\Delta MB &= \Delta C + \Delta R \\ &= -\text{ GH}10\text{m} + \text{GH}10\text{m} \\ &= 0\end{aligned}$$

Graphic illustration of sterilized foreign exchange intervention is shown in Fig. 12.1.

The sale of foreign assets to the public resulted in the central bank losing net international reserves, and the currency in circulation and money supply are reduced by—GH¢10 m. However, the central bank uses the GH¢10 m reserves gained from the sale of foreign assets to buy bonds from the public.

Thus, the net gained monetary base (GH¢10 m—GH¢10 m = 0) which is total reserves from both transactions, termed as sterilized foreign exchange intervention, is zero. In the first transaction, the sale of the foreign assets resulted in—GH¢10 m lost through currency in circulation, and the purchase of bonds worth GH¢10 m resulted in the reserves of the central bank rising by that amount. Therefore, the central bank loses net international reserves of—GH¢10 m and gains reserves from selling bonds which is worth GH¢10 m. The monetary base of the central bank

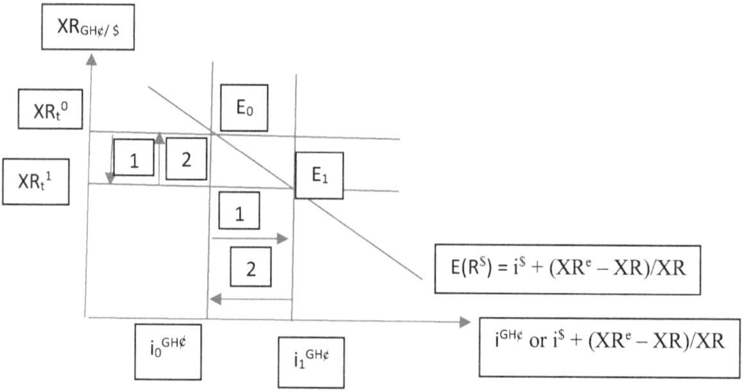

Fig. 12.2 Sterilized Intervention—Central bank's sale of foreign assets and purchase of bonds

and hence, the money supply nets out to zero, in the sterilized foreign exchange intervention.

Consequently, interest rate remains the same, and the money supply which contracted from the sale of the foreign reserves to cause interest rate to rise from $i_0^{GH¢}$ to $i_1^{GH¢}$, is reversed by the central bank's purchase of government bonds which increased the monetary base and the money supply to cause interest rate to fall and return to its original position $i_0^{GH¢}$. Thus, in the final analysis, sterilized intervention results in interest rate or the expected return remaining the same at its original position before the intervention, and the exchange rate remained unmoved at XR_t^0 as is shown in Fig. 12.2.

12.4 Operation of the Fixed Exchange Rate Regime

Suppose that the country's exchange rate is fixed to a par value determined by the US dollar which is the anchor currency at XR^{PAR}. Under a fixed exchange rate regime, the par exchange rate is determined by the central bank of the domestic country in agreement with the IMF. The intersection of the expected return of the domestic country, $i_0^{GH¢}$ and the expected return of foreign country, $i^{\$} + (XR^e - XR)/XR$, expressed

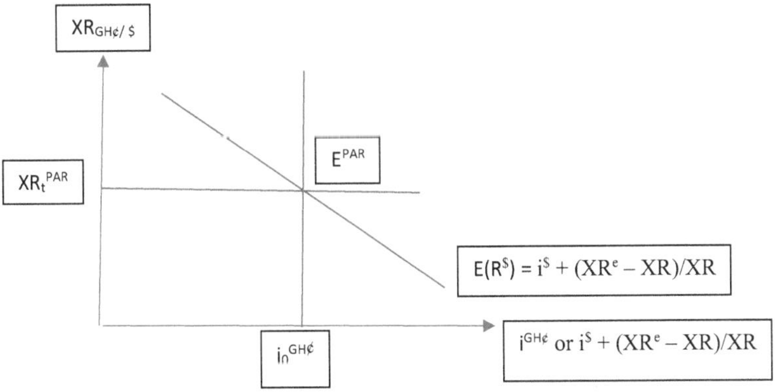

Fig. 12.3 Fixed exchange rate regime at its initial equilibrium

in GH¢s schedules, are used to determine the par valued exchange rate, XR^{PAR}, shown in Fig. 12.3.

12.5 Over-Valued Exchange Rate and Its Correction under a Fixed Exchange Rate Regime

For illustrative purpose, we shall consider a situation where a country, which is operating under a fixed exchange rate regime with the IMF and IBRD is experiencing an over-valued exchange rate. This situation is also shown in Fig. 12.4.

Suppose the country's exchange rate is fixed at E^{PAR} in equilibrium, where the expected return on domestic assets or deposits, $i_0^{GH¢}$ intersects the expected return of foreign assets or deposits $i^{\$} + (XR^e - XR)/XR$ denominated in GH¢ schedule at a par value of XR_t^{PAR} under the IMF's fixed exchange rate regime as shown in Fig. 12.4.

However, with the domestic exchange rate fixed at its par value of XR_t^{PAR}, if the country's current exchange rate determined by market forces moves to XR_t^1 at equilibrium E^1, then the domestic exchange rate is over-valued at the fixed exchange rate XR_t^{PAR} in equilibrium E^{PAR}.

How does the central bank correct the over-valued exchange rate XR_t^1 at E^1 under a fixed exchange rate regime?

The central bank of the domestic country can intervene the foreign exchange by using open market operation. This is achieved by selling

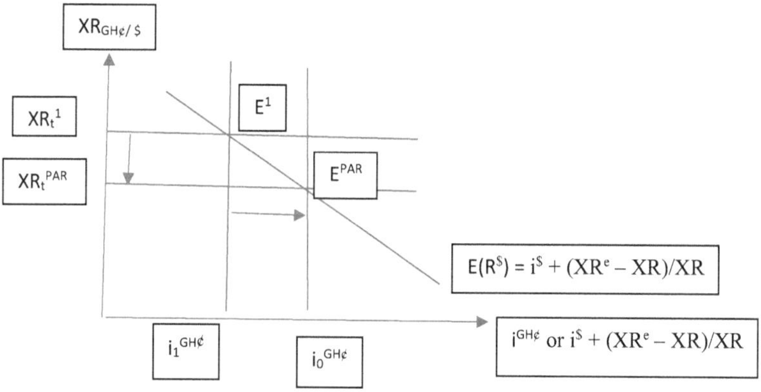

Fig. 12.4 Over-valued exchange rate under a fixed exchange rate regime

foreign assets/deposits or buying domestic currency to reduce the monetary base and subsequently the money supply. In so doing, the interest rate or domestic expected return rises from $i_1^{GH¢}$ and heads toward $i_0^{GH¢}$. The intervention process will continue till the fixed exchange rate regime is reached or upheld at XR_t^{PAR} on the expected return or interest rate $i_0^{GH¢}$.

Thus, the over-valued exchange rate is corrected by the central bank buying domestic currency or selling foreign assets. This results in the monetary base and subsequently the money supply contracting and domestic expected return or interest rate rising. The central bank's purchasing of domestic currency with foreign assets or deposits to correct the over-valued domestic currency, results in the domestic country losing net international reserves, which is not sustainable in the long run. If the country's net international reserves get exhausted, and the central bank cannot defend the depreciation pressure on the country's exchange rate anymore, then the central bank will have to devalue the exchange rate by resetting the par value at a lower value around XR_t^1 near equilibrium E^1 as shown in Fig. 12.4.

12.6 Under-Valued Exchange Rate and Its Correction under a Fixed Exchange Rate Regime

The exchange rate is fixed at the intersection of the domestic expected return $i_0^{GH¢}$ and foreign expected return $i^{\$} + (XR^e - XR)/XR$ denominated in GH¢s at an equilibrium E^{PAR} under a fixed exchange rate regime, where the domestic currency is fixed to the US dollar as the anchor currency.

In Fig. 12.5 market forces moved the exchange rate from its initial equilibrium E^{PAR} at the exchange rate XR_t^{PAR} on interest rate of $i_0^{GH¢}$ to a new equilibrium E^1, where domestic expected return $i_1^{GH¢}$ intersects the foreign expected return schedule $i^{\$} + (XR^e - XR)/XR$ denominated in GH¢s.

The current exchange rate of XR_t^1 at equilibrium E^1 makes the pegged exchange rate regime XR_t^{PAR} at equilibrium E^{PAR} under-valued as depicted in Fig. 12.5.

How does the central bank intervene in the foreign exchange market to correct the under-valued exchange rate?

The under-valued exchange rate XR_t^1, at the intersection of the domestic assets' expected return $i_1^{GH¢}$ and the GH¢ value of expected foreign assets/deposits return $i^{\$} + (XR^e - XR)/XR$ schedules, are in equilibrium at E^1. The central bank can correct the under-valued exchange rate at E^1 by buying foreign assets/deposits and/or selling domestic

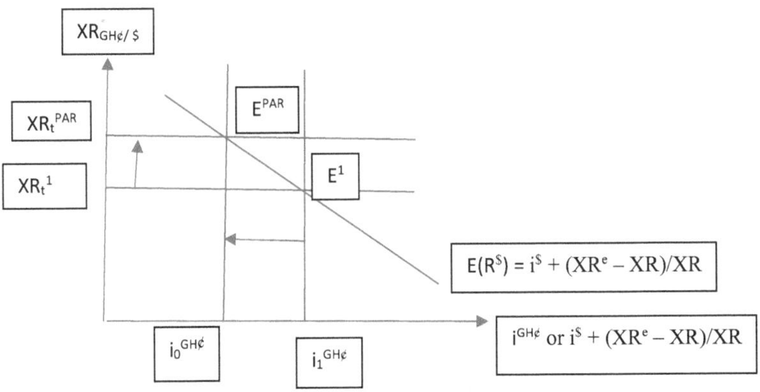

Fig. 12.5 Under-valued exchange rate under a fixed exchange rate regime

currency through open market operations to intervene in the foreign exchange market.

This will cause increase in the monetary base and subsequently the money supply, which will in turn cause a decrease in domestic interest rate or expected return. The process will continue till the domestic expected return or interest rate moves from $i_1^{GH¢}$ to $i_0^{GH¢}$ where the exchange rate XR_t^{PAR} is at equilibrium E^{PAR}. See Fig. 12.5.

The intervention described above is known as unsterilized intervention or (foreign exchange intervention). It results from the central bank's purposeful pursuit of foreign exchange intervention by either selling (or buying) foreign assets to reduce (or increase) the monetary base. Note that this type of foreign exchange intervention causes (a) the money supply to reduce (or increase), (b) interest rate to rise (or fall), and (c) the current exchange rate to appreciate (or depreciate). The outcome of this intervention activity on the monetary base is the same even if the members of the public use checks to pay for the central bank's sale of the foreign assets instead of using currency in circulation.

12.7 Foreign Exchange Rate and Policy

Thus, under a fixed exchange rate regime, the central bank intervenes in foreign exchange market to correct under-valued exchange rate by buying foreign assets/deposits or selling domestic currency. In the process the central bank accumulates net international reserves.

However, the accumulation of net international reserves causes appreciation of the domestic exchange rate, which makes exports of domestic goods expensive for foreigners to buy and imported foreign goods cheaper for domestic residents to buy. This translates to balance of payment surplus problems. The central bank resolves the problems associated with appreciation and accumulation of reserves by dismantling the fixed exchange rate regime and resetting the par value to a higher foreign exchange rate of the anchor currency. Thus, the under-valued exchange rate is now revalued.

Additionally, the central bank intervenes the foreign exchange market to correct over-valued foreign exchange rate under a pegged foreign exchange regime by selling foreign assets/deposits and/or buying domestic currency. In the process, the central bank loses net international reserves.

If the process which led to the over-valued foreign exchange rate repeat itself, the central bank will continue to prevent the depreciation threat of the exchange rate by repeating to sell the foreign assets/deposits and continue to lose reserves.

If the central bank reaches a point where its net international reserves dry out, then the country will have to devalue its currency by dismantling the standing or prevailing foreign exchange rate regime and enter a new arrangement with the IMF. The new arrangement will eliminate the depreciation pressure by changing the previously fixed exchange rate and pegging it to a lower exchange rate par value of the anchor currency. This means the under-valued exchange rate is devalued.

12.8 Caveat: Role of Perfect Capital Mobility and Speculation

12.9 Perfect Capital Mobility

How does the condition of perfect capital mobility impact the effectiveness of the central bank's sterilized intervention in the foreign exchange market (under a fixed exchange rate regime)?

Given that the domestic country is Ghana, $i_t^{GH¢}$ is the domestic interest rate, and i_t^F is foreign or the rest of the world's (ROW) interest rate. Under the condition of perfect capital mobility, if $i_t^{GH¢} < i_t^F$, there will be massive capital outflow from Ghana to the ROW; and if $i_t^{GH¢} > i_t^F$, there will be massive inflow of capital to Ghana from the ROW.

However, if $i_t^{GH¢} = i_t^F$, capital mobility will be stationary at zero. There will be no incentive for capital from the ROW to move to the domestic country, nor will there be any incentive for capital from domestic country to move to the ROW. In such circumstance, the direction of capital flow will be influenced by prevailing taxes, government policy restrictions, capital controls and other barriers to domestic and foreign or ROW's capital markets.

The absence of taxes on capital or capital gain taxes, government restrictions, and other barriers to domestic and foreign capital markets will not cause the par value of the exchange rate to remain at E^{PAR}. This is because, using sterilized intervention under such conditions of flexible exchange rate and absence of any barriers to capital mobility will not affect the expected return nor interest rate of the domestic country or the foreign country.

Consequently, pressure or threat of depreciation on a fixed exchange rate, XR^{PAR}, cannot be removed by sterilized intervention. In fact, depreciation pressure will quickly exhaust the net international reserves of the domestic country if the central bank continues to defend the fixed exchange rate with sterilized foreign exchange intervention. As a result, when the net international reserves go to zero, the country can only give in to such depreciation pressure by allowing the domestic currency to depreciate to find a lower exchange rate equilibrium with the ROW.

12.10 Speculation

How does a country cope with speculative attacks when it is operating a fixed exchange rate regime?

The fixed exchange rate regime is exposed to speculative attacks when the exchange rate of the domestic country is either over-valued or undervalued. Speculators massively sell off currencies that are either becoming or are weak, and massively buy currencies that are either getting or are stronger to make profit, and in so doing they cause sharper or destabilizing changes in the exchange rate. Most developing countries have experienced such destabilizing depreciation in their exchange rate. Examples of such experiences occurred in Jamaica in 1996–97, Mexico in 1994–95, Argentina 1997–1999, to name a few.

In 1994–95, during the peso crisis, the peso depreciated from $XR_0{}^M$ to $XR_1{}^M$ as the real interest rate or the expected return of the Mexican assets dropped from $i_0{}^M$ to $i_1{}^M$. This means that had events occurred without the activities of speculative attacks, the central bank of Mexico would have required to buy a smaller volume of Mexican pesos to raise the interest rate of pesos back to $i_0{}^M$ and close the $i_1{}^M - i_0{}^M$ gap and return the exchange rate from $XR_1{}^M$ back to its original position, $XR_0{}^M$. See Fig. 12.6.

However, because of speculative attacks, the foreign currencies or dollars sold by speculators were so huge that the Mexican interest rate initially fell by a huge amount, which caused the Mexican real interest rate to fall to $i_1{}^{M'}$ at the exchange rate of $XR_1{}^{M'}$. Consequently, the central bank of Mexico had to spend more foreign reserves to contract the pesos in circulation to raise the Mexican interest rate to close the large interest rate gap, $i_1{}^{M'} - i_0{}^M$, to bring the peso exchange rate back to $XR_0{}^M$ at the initial equilibrium E_0 on real interest rate $i_0{}^M$.

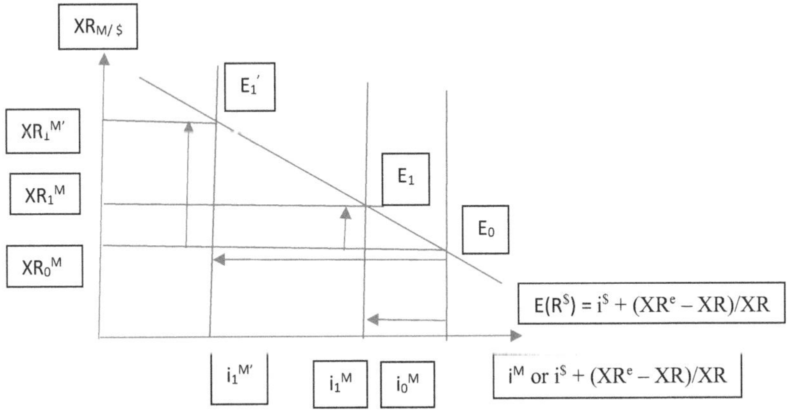

Fig. 12.6 Effect of speculative attacks on the Mexican Peso during the peso crisis

During the peso crisis in Mexico, speculative attacks on the Mexican peso resulted in more than 25 percent depreciation in December 1994. Mexico's foreign reserves of \$25.9 billion in the first quarter of 1994 fell to \$6.3 billion at the close of 1994, below the central bank of the country's required minimum threshold of tolerance of \$10 billion. Consequently, it could not support sterilized interventions to defend the peso from attacks of speculators. It should be noted, although, that the central bank had used sterilized intervention to defend the peso successfully in 1993 from speculative attacks when the country had adequate net international reserves during that time. See Ghartey (2009, p.77), Calvo and Mendoza (1996), Edwards (1996), and Sachs, Tornell, and Velasco (1996).

However, the Mexican peso crisis, otherwise known as the Mexican balance of payments crisis, resulted in the country's short-term interest rate (or expected return) being raised from 15 percent to about 32 percent by the central bank of Mexico. Consequently, the peso was devalued at the end of December 1994 by about 14 percent. At the same time, the IMF and the Clinton administration supported the central bank by giving Mexico about \$52 billion to ward off the destabilizing activities of speculators—the main winners in the crisis—which were draining the country's net international reserves. Many foreign investors also became casualties of the peso crisis, and speculators in the country initiated massive foreign assets capital flight to abroad.

The reverberations of the peso crisis, which was dubbed as the Tequila effect, extended beyond the borders of Mexico to countries as far as Argentina and Brazil in South America in 1999, Thailand, and South Korea in East Asia in 1997–98, Russia in 1998, and Eastern Europe in the late 1990s.[1]

12.11 Summary

Foreign exchange market intervention by the central bank using the money supply to calm daily fluctuations in exchange rate is discussed.

The physiology of the foreign exchange market by the central bank using the money supply as a policy instrument is examined from the perspective of unsterilized foreign exchange intervention, and sterilized intervention by trading foreign assets and bonds to influence the money supply.

Foreign exchange intervention is used by central banks to correct over-valued and under-valued exchange rates of countries that have fixed their exchange rate under the IMF's fixed exchange rate regimes.

Speculative attacks are discussed especially under a fixed exchange rate regime. The effectiveness of central bank's sterilized interventions is discussed when there is perfect capital mobility.

12.12 Problems

12.1 Suppose the par value of Nigerian's exchange rate was under-valued during the Bretton. Woods fixed exchange rate regime era. What intervention policy can the central bank of Nigeria employ? Discuss the effect the intervention will have on Nigerian's net international reserves and the money supply.

12.2 (12.2) Central bank of Mexico has pegged the peso to the US dollar and has committed to a fixed dollar/peso exchange rate. Using graphs of the market for peso assets (or foreign exchange) show and explain how the peg should be maintained if

[1] See Krugman and Obstfeld (2000), and Salvatore (2010).

a shock in the US economy forces the Federal reserve to pursue contractionary monetary policy.

How effective is the central bank of Mexico in solving the domestic economic problem to defend the pegged exchange rate?

12.3 (12.3) "In a clean floating exchange rate regime, the foreign exchange market has no direct impact on the money supply."

Is this statement True, False, or Uncertain?

Explain whether monetary policy is ineffective on the clean floating foreign exchange market.

12.4 "If a country wants to keep its exchange rate from changing, it must surrender some control over its money supply,"

With the aid of appropriate model explain whether the statement is True, False, or Uncertain?

12.5 The central bank of Belize has decided to increase the value of the Belizean dollar against the dollar. Assuming the role of economic advisor, how will you advise the central bankof Belize to intervene the foreign exchange market to accomplish this objective?

If the central bank of Belize wants the money supply to remain the same after the foreign exchange market intervention, what type of intervention should they conduct? Explain how it will work.

12.6 When a central bank pegs its exchange rate, it also sacrifices its ability to autonomously set domestic monetary policy. In such situation, the central bank foregoes its ability to use monetary policy to fend off wage-price inflation. The argument can be summarized as follows:

> Suppose workers demand higher wages and employers give in, but that the employers then raise output prices to cover their higher costs. Now the price level is higher and real balances are momentarily lower, so to prevent an interest rate rise that would appreciate the currency, the central bank must buy foreign exchange and expand the money supply. This action accommodates the initial wage demands with monetary growth and the economy moves permanently to a higher level of wages and prices. With a pegged exchange rate there is thus no way of keeping wages and prices down.

Do you agree with the above argument? If yes, why and if no, why not? Explain your answers.

12.7 Let the central bank of a small country be faced with a rise in the world interest rate, i^F.

What will happen to its (i) international reserves holdings? (ii) money supply? Will it offset either of these effects through open market operations?

Selected References

Dornbusch, Rudiger, Fischer, Stanley, and Sparks, Gordon, R. (1982), *Macro Economics*, (New York: McGraw-Hill Ryerson Limited).

Husted, Steven, and Michael Melvin (1993). *International Economics*, (New York: Harper Collins College Publishers).

Krugman, Paul R., Maurice Obstfeld (2000). *International Economics: Theory and Policy*, (New York: Addison-Wesley Longman).

Krugman, Paul R., Maurice Obstfeld, and Marc J Melitz (2015). *International Economics: Theory and Policy*, (New York: Pearson).

McCallum, Bennett T. (1989), *Monetary Economics: Theory and Policy*, (New York: Macmillan Publishing Company).

Mishkin, Frederic S. (2016), *The Economics of Money, Banking, and Financial Markets*, (New York: Pearson).

Salvatore, Dominick (2010), *International Economics* (New York: John Wiley & Sons, Inc.).

CHAPTER 13

The Open Economy Trilemma and Exchange Rate Regimes

Learning outcomes

Readers of this Chapter, should be able to have acquired clear knowledge and understanding of the materials, among others, to do the following:

(1) Define the following terms and concepts:

- (i) international currency area
- (ii) interregional currency area
- (iii) international macroeconomic impossibility trinity
- (iv) seigniorage
- (v) optimum currency area
- (vi) currency union
- (vii) dollarization
- (viii) currency-board
- (ix) inflation targeting

(2) List and differentiate variants of fixed exchange rates, and types of currency areas.
(3) Distinguish features of inflation targeting and currency-board.
(4) Determine advantages of inflation targeting, dollarization, and exchange rate targeting.
(5) Illustrate the adjustment process in the international currency area with fixed exchange rates

E. E. Ghartey, *International Macroeconomics and Finance*,
https://doi.org/10.1007/978-3-032-04145-6_13

(6) Illustrate the adjustment process in the interregional currency area with a single currency
(7) Illustrate the adjustment process in the situation of regional currency area under floating exchange rates. (Hint: Use the assumptions of Mundell (1961)).

13.1 Introduction

The open economy monetary policy trilemma is a concept which evolved from currency carry trade. It was said to have been developed independently by Robert A. Mundell and John M. Fleming in the early 1960s. It is also known as the impossibility trinity. The impossibility trinity concept which is based on uncovered interest rate arbitrage parity condition, is explained as the interest rate differential between domestic interest rate and foreign interest rates, being equal to the expected depreciation, or appreciation of domestic exchange rate.

Thus, if the domestic interest rate is 10 percent and the foreign interest rate is 8 percent, investors will be attracted to invest in the domestic country. In such circumstance, a country cannot allow free flow of funds between itself and the rest of the world, and at the same time fix or peg its exchange rate. If it attempts to do so, the inflow of external funds into the domestic country will cause a balance of payment surplus, which will stress the pegged rate to the point of causing its currency to be over-valued and cause unemployment to violate the essence of the pegged exchange rate.

13.2 The Impossibility Trinity

Discussion on the physiology of a fixed exchange rate regime and its benefit to countries, suggests that countries which tie their exchange rate to an anchor currency, cannot enjoy the benefit of monetary autonomy and free mobility of its capital with the rest of the world.

A smaller country may choose to fix its currency to an anchor currency so that it can enjoy some of the benefit a strong and stable exchange rate bestows on a large country, such as stable exchange rate and low inflation.

The Bahamas, and the Eastern Caribbean Currency Union (ECCU)[1] (and to some extent Belize and Barbados) have fixed their currencies to the US dollar. Under such condition and situation, when the US government raises its interest rate to reduce the expected inflation in the country, and this causes appreciation of the US dollar, these countries' interest rate will fall which will cause their national currencies to depreciate. Their central banks will have to use sterilized intervention consisting of selling their foreign assets and buying their respective domestic currencies to cause their exchange rates to rise to defend the depreciation threat to their respective exchange rates.

Unfortunately, continuous dependence on the use of sterilized intervention to defend the pressure of depreciation on their over-valued exchange rate will result in the countries continuously losing their net international reserves till they dry out. When that occurs, these countries will then have to devalue their respective exchange rates by fixing their respective currencies to a lower par value.

These countries cannot afford to maintain independent monetary policy by always losing their foreign reserves or assets in their attempt to continuously use sterilized intervention to defend their respective exchange rates against depreciation pressure.

Thus, generally, a country cannot simultaneously fix its exchange rate to a large country, maintain free financial flows (or perfect capital mobility), and adhere to monetary policy independence. In the above discussion, the countries can only maintain fixed exchange rate and free financial flows, but they cannot conduct independent monetary policy, since changes in interest rates which emanates from monetary policy autonomy of their central banks, is not possible.

It is for this reason that the impossibility trinity says it is impossible for country's central banks or monetary authorities (MA) to implement

[1] The Eastern Caribbean Currency Area comprises of members of the Caribbean Community (CARICOM) from Antigua and Barbuda, Dominica, Grenada, Saint Kitts and Nevis, Saint Lucia, and Saint Vincent and the Grenadines. They are referred to as the Eastern Caribbean Currency Union (ECCU) as they have adopted a common currency, which is the US dollar, and fixed their exchange rates to determine their trade relationships in goods, services, and capital with each other. However, they have foregone their monetary policy autonomy and relegated it to the Eastern Caribbean Central Bank (ECCB), which is headquartered in Saint Kitts and Nevis, to conduct aggregate demand policies to influence production and expand employment in member countries in the union.

simultaneously the following three monetary policy objectives or options in a carry trade, namely:

(a) to peg its exchange rate,
(b) to maintain free flow of funds (FFF) or complete capital movement between countries, and
(c) to administer monetary policy autonomy (MPA).

The impossibility trinity or trilemma says that central banks can only implement or choose only two of the above three policy options listed in the trilemma simultaneously. See Panel 13.1.

If central banks choose to simultaneously implement both free flow of funds and independent monetary policy, they cannot peg their exchange rate. Such a dual policy choice is consistent with floating exchange rate. If monetary authorities (MAs) choose to pursue independent monetary policy, they can only float their exchange rate. Otherwise, the MAs can implement a pegged exchange rate and pursue independent monetary policy simultaneously to manage fluctuations in their interest rate, while foregoing free flow of funds. Such a dual policy choice has been adopted by China, and it is consistent with only capita controls.

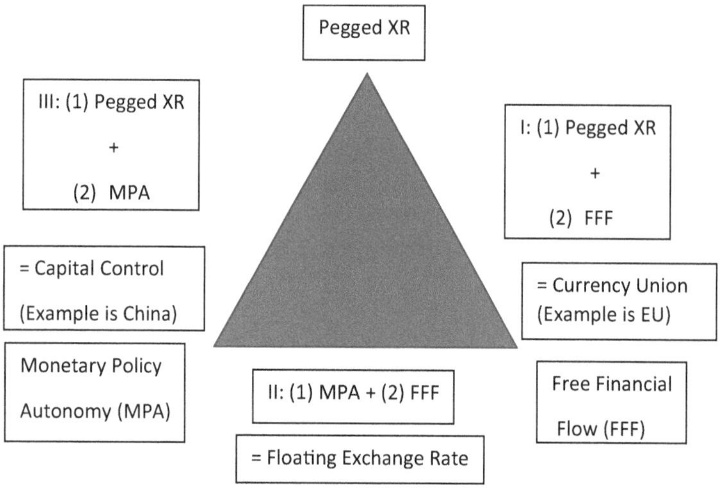

Panel 13.1 International macro-and-monetary economic impossibility trinity

In fact, a country which fixes its exchange rate cannot simultaneously practice a free flow of funds among countries while maintaining its monetary autonomy. The adoption of the monetary or currency union by the 11 European countries in 1999 was tantamount to the Euro Zone countries adopting a fixed exchange rate and free flow of funds (or) capital among its members, while foregoing the practice of monetary policy autonomy/independent policy among its members.[2] Most countries outside the Euro Zone which are members of the IMF, have adopted managed floating exchange rate, which is a form of pegged exchange rate to impose monetary discipline in their central banks, to ensure that they practice monetary independence.

This choice of fixed exchange rate and monetary policy autonomy became popular among countries in the world during the second United Nations Monetary and Financial Conference which was organized in Bretton Woods, New Hampshire, when the IMF was formed. Thus, it lasted throughout the period before the end of World War II on July 1–22, 1944, until it was abolished in 1971 when the US terminated the conversion of dollars into gold. During this period, the world economies recorded consistently higher global economic growth than what was experienced in the period after 1971. The IMF introduced the Special Drawing Rights (SDRs) to complement official reserves in the BOPs account. Thus, the official reserves at that period comprised of (1) gold, (2) SDRs, which are referred to as international money and are valued as the weighted average of various convertible currencies in the IMF, (3) reserve position in the IMF, and (4) convertible foreign currencies which is predominantly US dollars.

In 1973, the world experienced a generalized free floating exchange rate which survived the oil price hikes of Oil and Petroleum Exporting Countries (OPEC) in the 1970s. In mid-1974, the IMF re-defined the unit of SDRs in terms of gold or dollars. The Jamaica accords[3] of 1976

[2] In January 1999 when the 11 members of the European Monetary Union (EMU), comprising of Austria, Belgium, Finland, France, Germany, Ireland, Italy, Luxembourg, Netherlands, and Portugal, adopted the euro and a common monetary policy to become European Union, their monetary policy control was handled by (Bundesbank) European Central Bank with headquarters in Frankfurt. The foreign exchange rate then was set at €1 = $1.17.

[3] Jamaica Accords commenced full operation (or was ratified) in 1978 when President Nixon abolished the official gold standard or conversion of price of an ounce of gold for 1 SDR or $35, and was replaced with IMF's agreement to managed float.

resulted in a committee of the IMF board of governors floating the price of gold, with respect to the US dollar and other currencies. In 1981, the IMF defined the SDR as the weighted average of five countries, which comprised of the US, Germany, Japan, France, and UK.

It is for this reason, among others, that in November 1993, the Euro Zone countries opted to form the European Union to (1) curb fluctuations in their exchange rate, (2) maintain monetary discipline to stabilize their inflation rate, and (3) enhance and expand their economic growth in Europe.

On, the other hand, most-smaller Eastern Caribbean countries, based on the size of their countries, adopted currency union, known as the Eastern Caribbean Currency Union (ECCU), which meant they forfeited their independent monetary policy autonomy, so that they could gain some of the benefits a collective currency union bestows on them. The Bahamas, on the other hand, dollarized or pegged its foreign exchange rate on a one-to-one basis to the US dollar. Thus, the ECCU members forwent their monetary policy autonomy to gain the benefits of a large country from their anchor currency—in this case the US dollar.

Thus, in this chapter we have discussed three policy options (namely: monetary autonomy or independence; free financial flow or capital mobility; and stable or pegged exchange rate) of central banks, which are known as the open economy monetary policy trilemma or trinity, which are linked to carry trade. We then concluded the discussion by identifying the policy pairs which can be implemented simultaneously by central banks.

13.3 Exchange Rate Regimes

The managed float which emerged in 1973 raised the question: how does a country choose an optimal exchange rate regime in an era of the Bretton Woods experience and post Jamaican accords?

There are typically two exchange rate regimes. These are floating exchange rate and fixed exchange rate. The fixed exchange rate has five variants. These are (i) inflation targeting, (ii) dollarization, (iii) currency or monetary union, (iv) exchange rate targeting, and (v) currency-board.

13.4 Inflation Targeting

The primary long-run goal of monetary policy is stable prices, and inflation targeting is a nominal anchor that ties down prices to stabilize inflation.

13.5 Features of Inflation Targeting

There are several features of inflation targeting, among which are the following:

(i) Public announcement of medium-term objectives or targets of inflation. For instance, the Governor of a central bank in such countries may publicly set the inflation target typically as either a range between say 3 to 5 percent per annum, or target of 3 or 4 or 5 percent per annum, etc.
(ii) The Governor of the central bank publicly announces say five years as the term or period the central bank intends to achieve the inflation target of the country.
(iii) The Governor of the central bank must publicly set up institutional commitment of the central bank to achieve stable prices stated in the inflation targeting document. This might require that the Governor of the central bank sets up monetary policy committee comprising of representatives from all walks of life, to develop a monetary policy target such as the monetary policy rate, with a goal of achieving a desired inflation rate target over a specific period.
(iv) Uses information inclusive approach and mathematical model which involves several variables, and communications from several public and private sources to make decisions about monetary policy to achieve stable prices, and to obtain the stated inflation rate target over the stated period.
(v) Increases transparency in making decision on monetary policy strategy through communication with the public, stakeholders, and professionals in the country.
(vi) Augments and intensifies the accountability of the central bank to achieve inflation targeting objectives with the cooperation, and sound fiscal commitment of the Minister of Finance of the nation.

13.6 Advantages of Inflation Targeting

There are several advantages of inflation targeting for an economy, among which are the following:

(a) Inflation targeting reduces time inconsistency problem.[4] It specifically targets a numerical value for inflation which the central bank employs its expansionary monetary policy to achieve. Consequently, the central bank is not entrapped to employ a repeated expansionary monetary policy in a time inconsistency problem, where the central bank employs monetary expansion policy each time the country faces high unemployment, in a never-ending fashion.

(b) Inflation targeting brings transparency into the management of the economy. It requires that the targeted inflation rate policy is announced, so that members of the public become aware and well-informed about the inflation targeting policy. Typically, the inflation targeting policy in relation to the central bank and its governor are enshrined in the constitution of the country. The central bank also informs the public and institutions about the numerical value of the inflation rate it has targeted, and the method it has employed to achieve that inflation target. The members of the public are reached daily through the media, seminars, news report, and other forms of public education to elicit their participation in achieving the long-run goal of the inflation target.

(c) Inflation targeting promotes increased accountability in monetary policy. It assists the central bank to reach its goals through the monetary policy. In New Zealand, the central bank governor's performance in meeting the inflation targeting goal is tied to his/her success in achieving the stipulated inflation targeting, which is enshrined in the constitution of the nation pursuing the inflation target. This constitutional requirement stipulation and the central bank's adherence of sound monetary policy conduct which is announced and reported in the news media, and other sources

[4] A policy is time consistent if an action planned at time t for implementation at time t + 1 proved to be optimal for implementation when time t + 1 arrives. However, if at time t + 1 the policy fails to respond as originally planned, then the policy is said to be time inconsistent. See Carl Walsh (1998).

like posters, and TV news win the public's support, and make the entire process transparent to the citizenry.

(d) Inflation targeting is very much aligned with democratic principle. The governor of the central bank, other banking officials, and nonbanking representatives and government officials are chosen by the Governor of the central bank with the tacit support of Minister of Finance to form a monetary policy committee, with the responsibility to set monetary policy goals and to conduct monetary policy. The monetary policy committee members are chosen from all walks of life, namely, academia, businesses, and banks, to name a few. As such, the decisions of the monetary policy committee are representational of the entire economy in the country.

(e) Inflation targeting policy improves the conduct of monetary policy. The sound and transparent monetary policy employed to curb inflation gains the confidence of the entire society, as it is arrived at by a democratically elected and informed members of a monetary policy committee across the entire country. The backing of the representational members of the monetary policy committee gains the confidence of the entire society, and this removes any time inconsistency problem from the monetary policy committee's decisions, and it stamps out time inconsistency problem which had plagued past decisions of monetary authorities in economies.

13.7 Dollarization

Dollarization is a variants of fixed exchange rate regime. Other fixed exchange rate variants are currency union, and currency-board. Dollarization is another term for currency substitution. If a small island economy adopts the US dollar as its legal tender currency, then even though the small island country has its own currency, the country's use of the foreign currency is termed as dollarization. A few currencies have served as dollarization. Among the currencies that are considered as 'dollars' in international finance and banking are the US dollar, the European euro, the British pound sterling, the Chinese yuan renminbi, to name a few.

13.8 Advantages of Dollarization

(i) Dollarization provides a much stronger, permanent, and irrevocable commitments for the dollarized country, than a currency-board which can either be abandoned by the currency-board country or replaced with other currencies or reset the currency par values or even adopt a flexible exchange rate regime.

(ii) Dollarization tends to align or promote economic, financial, and banking integration of the dollarized country with the economy of the developed foreign reserve or anchor currency country which has been adopted for dollarization, and the global economy. It accelerates the convergence of the dollarized country's economy with developed economies whose currency has been adopted. It also makes it difficult to insulate the domestic country's financial and banking system from the rest of the world. Rather, it facilitates the integration of the dollarized country with the developed country whose currency has been adopted for the dollarization like the US, and the rest of the world. This results in the dollarized economy's interest rates, prices, inflation, and interest spread reducing to either the level of the developed country like the US or near it.

(iii) Dollarization provides countries a means to eliminate completely devaluation or currency risk, and attendant inflation and associated threat, since the dollarized currency is stable, strong, and irrevocable. However, although it cannot fully remove default or sovereign risk, dollarization reduces suspension or disruption in making payment on foreign debt, which is indirectly influenced by future foreign exchange disturbances.

(iv) It removes any expectation of sudden risk associated with exchange rate adjustments which originates from instability in international capital flows and currencies, which are driven by depreciation or devaluation, and changes in interest rates. It is also a mechanism by which currency and balance of payments crises can be averted.

(v) In smaller developing countries, foreign exchange reserves tend to be inadequate in banks. This makes it difficult for central banks to operate as a lender of last resort. The problem even increases when there are massive withdrawals of funds because of bank panics.

However, in a dollarized economy, where the confidence of depositors is firmly established, there are no currency mismatches in position of banks, and because the country's monetary assets are dollarized, bank runs become rare in occurrence. The dollarized country requires a much smaller foreign exchange reserves to adequately back up the central bank's reserves requirements to support depositors. Consequently, dollarization enhances the central bank's role as a lender of last resort.

(vi) Dollarization also completely assists in eliminating speculative attacks in the dollarized country. This is because the dollar is irrevocable and remains the same in value over time, barring depreciation or devaluation and inflation risk.

(vii) With proper currency matching of bank positions and depositors being highly confident of the banking system, a full dollarization can provide a good basis for the financial sector; and reduce administrative costs, level of interest rates, inflation, risk premium, and interest spread in the dollarized economy.

13.9 Disadvantages of Dollarization

There are few disadvantages associated with dollarization. These disadvantages can be summarized as follow:

(i) A country that adopts dollarization foregoes completely its monetary and exchange rate policy autonomy. Unlike central banks, it cannot use monetary policy to conduct demand management policies to achieve most economic goals, and inflation finance its economy.

(ii) A country that dollarizes loses its seigniorage, which is the profit or revenue accruing to the monetary authority of the country which prints or exercises the right and issues legal tender or currency or the dollar. The dollarized country transfers its seigniorage to the country which it transfers or replaces its currency with its dollar, such as the US.

(iii) Dollarization results in loss of lender of last resort function of the central bank, as the replacement of the domestic country's currency with the foreign currency means absence of central bank in the dollarized country. Consequently, the dollarized country cannot use the discounting process at the discount window. This means that during financial distress, the central bank cannot extend discounting lending to financial institutions in the domestic economy.

(iv) (Dollarization which means replacement of national currency with foreign currency can erode political pride of the nation. It also deprives the dollarized country of its international prestige and pride which ownership of national currency bestows to the currency issuing country. The absence of the domestic currency also means that the nation cannot print money to finance fiscal spending to promote economic growth.

13.10 Currency or Monetary Union

Currency union, which is also known as monetary union, is a union formed by a group of countries which come together to fix their exchange rate in relations to each other by adopting a common currency.

Balance of payments (BOPs) crises are important perennial problem which threatens most developing and emerging market economies under the Bretton Woods System of fixed exchange rate, where inflexible wages and prices dislocate the equilibrium adjustment mechanism by inhibiting the terms of trade from performing their natural role of adjusting the economy.

Under a flexible exchange rate regime, depreciation is used to solve BOPs deficit problem instead of allowing the economy to be saddled with unemployment problem, and appreciation is used to solve inflation problem which originate from BOPs surplus problem.

Should the Jamaican dollar be allowed to float against all currencies or fixed to the dollar? Should currencies of the Caribbean Single Market Economies (CSME) be fixed to the dollar? Should the CSME float their respective currencies against a reserve currency like the dollar or euro or yuan? Should the CSME float a single representative currency for its members against a reserve currency?

What is the optimum currency area of the CSME or West Africa Monetary Zone (WAMZ) or Economic Community of West African States (ECOWAS) Single Market Economies (ESME)? Is there an optimum currency area domain for single currency, such as the Belize dollar, and currency union for the CSME? What is the optimum currency area of a country such as Ghana or currency union such as ESME?

The discussions below attempt to provide some answers to the above questions.

13.11 Types of Currency Areas

There are two types of currency areas. These are international currency area and interregional currency area. The international currency area is a currency area comprising of a single currency, which is fixed to a reserve currency, such as the dollar or yuan or euro, or is floated against international currencies. The interregional currency area is a currency area which comprises of more than one currency areas.

The adjustment process by which a deviation from equilibrium is corrected, assists in determining which of the two types of the currency areas is the optimum currency area domain for a single country with a single currency under a fixed exchange rate, and interregional currency area under either a flexible or fixed exchange rate. See Robert A. Mundell (1961).

13.12 Illustrative Hypothetical Examples

Most countries have a central bank which issues a single currency to serve as an interregional means of payment system with elastic supply. However, the ESME which plans to issue the eco as the currency in ESME currency area, has more than one central bank, so the means of payment in that region will have to be agreed upon by all central banks constituting the WAMZ region. Any central bank in the ESME currency area which attempts to increase its money supply faster than its counterparts, without incorporating the rate which monetary liabilities is growing in the currency area, will lose reserves. It will also fail to convert its money supply which will impair the convertibility of the currency area?

Thus, the adjustment within a currency area which comprises of a single currency, and a currency area which comprises of more than one currency are different. Adjustments within an interregional currency area, and international currency area which has a fixed exchange rate, are different.

In the tradition of Mundell (1961), and for illustrative purpose, we assume the following:

(a) Two simple models comprising of interregional model (Y) and international model (X).
(b) The economies in models X and Y are initially operating at the full employment and the balance of payments are in equilibrium before adjustment.
(c) The money wages and prices are sticky downwards and can be reduced in the short-term by increasing unemployment, which means it exhibits a Phillips curve type of relationship.
(d) The monetary authorities employ monetary policy to avert inflation.

Example 1: Suppose there are two cases. The first case (X) illustrates a situation where a country adjusts within an international currency area comprising of several countries with independent currencies which have fixed exchange rates. The second case (Y) is a situation where a country which belongs to a regional currency area, share a common currency which adjusts within an interregional currency area.

13.13 Adjustment Process in the International Currency Area with Fixed Exchange Rates

Suppose that the international demand shifts from country X's goods and services to goods and services of country Y. What happens in the adjustment process? Assume that each country has its own currency, p_x is the price of goods and services of country X, and p_y is the price of goods and services of country Y. Terms of trade in country Y is (p_y/p_x).

The shift in demand from goods and services in country X to goods and services in country Y results in a fall in goods and services of country X and increase in goods and services of country Y. Unemployment in country X increases which results in balance of payments deficit there, while overemployment which results from increase in demand for goods and services in country Y, results in balance of payments surplus and inflation pressure in country Y.[5]

[5] Unemployment is actual real output being less than the full employment or the natural rate of employment or the natural real output or employment, and overemployment is actual real output or employment being greater than the full employment or natural rate of employment or natural real output.

The increase in demand for country Y's goods and services pushes up prices of those goods and services from p_y to $p_y{}'$, and the reduced demand for country X's goods and services causes prices of those goods and services p_x to fall to $p_x{}'$. Thus, the terms of trade of country X improves from (p_x/p_y) as it falls to $(p_x{}'/p_y{}')$ in country X and rises in country Y.

Country X cannot reduce prices because money wages and prices are sticky downward. Any attempt of country Y to contract monetary policy to hike up real interest rate to reduce credit in country Y will worsen the adjustment problems of country X. Country X cannot reduce its real income to improve its terms of trade. The solution to the depressed economic condition is better resolved by country X decreasing its employment and output to improve its terms of trade. This is because leaving the burden of adjustment problem to the balance of payments surplus country Y will depress the world economy under a fixed exchange rate or currency area with many separate currencies, which Mundell referred to as an international currency area. See Mundell (1961, p.658).

13.14 Adjustment Process in the Interregional Currency Area with a Common Single Currency

A country in a currency area, such as ESME, shares a common currency, namely: eco, with countries in West African Monetary Zone (WAMZ). The following explains its adjustment process.

Suppose demand shifts from goods and services of country X (Ghana) to goods and services of country Y (Gambia) where both countries belong to ESME and use a common currency, eco, within a closed common currency area. Here, eco is a common currency in use in the common currency area. Assuming that the economy was at equilibrium before the shift in demand. What will happen between country X and Y or the world economy?

The effect of the shift in demand for goods and services from country X (Ghana) to country Y (Gambia), where both countries belong to the ESME, with the assumptions in Section 13.14 above holding good, will cause BOPs deficit and unemployment in country X (Ghana); and the increase in demand for goods and services of country Y (Gambia) will cause overemployment, and BOPs surplus which will trigger inflationary pressure in country Y (Gambia).

Country X (Ghana) cannot expand its money supply to prop up its spending within the interregional currency area, because it does not have a central bank, as the ESME currency area has its own central bank or monetary authority.

However, because both countries belong to an interregional currency area where the countries use the same single currency, their response to the shift in demand will lead to inflation in country Y (Gambia). Note that without country X (Ghana) propping up its demand by expanding the money supply, and leaving the economy to market forces, will result in overemployment and inflation pressure which will cause price of country Y's goods and services p_y to increase to $p_y{}'$. Consequently, the terms of trade $(p_x/p_y{}')$ improves in favor of country X to complete the adjustment in the world economy since $(p_x/p_y{}') < (p_x/p_y)$.

13.15 Summary

A currency area comprising of several countries which share a common single currency, the adjustment process will require that the monetary authority or the central bank sets the inflation rate in the BOPs surplus country to ensure unemployment in the BOPs deficit country.

A currency area which comprises of several countries, with each country having its own currency, the adjustment process ensures that the BOPs surplus country employs expansionary monetary policy to reduce the real interest rate to cause the BOPs deficit country's employment to grow and reduce its unemployment.

Thus, in both case (1) international currency area and case (2) interregional currency area, the shift in demand from one country to another country will result in unemployment in country X and inflation in country Y, which will violate BOPs equilibrium. In both international and interregional currency areas, monetary authorities cannot avert both inflation and unemployment among member countries.

13.16 Currencies of Countries under Flexible Exchange Rates

Suppose there is a demand shift from goods and services of country A to goods and services of country B. This will result in a fall in demand which will cause unemployment in country A, while the increase in demand will cause inflation in country B. There will also be an imbalance in BOPs, with country A experiencing BOPs deficit and country B experiencing BOPs surplus.

Under flexible exchange rate regime, depreciation in country A will solve the BOPs deficit, and unemployment in country A, and appreciation in country B will solve the BOPs surplus, overemployment, and inflation in country B.

Thus, variable exchange rates indicate (or are consistent with) the existence of several global currencies.

Examples

Suppose there are two countries, namely Nigeria and South Africa. South Africa's currency is the rand and Nigeria's currency is the naira. These currencies are separate, but they fluctuate against each other. Suppose for simplicity that these two countries exist on the globe. Suppose the world is split up into two sectors. One-sector is the South, and the other sector is the North. The line which splits up the globe into two sectors does not share any boundaries nor are they in any way related with the two countries.

The Northern sector's industry produces oil and related product, and the Southern sector produces diamonds and related product. If productivity in the oil sector increases to cause demand for diamond to increase in the South, the supply of oil will exceed its demand in the North. Consequently, the excess supply of oil will result in increase in unemployment in the North. Furthermore, the excess demand for diamond will cause inflation threat in the South. Bank reserves will flow from the North to the South.

Central banks in both Nigeria and South Africa will resolve the unemployment in the North by implementing an expansionary monetary policy and fight the inflation pressure threat by using a contractionary monetary policy in the South. It should be noted that although the inflation threat in the South and the unemployment in the North result in external disequilibrium in the world, they cannot lead to BOP surplus in the North and BOPs deficit in the South.

However, both Nigeria and South Africa can curb inflation threat by contracting the money supply in the South, and unemployment problem can be solved by expanding monetary policy in the North. Unemployment can be solved in the North by both countries at the expense of inflation threat. Inflation threat pressure can be curbed by both countries in the South but at the expense of unemployment. In both Northern and Southern sectors or regions, both unemployment and inflation cannot be solved simultaneously.

The floating exchange rate cannot be used to solve BOPs disequilibrium problem between the Northern and Southern sectors or regions of the globe. However, the floating exchange rate can be used to solve BOPs disequilibrium problems in both countries. The flexible exchange rate cannot be used to solve a currency union problem. Currency union requires a common currency or group of countries with single currencies which are tied by fixed exchange rates.

13.17 Regional Currency Areas under Floating Exchange Rates

The main question which remains is as follows:

Is there a justification for a floating exchange rate?

The answer is yes, there is. We shall illustrate the case for regional currency area under floating exchange rates by using the discussion of adjustment of the world in the preceding sections. We have modified the example in Mundell (1961) to reflect the case which is elucidated below.

Let the world's currencies consist of Southern cedis and Northern cedis. Thus, there are now no naira and rand currencies.

(i) Under a fixed exchange rate regime:

Under a fixed exchange rate regime, the Southern cedis will be fixed to the Northern cedis. The adjustment process follows a shift in demand from Northern oil to Southern diamond. The result is analogous to the adjustment process in the interregional currency area under a common or single currency discussed above. See previous Sections 13.14–13.16.

(iia) Under a floating exchange rate regime:

However, under a floating exchange rate, if there is a shift in demand for diamond in the South from oil in the North, it will not result in excess demand for diamond in the South and excess supply of oil in the North. Consequently, there will be no inflation threat in the South and unemployment in the North. Rather, the Southern cedis facing the excess demand will appreciate relative to the Northern cedis, and the Northern cedis facing the excess supply will depreciate relative to the Southern cedis. The balance of payments equilibrium will be reestablished, as central banks of both regions implement appropriate monetary policy changes to ensure that equilibrium interest rate is maintained, with equilibrium real exchange rate between the Northern and Southern regions, and equilibrium prices, real output, and employment. See Chapter 10.

Thus, floating exchange rates case rests on regional currencies but not on national currencies or group of countries with different single currency. According to Mundell, the region becomes the optimum currency area.

(iib) Under the gold standard

An alternate view to the analysis above, from the perspective of the gold standard which most countries in the world adopted dating back from 1929, yield similar outcome discussed in early Chapters. From 1929 and thereafter, countries which experienced depression transferred their depression experience to other foreign countries through the external trade multiplier. Depression in countries spread to other countries in Europe, Latin American, and even Africa, and it continued to the end of Second World War which spanned 1939–1945.

The Bretton Woods system emerged in 1945, when the world system was moved from the gold standard to the US dollar which replaced it and served as a common currency regime in a world of multiregional currency; depression continued to be transferred from one country (or region) to other countries (or regions). Similarly, BOPs deficit problem was transferred from one country to other foreign countries through the foreign trade multiplier. Thus, interregional BOPs problem was invisible as it reflected or was subjected to the self-adjusting effect of interregional flows of money. The BOPs disequilibrium adjustment transferred international reserves from the BOPs deficit country to the BOPs surplus country. See Mundell (1961), Krugman and Obstfeld (2000). See also Chapter 10, Section 10.6.[6]

[6] This effect can be likened to the currency crises, dubbed as the Tequila effect, which spread from Mexico in the mid-1990s to South America, Eastern Europe, and East and

13.18 Exchange Rate Targeting

It is a monetary policy strategy of fixing the value of the domestic currency to a commodity such as gold during the gold standard Bretton Woods period. See the last paragraph of Chapter 10, Section 10.4. However, in recent times, the domestic currency is fixed to an anchor country, which is usually a large country with a low inflation like the US or the UK during the colonial era or Germany in the Euro Zone during the inception of the European Union.

An alternative to exchange rate targeting is crawling peg or target, where a currency is allowed to depreciate consistently and steadily to ensure that the country pegging to the large economy and low inflation anchor country, can maintain it closer to the inflation of the anchor country's currency.

13.19 Advantages of Exchange Rate Targeting

(1) Exchange rate targeting provides a nominal anchor to maintain inflation by tying the country which is pegging its currency to the exchange rate of international traded goods, while fixing the domestic price of these goods to the exchange rate target. If the exchange rate targeting is credible, the inflation expectations is set to the inflation of the anchor country.

(2) It provides an automatic rule to guide the conduct of monetary policy to mitigate time-inconsistency problem inherent in the central bank's attempt to employ temporary monetary expansion to mitigate low output or high unemployment.

(3) The benefit of exchange rate targeting when the targeting country's exchange rate is fixed to a low exchange rate and inflation rate, and a high growth large anchor country, outweighs the loss of its monetary policy autonomy. This renders it impossible for the targeting country to use discretionary monetary policy to deal with domestic concerns.

(4) It is simple, has clarity, and can be easily understood by the public.

South-East Asia in the early 2000, although during that time the world was no longer on gold standard, and all affected countries were members of the IMF.

(5) Most developed economies use the long-run interest rate movement to determine whether monetary policy is expansionary or not. Thus, a low or declining long-run interest rate can inform the market that monetary policy is expansionary.

However, most emerging and/or developing countries do not have long-term bonds, consequently, an important signal on the direction of monetary policy movement is absent. In emerging or developed countries, the depreciation of domestic currency serves as an indication of the central bank's pursuit of expansionary monetary policy. This often results in the public pressurizing the central bank to apply breaks on excessive monetary expansion.

The public's expression of fear of depreciation, serves as a constraint on the central bank, to limit it from committing time inconsistency problem in conducting monetary policy. In most countries or developing countries, depreciation tends to cause inflation[7]: since inflation is almost always caused by expansionary monetary policy. In fact, depreciation often indicates that the central bank is pursuing an expansionary monetary policy. This results in the public's dissatisfaction which is expressed by unions demanding higher wages; and sellers and public transport owners hiking up prices and fares.

Government which are responsive to public opinions tend to blame their central banks. Central banks which are pursuing exchange rate targeting in emerging economies use depreciation as an indicator that the central bank is following a loose monetary policy and is therefore committing a time inconsistency problem.

(6) Exchange rate targeting permits economies which are contiguous or connected with each other or share borders to form economic integration. Unfortunately, such reason based on contiguous of boundaries cannot explain the experience of small island economies in the Caribbean, and anglophone countries in West Africa, as they are surrounded by francophone countries.

Exchange rate targeting in emerging market economies have been used to curb or reduce inflation. Mexico reduced its high inflation which exceeded 100%, a hyperinflation, in 1988–1993 by adhering to exchange rate targeting.

[7] See Ghartey (2019).

13.20 Disadvantages of Exchange Rate Targeting

(1) The principal problem associated with the exchange rate targeting is that all shocks which negatively affect the anchor country, automatically affect the small country which is pursuing the exchange rate targeting, by pegging its currency to the anchor country's exchange rate.

(2) The principal problem in the light of the fact that capital is mobile, is that the country which has adopted the exchange rate targeting tends to forego its use of monetary policy to meet its macroeconomic and aggregate demand problems. Consequently, it cannot employ monetary policy independently to solve its idiosyncratic shocks (which are independent of large and low anchor country), the smaller country has targeted with its currency. As mentioned earlier, Mexico used exchange rate targeting to reduce its hyperinflation in 1988 to a single digit inflation in 1994.

(3) Exchange rate targeting exposes countries to speculative attacks on their national currencies. This problem tends to be problematic for emerging market economies. Argentina in 2002, East Asia in 1997, and Mexico in 1994 were driven into financial crises which were made worse by speculative attacks which drove their economies into near financial collapse.

(4) Thus, although it could be argued that because most emerging economies have not developed proper financial and institutional mechanism in their countries to effectively allow their monetary policy to be employed successfully in mitigating external shocks, adopting exchange rate targeting, which subject emerging economies to the discipline of the anchor country like the US, extend the benefit of the gains from monetary discipline of the US, the anchor currency, to the emerging economies which may far exceed the loss of the targeted country's monetary policy autonomy.

(5) Exchange rate targeting can weaken the integrity and accountability of policymakers, especially in emerging market economies. The fact is, exchange rate targeting fixes the exchange rate, which is more pronounce in emerging market. Thus, it removes an important signal which assists policymakers and market participants from being informed on the direction of economic policy, whether it

is more expansionary or not. Thus, it limits or reduces time-inconsistency problem associated with the central bank's tendency to engage in expansionary or loose monetary policy. It should be noted though, that issues that relate to exchange rate targeting, which are very common in emerging economies, are not important features in most developed countries. It is for this reason that exchange rate targeting is not a very common feature in developed countries, as they prevail in emerging economies.

13.21 The Currency-board

Currency-board originated in Britain. The first currency-board was established in Mauritius in 1849. The West African Currency Board was established in 1912 for four West African countries, namely: Gambia, Ghana, Nigeria, and Sierra Leone. Currency-boards were also established in British Colonies in Asia, the Caribbean, the Pacific islands, and other African countries.

Orthodox currency-boards have been and are in existence in Bermuda and Cayman Islands. The IMF has classified Eastern Caribbean Central Bank as a currency-board, although as a central bank it maintains between 60–90 percent of its monetary base in foreign reserves or the anchor currency or reserve currency which is the US dollar. It should be noted that typical currency-board's reserves are generally between 100 to 110 percent of its coins and notes for public transaction purposes set by law. Other countries with currency-board arrangement in accordance to recent IMF's classification of exchange rate arrangements are Bulgaria, Estonia, and China-Hong Kong SAR.

A currency-board is a monetary authority which issues notes and coins which can be converted into a reserve currency at a fixed rate on demand. Although a currency-board does not accept deposits, its reserves are low-risk interest-bearing bonds and other assets which are denominated in the foreign anchor currency. It generates profits commonly known as a seigniorage which is the interest earned on its reserve assets minus the expense of the maintenance liabilities (or its notes and coins in circulation).

Monetary authorities of a currency-board pay all their profits to the government after they have covered their expenses and maintained their reserves at the level set by law. As an orthodox currency-board, it does not possess any discretionary power to conduct monetary policy to influence monetary targets, as only market forces determine its money supply. See Owen F. Humpage and Jean M. McIntire (1995), and Steve H. Hanke, Lars Jonung, and Kurt Schuler (1993).

13.22 Features of Currency-Board

Principal features of a currency-board are

(i) A currency-board country chooses a currency which commands a universal acceptance throughout the world and is generally expected to be stable as its anchor currency. Among currencies that have been chosen as currency-board currencies are the US dollar, the British pound, and occasionally the German mark. Central banks do not issue anchor currency. In the past, a few countries have used gold and silver as anchor currencies.

(ii) A currency-board's notes and coins are ensured to be convertible into an anchor currency to keep full and unlimited conversion of the currency-board currency at a fixed exchange rate upon demand.

(iii) Currency-boards do not convert bank deposits into currency-board notes. Only banks make such conversion. Currency-boards can only issue coins and currency-board notes.

(iv) A currency-board in an orthodox system can convert unlimited coins and notes into the anchor currency. It is not restricted from converting current account (goods, services, and unilateral transfers) transactions and capital account (financial assets such as bonds, stocks, etc.) transactions.

(v) Reserves of currency-boards are sufficient to ensure that all owners of currency-board notes and coins can convert them into the reserve currency. Currency-boards usually hold 105 to 110 percent reserves against its liabilities instead of 100 percent reserves. This means it uses between 5 to 10 percent of its reserves as a reserve buffer to protect the currency-board when its reserves decrease due to the possibility of its bonds dropping in value.

(vi) Coins and notes of currency-board country unlike bonds and deposits of banks do not earn or attract interest. The profit of the issuer of currency-board notes and coins—or the monetary authority—is equal to the difference between interest earned on reserves and the expenses incurred from minting currency-board coins and printed currency-board notes used by the public.[8] Typically, the expenses are one percent of the assets or GDP per year. The monetary authorities' net worth increases when the currency-board's notes and coins wear out or are destroyed. This is because the value of assets of the currency-board's country remains the same, whereas its liabilities decrease when the currency-board's notes and coins wear out and are destroyed or replaced. Generally, after paying all expenses of the currency-board's country, its leftover profit is one percent of the GDP per year.

The currency-board's country gains its seigniorage if it uses the currency-board's own coins and notes as the currency of the currency-board country instead of the anchor currency (as is done by The Bahamas). The seigniorage of the currency-board country will be lost if the foreign anchor currency such as the US dollar, UK pound, etc., is used as the reserve currency of the currency-board country. Additionally, using the currency of currency-board country in the country of the currency-board boosts the national pride of its citizenry.

(vii) A currency-board does not have discretionary powers. Hence it cannot employ monetary policy to achieve interest rate targets. Its main function is to serve as a mechanism to exchange currency-board notes and coins for the anchor currency at a fixed exchange rate on demand. An orthodox currency-board unlike central banks cannot lend to government nor companies nor banks. A government in currency-board country finance its country's fiscal expenditure through either taxation or borrowing. Consequently, it cannot create inflation through either money printing or by sterilizing the budget deficit of the currency-board country.

The central bank of a country with the currency-board cannot print money, so it cannot cause inflation. It also cannot serve as lender of last resort because of its inability to create money which is a function of inflation.

[8] Note that the minting of currency-board coins and printing of currency-board notes are not the same as the central bank's minted coins and printing of notes which are constituents of monetary aggregates or the money supply.

An orthodox currency-board cannot exercise discretionary monetary policy, so it cannot change the level of interest rate. It does not have monetary policy authority to employ open market operation or use the discounting process at the discounting window of the central bank to target inflation or alter the interest rate level. In fact, the orthodox currency-board passively relies on the self-correction mechanism of market forces to automatically determine the goals of monetary policy in the currency-board country.

The central bank's commitment to a fixed exchange rate is relatively weaker than the commitment of the currency-board to a fixed exchange rate. This is because the latter's commitment to a fixed exchange rate is automatically subject to the control of the anchor country, and it is independent of the central bank and government of the country. It must be noted that the commitment of central bank of the country is subject to the government who nominates the governor of the central bank of the country.

(viii) The fact that the exchange rate of a currency-board country is deliberately fixed to the anchor currency country with low inflation and healthy economy aligns its interest rate and inflation rate to either the low level of the anchor currency country or close to it. Thus, although prices and inflation in the currency-board country are initially very high, with time its prices and inflation drop gradually to the low level of the anchor currency country.

(ix) This path which the currency-board country travels from its initial high prices and inflation level which gradually drops to the low prices and inflation level of the anchor currency country has been experienced by currency-board country like Argentina in the late 1990s, and even high inflation country like Mexico in the late 1980s. Historically, most currency-board countries adopt stable currencies like the US dollar, the UK pound, and the German mark as anchor currencies, because they have common characteristics of being low inflation and healthy economies.

13.23 Fractional-Reserve Operation of Currency-Board

The money supply has been derived in Chapter 5, see Section 5.8. The money supply for currency-board is derived below to highlight on the effect of money supply and monetary policy in a currency-board operating country. We shall also compare the effect of money supply, and the conduct of monetary policy in a currency-board country with countries which maintain and operate central bank.

In a currency-board country, commercial banks operate fractional reserve basis. There is no legal reserves requirement as banks determine the amount and composition of their reserves by relying on (i) the size and velocity of deposits, (ii) clearing obligations, (iii) the public's relative demand for notes, and (i) the opportunity cost (or interest rate) of reserves held.[9]

The public holds currency-board notes (C) and commercial bank deposits for transaction purposes (DD). Let M be the money supply, and MB be the monetary base of the currency-board.

M = currency-board notes held by the public + commercial bank deposits in currency-board country

MB = currency-board notes held by the public for transaction purposes (C) + currency-board notes held by commercial banks or in reserves against deposits (R).

C = CNP = currency-board notes of the public

DD = CNR = currency-board notes in reserves

r = average currency-board reserves-to-deposit ratio (or required reserve ratio)

= average reserve (R)/deposits (DD)

c = average ratio of currency-board notes to deposits held by individuals or the public

= average notes (C)/deposits (DD)

Thus,

$$M = C + DD \tag{13.1}$$

$$MB = C + R \tag{13.2}$$

[9] See Owen F. Humpage and Jean M. McIntire (1995).

r = R/DD and

$$c = C/DD$$

Equation (13.1) becomes:

$$M = (C + DD) = (C/DD + DD/DD).DD = (c + 1).DD \quad (13.3)$$

$$MB = (C/DD + R/DD).DD = (c + r).DD \quad (13.4)$$

But from equation (13.4)

$$DD = MB/(c + r) \quad (13.5)$$

Substituting for DD in equation (13.5) for DD into equation (13.3) yield

$$M = [(c + 1)/(c + r)].MB \quad (13.6)$$

where, the currency-board money multiplier (mm) is

$$mm^{CB} = [(c + 1)/(c + r)]$$

Thus, the mm^{CB} of the currency-board country which is [(c + 1)/(c + r)] is greater than the mm of the central bank which is [(c + 1)/(c + r + e)], where e is excess reserve ratio. Cf. equation 5.6.

The fundamental balance of payment identity reported in Section 2.7 of Chapter 2 is as follows:

$$BOP = CAB + K\left(i - i^F\right) = IR$$

where,CAB = Current account balance, IR = international reserves$K(i - i^F)$ = capital flow of domestic countryIf $i = i^F$, $K = 0$ the capital flow is zero and the capital account is in a balance.If $i > i^F$, $K_1 > 0$ and the capital inflow is perfect, then $K \rightarrow \infty$.If $i < i^F$, $K_2 < 0$ and the capital outflow is perfect, then $K \rightarrow -\infty$.We have assumed here that there is perfect mobility of capital in and out of the domestic country. The rest of the notations maintained the definitions used in earlier chapters.

13.24 Contrasting Currency-Board versus Central Bank

In Panel 13.2 Section A, the balance sheet of the currency-board country indicates that the currency-board notes with the public and commercial bank notes cannot exceed the foreign exchange or international reserves of the currency-board country. The currency-board also connects the foreign exchange reserves of the currency-board to the overall balance of payment through the BOPs identity below:

$$CAB + K\left(i - i^{F}\right) = IR$$

This permits us to express equation (13.6) as

$$M = mm.MB$$

$$M = mm.\left[CAB + K\left(i - i^{F}\right)\right] \quad (13.7)$$

$$M = mm.IR \quad (13.8)$$

If

$$M = mm.\left[CAB + K\left(i - i^{F}\right)\right] < 0$$

Panel 13.2 T-account of the currency-board and central bank[10]

A: T-account of currency-board	
Assets	Liabilities & Net Worth
Foreign exchange reserve (IR)	Currency-board notes with the public (C)
Liquid reserve account	Commercial bank notes (R)
Investment reserve account	
Surplus reserve account	
B: T-account of central bank	
Assets	Liabilities & Net Worth
Foreign reserves (IR)	Monetary base: C + R
Gold & SDR	
Domestic Credits (DC): Loans and Securities	Coins in circulation

[10] See also Humpage and McIntire (1995).

it means that the BOPs deficit results in the currency-board losing foreign reserves, all other things being equal. The monetary base also contracts and so does the money supply. If we accept Friedman's dictum that inflation is almost always and everywhere a monetary phenomenon, then because the money supply contracts, inflation too will contract, all things being equal. The reduction in prices results in businesses contracting and unemployment increasing in the currency-board country.

Again, if

$$M = mm.\left[CAB + K\left(i - i^F\right)\right] > 0 \tag{13.9}$$

which means that the BOPs surplus results in the currency-board gaining foreign reserves. The monetary base also expands and so does the money supply. Again, using Friedman's dictum that almost always and everywhere inflation is a monetary phenomenon, we find that the increase in the money supply drives up inflation too.

A currency-board country cannot rely on its current account surplus to expand its money supply. Emerging market economy can have current account deficit and still have a larger net capital-account inflows to dwarf the former to make the overall BOPs a surplus.

Equation (13.9) shows that to the extent that the currency-board country runs a BOPs surplus, the money supply in the currency-board country will increase.

The currency-board country can increase its reserves if the reserve currency country or the anchor currency country increases its money supply more than the demand of its citizens. This will cause the interest rate in the reserve currency or anchor currency country to fall. Prices will increase in the reserve currency country to initiate arbitrage trading which will result in a fall in prices of the currency-board country. This will result in an increase in the demand for goods and services from the currency-board country. The increase in interest rates in the currency-board country also attracts more capital inflow from the reserve or anchor currency country.

The increase in demand for exports of goods and services from the currency-board country improves the balance of payment by reducing its balance of payment deficit position and moving it into a surplus. Capital inflows improve net international reserves. Thus, the reserves of the currency-board country can be increased by self-correction mechanism of supply and demand, although this happens automatically and not by discretionary monetary policy.

However, contrary to the money supply of the currency-board, the money supply of the central bank, which is developed and extensively discussed in Chapter 5, especially Section 5.8, when we assume away the excess reserve ratio (e), is reported in Section B of Panel 13.1 and it is shown as

$$M = [(1 + r)/(r + c)].[(IR + DC)] \tag{13.10}$$

where, DC are domestic credits and generally comprise of loans to banks and securities of the Treasury. The central bank can respond to changes in international reserves by sterilizing its effects on domestic money supply. This is done by conducting an offsetting monetary policy operation from the monetary base as follows:

$$-\Delta IR = \Delta DC$$

In the previous chapters, we discussed that the net international reserves of the central bank are constrained by its ability to sustain reserve losses emanating from the balance of payments deficit. Per the account of the monetary approach to the balance of payments presented in Chapter 11, the central bank's sterilization of balance of payments disequilibrium through open market operation is limited to the central bank's available volume of the net international reserves. However, if the balance of payments problem is long-term or originates from speculators, then the size of the net international reserves required to successfully sterilize increases. In the event where the net international reserves are inadequate to support sterilization, activities of speculators can drain international reserves and often result in capital flight.

Finally, it is inadvisable for currency-boards to engage in treasury instruments trading to promote their participation in fiscal activities, and to permit them from assuming the role of discretionary monetary policy. It is argued that countries which purposefully adopted currency-boards to fight inflation have now replaced their currency-boards with central banks to regain their authorities to conduct discretionary monetary policy, and to support fiscal activities which currency-boards cannot undertake.

A currency-board country cannot serve as a lender of last resort. This is because an orthodox currency-board country's monetary authorities do not hold reserves against commercial bank deposits, so they do not have any authority to use discretionary monetary powers. Consequently, they cannot conduct discounting process at discount windows, as they do not have any authority to use the discounting process to serve as a lender of last resort. See Humpage and McIntire (1995), Hanke (2002), and Hanke et al. (1993).

13.25 Summary

Carry trade is also known as uncovered interest rate parity condition. The central bank employs monetary policy to set up the differential between domestic and foreign interest rates which is equal to the change in expected exchange rate of the national currency to produce a stabilizing effect to achieve internal stability. The impossibility trinity which states that a central bank cannot simultaneously fix its exchange rate, maintain free capital flows, and enjoy monetary autonomy to independently conduct monetary policy, emerges from the carry trade.

Two types of exchange rates are floating exchange rate and fixed exchange rate. Five variants of fixed exchange rates are inflation targeting, dollarization, currency union, exchange rate targeting, and currency-boarding.

The primary long-run goal of monetary policy is stable prices, and inflation targeting is a nominal anchor that ties down prices to stabilize inflation. It entails as its features public announcement of medium-term objectives or targets of inflation. It widens transparency in making decision on monetary policy strategy through communication with the public and stakeholders. It strengthens the accountability of the central bank to achieve inflation targeting objectives.

Inflation targeting is very much in line with democratic principle. The governor of the central bank, and other banking officials are chosen by the government to form a monetary policy committee, with the responsibility to set monetary policy goals and to conduct monetary policy. Monetary policy committee members are chosen from all walks of life, namely, academia, businesses, and banks, to name a few. As such, the decisions of the monetary policy committee are representational of the entire economy in the country.

Dollarization occurs when a small country adopts a hard currency such as the US dollar or yuan renminbi, to name two, as its vehicular currency or legal tender to conduct its international transactions. Dollarization facilitates the integration of the dollarized country with the developed country whose currency has been adopted for the dollarization like the US, and the rest of the world. Dollarization provides countries a means to eliminate completely devaluation or currency risk, and attendant inflation and associated threat, since the dollarized currency is stable, strong, and irrevocable.

Dollarization enhances the central bank's role as a lender of last resort. It also completely assists in eliminating speculative attacks in the dollarized country. A country that adopts dollarization foregoes completely its monetary and exchange rate policy autonomy. A country that dollarizes loses its seigniorage, which is the profit or revenue accruing to the monetary authority of the country which prints it. The dollarized country transfers its seigniorage to the country which it transfers or replaces its currency with its dollar.

Dollarization results in loss of lender of last resort function of the central bank, as the replacement of the domestic country's currency with the foreign currency means absence of central bank in the dollarized country. This means that during financial distress, the central bank cannot extend discounting lending to financial institutions in the domestic economy. It also deprives the dollarized country of its international prestige and pride which ownership of national currency bestows to the currency issuing country.

Currency union, which is also known as monetary union, is a union formed by a group of countries which come together to fix their exchange rate in relations to each other by adopting a common currency.

Under a flexible exchange rate regime, depreciation is used to solve BOPs deficit problem instead of allowing the economy to be saddled with unemployment problem, and appreciation is used to solve inflation problem which originate from BOPs surplus problem.

There are two types of currency areas. These are international currency area and interregional currency area. The international currency area is a currency area comprising of a single currency, which is fixed to a reserve currency, such as the dollar or yuan or euro, or is floated against international currencies. The interregional currency area is a currency area which comprises of more than one currency areas.

A currency area which comprises of several countries, with each country having its own currency, the adjustment process ensures that the BOPs surplus country employs expansionary monetary policy to reduce the real interest rate to cause the BOPs deficit country's employment to grow and reduce its unemployment.

Under flexible exchange rate regime, depreciation in country A will solve the BOPs deficit, and unemployment in country A, and appreciation in country B will solve the BOPs surplus, overemployment, and inflation in country B.

Exchange rate targeting is a monetary policy strategy of fixing the value of the domestic currency to a commodity such as gold during the gold standard Bretton Woods period. It provides a nominal anchor to maintain inflation by tying the country which is pegging its currency to the exchange rate of international traded goods, while fixing the domestic price of these goods to the exchange rate target. If the exchange rate targeting is credible, the inflation expectations is set to the inflation of the anchor country.

It provides an automatic rule to guide the conduct of monetary policy to mitigate time-inconsistency problem inherent in the central bank's attempt to employ temporary monetary expansion to mitigate low output or high unemployment. Exchange rate targeting exposes countries to speculative attacks on their national currencies.

Exchange rate targeting can weaken the integrity and accountability of policymakers, especially in emerging market economies. Exchange rate targeting exposes countries to speculative attacks on their national currencies. Exchange rate targeting in emerging market economies have been used to curb or reduce inflation. It limits or reduces time-inconsistency problem associated with the central bank's tendency to engage in expansionary or loose monetary policy.

Exchange rate targeting can weaken the integrity and accountability of policymakers, especially in emerging market economies. The fact is, exchange rate targeting fixes the exchange rate, which is more pronounce in emerging market. It removes an important signal which assists policymakers and market participants from being informed on the direction of economic policy, whether it is more expansionary or not.

Thus, it limits or reduces time-inconsistency problem associated with the central bank's tendency to engage in expansionary or loose monetary policy. It should be noted though, that issues that relate to exchange rate targeting, which are very common in emerging economies are not important features in most developed countries. It is for this reason that exchange rate targeting is not a very common feature in developed countries, as they prevail in emerging economies.

A currency-board is a monetary authority which issues notes and coins which can be converted into a reserve currency at a fixed rate on demand. Although a currency-board does not accept deposits, its reserves are low-risk interest-bearing bonds and other assets which are denominated in the foreign anchor currency. It generates profits commonly known as a seigniorage which is the interest earned on its reserve assets minus the expense of the maintenance liabilities (or its notes and coins in circulation).

Currency-boards do not convert bank deposits into currency-board notes. Only banks make such conversion. Currency-boards can only issue coins and currency-board notes. The central bank of a country with the currency-board cannot print money, so it cannot cause inflation. It also cannot serve as lender of last resort because of its inability to create money which is a function of inflation.

13.26 Problems

(13.1) The central bank of Nigeria has just sold dollars in the foreign exchange market, without not sterilizing its intervention, what will be the impact on international reserves, the money supply, and the exchange rate?

(13.2) Suppose the world is under the gold standard, and the productivity of South Africa has dropped relative to the productivity of Kenya: (i) What would happen to the money supply in the two countries? (ii) Do you expect the changes in the money supply to preserve a fixed exchange rate between Kenya and South Africa? Explain your answer.

(13.3) A country's par exchange rate was under-valued during the Bretton Woods era of fixed exchange rate. What kind of intervention would that country's central bank be compelled to undertake, and what effect would it have on its interventional reserves and the money supply? Explain in the context of a large balance of payments deficit, how it contributes to a country's unemployment?

(13.4) The impossibility trinity is consistent with the following assertion: "A country that wants to keep its exchange rate stable must give up some control over its money supply." Is the statement true, false, or uncertain? Explain your response in some detail.

(13.5) Explain whether balance of payments surplus can force some countries to embark on an expansionary monetary policy?

(13.6) Is inflation possible under the gold standard? Yes or No. Explain your answer in some detail.

(13.7) Under a pure floating exchange rate system, there is no direct effects between the foreign exchange market and the money supply. Explain.

Will you conclude that the foreign exchange market has no effect on monetary policy?

(13.8) Discuss four key advantages and five key disadvantages of exchange rate targeting.

(13.9) "Balance of payments deficits always cause a country to lose international reserves."

Discuss the validity or falsity of the statement.

(13.10) Is inflation possible under the gold standard? Explain your answer.

(13.11) Explain how exchange rate targets cause speculative attacks on currency.

(13.12) Discuss advantages of currency-board over the exchange rate targeting monetary policy.

(13.13) "The multiplier of the currency-board is greater than the multiplier of the central bank." Is the statement True or False or Uncertain? Explain your answer in some detail.

(13.14) Suppose two countries, namely: Ghana and Gambia belong to ECOWAS single market economy (ESME), and they use a common currency known as eco in a closed common currency area. Given there is a shift in demand from Ghana's goods and services to Gambia's goods and services. Assuming that the economy was at equilibrium before the shift in demand, and the economy was operating at full employment, and the balance of payments was balanced before the shift in demand. Discuss the adjustment process between Ghana and Gambia, and in the ESME?

Selected References

Bernanke, Ben S. and Frederic S, Mishkin (1997). "Inflation Targeting: A New Framework for Monetary Policy?" *Journal of Economic Perspectives*, 11(2): 97–116.

Berg, Andrew and Eduardo Borensztein (2000). "The Pros and Cons of Full Dollarization," IMF Working Paper WP/00/50 (Washington DC: International Monetary Fund).

Cohen, Benjamin J. (2000). "Dollarization: Pros and Cons," University of California at Santa Barbara, (Unpublished Working Paper).

Feenstra, Robert C. and Alan M. Taylor (2008). *International Macroeconomics*, New York: Worth Publishers.

Ghartey, Edward E. (2019), "Asymmetries in exchange rate pass-through and monetary policy principle: Some Caribbean empirical evidence," North American Journal of Economics and Finance, 47, 325-335.

Hanke, Steven H. (2002). "Currency Boards," *The Annals of the American Academy*, 579: 87-105.

Hanke, Steve H. (2002). "On dollarization and currency boards: error and deception," *Policy Reform*, 5 (4): 203-222.

Hanke, Steve H., L. Jonung, and Schuler, K. (1993). *Russian Currency and Finance*, London: Routledge.

Humpage, Owen F. and Jean M. McIntire (1995), "An Introduction to Currency Boards," *Economic Review, Federal Reserve Bank of Cleveland*, Issue Q11, 2-11.

Husted, Steven. and Michael Melvin (1993). *International Economics*, (New York: Harper Collins College Publishers).

Krugman, Paul R., and Maurice Obstfeld (2000). *International Economics: Theory and Policy*, (New York: Addison-Wesley, Longman, Inc.).

Mishkin, Frederic S. (2016). *The Economics of Money, Banking, and Financial Markets*, (New York: Pearson).

Mundell, Robert A. (1961). "A Theory of Optimum Currency Areas," *American Economic Review*, 51 (4), September: 657–665.

Salvatore, Dominick (2010). *International Economics*, (New York: John Wiley & Sons Inc.).

Walsh, Carl E. (1998), *Monetary Theory and Policy*, (New York: The MIT Press).

Bibliography

Ahking, F, W. (1984). "International currency substitution: A reexamination of Brittain's econometrics evidence," *Journal of Money, Credit, and Banking*, 16: 546–556.

Alexander, S. S. (1952). "Effects of Devaluation: a Simplified Synthesis of Elasticities and Absorption Approach," *American Economic Review*, 49, 22–42.

Allais, Maurice (1947). E'conomie et interet, (Paris: Librairie des publications officielles).

Apergis, N. and Miller, S. (2006), "Consumption asymmetry and the stock market: Empirical Evidence." *Economics Letters,* 93 (3), 337–342.

Arango, S. and Nadiri, M.I. (1981). "Demand for money in open economies," *Journal of Monetary Economies*, 7: 69–83.

Bahmani-Oskooee, Moshin. T. (1991). "The demand for money in an open economy: The United Kingdom," *Applied Economics*, 23: 1037–1042.

Bahmani-Oskooee, M. and D. Bernstein (1999). "Exchange Market Pressure during the Current Managed Float," *Applied Economic Letters*, 6, 585–588.

Barro, Robert. J. (2001). *Macroeconomics,* New York: The MIT Press.

Baumol, William J. (1952). "The Transactions Demand for Cash: An inventory theoretic approach," *Quarterly Journal of Economics*, 66 (4): 545–556.

Bernanke, Ben S. and Frederic S, Mishkin (1997). "Inflation Targeting: A New Framework for Monetary Policy?" *Journal of Economic Perspectives*, 11(2): 97–116.

Berg, Andrew and Eduardo Borensztein (2000). "The Pros and Cons of Full Dollarization," IMF Working Paper WP/00/50 (Washington DC: International Monetary Fund).

E. E. Ghartey, *International Macroeconomics and Finance*,
https://doi.org/10.1007/978-3-032-04145-6

Blanchard, Olivier J. and Lawrence H. Summers (1987). "Hysteresis in unemployment," *European Economic Review*, 31, 288–295.

Borenstein, S., Cameron, C. and Gilbert, R. (1997), "Do gasoline prices respond asymmetrically to crude oil price changes?" *The Quarterly Journal of Economics*, 112 (1), 305–339.

Cagan, Phillip (1956). "The Monetary Dynamics of Hyperinflation," in *Studies in the Quantity Theory of Money*, edited by Milton Friedman (Chicago: University of Chicago Press).

Clower, R.W. (1967), "A reconsideration of the micro-foundations of Monetary theory," *Western Economic Journal*, 6 (1), 1–9.

Cohen, Benjamin J. (2000). "Dollarization: Pros and Cons," University of California at Santa Barbara, (Unpublished Working Paper).

Connolly, M. and J. D. da Silveira (1979). Exchange Market Pressure in Postwar Brazil: an Application of the Girton-Roper Monetary Model," *American Economic Review*, 69 (3), 448–454.

Croushore, Dean. (1993). "Money in the utility function: Functional equivalence to a shopping-time model," *Journal of Macroeconomics*, 15 (1): 175–182.

Cuddington, J. T. (1983). "Currency substitution, capital mobility and money demand," *Journal of International Money and Finance*, 2: 111–133.

Dornbusch, R. (1973). "Devaluation, Money, and Non-traded Goods," *American Economic Review*, 63, 871–880.

Dornbusch, R. (1976). "Expectations and Exchange Rate Dynamics," *Journal of Political Economy*, 86 (6), December, 1161–1176.

Dornbusch, Rudiger, Fischer, Stanley, and Sparks, Gordon, R. (1982). *Macro Economics*, (New York: McGraw-Hill Ryerson Limited).

Dornbusch, R. and Stanley Fisher (1987), Macroeconomics, (New York: McGraw-Hill, Inc.).

Engle, R.F. and C.W.J. Granger (1987). "Cointegration and error-correction: representation, estimation and testing," *Econometrica*, 55: 251–769.

Feenstra, Robert C. and Alan M. Taylor (2008). *International Macroeconomics*, (New York: Worth Publishers).

Fisher, Irving (1930). *The Theory of Interest*, (New York: Macmillan).

Fleming, J.M. (1962). "Domestic Financial Policies under Fixed and under Floating Exchange Rates," *IMF Staff Papers*, November.

Frenkel, J. A. and H. G. Johnson, eds., (1976). *The Monetary Approach to the Balance of Payments*, (University of Toronto Press, Toronto).

Friedman, Milton (1968). "The role of monetary policy," *American Economic Review*, 58, March, 1–17.

Ghartey, Edward E. (1987). "Devaluation as a balance of payments corrective measure in developing country: a study relating to Ghana," *Applied Economics*, 19 (7): 937–947.

Ghartey, Edward E. (1998). "Monetary Dynamics in Ghana: Evidence from Cointegration, Error Correction Modelling, and Exogeneity," *Journal of Development Economics*, December, 57 (2): 473–486.

Ghartey, Edward E. (2002). "Exchange Market Pressure and Optimal Foreign Exchange Regime in Jamaica," *Social and Economic Studies*, 51 (2), 49–62.

Ghartey, Edward E. (2004). "Random Walk as a Universal Test of Weak-Form Foreign Exchange Market Efficiency: A Proof," *Frontiers in Finance and Economics*, 1 (1): 37–45.

Ghartey, Edward E. (2009). "The Mid 1990s Peso Crisis in Mexico: An Application of the Girton-Roper Model," *Frontiers in Finance and Economics,* 6 (1), 73–92.

Ghartey, Edward E. (2018), "Exchange Rate Principles in Especially Developing Countries," Presidential Address, AFEA/ASSA/AEA Annual Meeting, Philadelphia, January 5.

Ghartey, Edward E. (2019), "Asymmetries in exchange rate pass-through and monetary policy principle: Some Caribbean empirical evidence," North American Journal of Economics and Finance, 47, 325–335.

Girton, L. and D. Roper (1977). "A Monetary Model of Exchange Market Pressure Applied to the Postwar Canadian Experience," *American Economic Review*, 67 (4), 537–548.

Granger, C.W.J. and Yoon, G. (2002). "Hidden Cointegration," unpublished manuscript, University of California, San Diego.

Hanke, Steven H. (2002). "Currency Boards," *The Annals of the American Academy*, 579: 87–105.

Hanke, Steve H. (2002). "On dollarization and currency boards: error and deception," *Policy Reform*, 5 (4): 203–222.

Hanke, Steve H., L. Jonung, and Schuler, K. (1993), *Russian Currency and Finance*, (London: Routledge).

Harberger, A. C. (1950). "Currency Depreciation, Income, and the Balance of Trade," *Journal of Political Economy*, 58, 47–60.

Hausman, J.A. (1978). "Specification tests in econometrics," *Econometrica*, 46: 1251–1272.

Hendry, David F. and Neil R. Ericsson (1991). "An econometric analysis of U.K. money demand in monetary trends in the United States and the United Kingdom by Milton Friedman and Anna J. Schwartz," *The American Economic Review*, 8 (1): 8–38.

Heung, Cheung J. (1999), "Money demand in an open-economy shopping time model: An out-of-sample-prediction application to Canada," *Journal of Economics and Business*, (51): 489–503.

Hicks, John R. (1937), "Mr. Keynes and the 'CLASSICS' a suggested interpretation," *Econometrica*, 5 (2), April: 147–159.

Hume, D. (1963). *Essays: moral, political, and literary*, (Oxford University Press, London).

Humpage, Owen F. and Jean M. McIntire (1995), "An Introduction to Currency Boards," *Economic Review, Federal Reserve Bank of Cleveland*, Issue Q11, 2–11.

Husted, Steven and Michael Melvin (1993), *International Economics*, (New York: Harper Collins College Publishers).

Institute for Capacity Development (2013), *Financial Programming and Policies*, International Monetary Fund.

Johnson, H.G. (1977). "The Monetary Approach to the Balance of Payments: A Non-technical Guide," *Journal of International Economics*, 7, 251–68.

Keynes, John M. (1936), *The General Theory of Employment, Interest, and Money*, (London: Macmillan Press).

Kim, I. (1985). "Exchange Market Pressure in Korea: An Application of the Girton-Roper Monetary Model," *Journal of Money, Credit, and Banking*, 17(2), 258–263.

King, Robert T., Charles L. Plosser and Rebelo, S. T. (1988). "Production, growth, and business cycles: I. The basic neoclassical model," *Journal of Monetary Economics*, 21, 2–3: 195–232.

King, Robert G. and Charles I. Plosser (1984). "Money, credit, and prices in a real business cycle," *American Economic Review*, 74, June, 363–80.

Krugman, Paul R. and Maurice Obstfeld, (2000). *International Economics: Theory and Policy*, (New York: Addison-Wesley, Inc.).

Krugman, Paul R., Maurice Obstfeld, and Marc J Melitz (2015). *International Economics: Theory and Policy*, (New York: Pearson).

Kydland, Finn E. and Edward C. Prescott (1982). "Time to build and aggregate fluctuations," *Econometrica*, 50, November, 1345–70.

Levantakis, John A. (1993). "Modelling money demand in open economies over the modern floating rate period," *Applied Economics*, 25: 1005–1012.

Long, John B. and Charles I. Plosser (1983). "Real business cycles," *Journal of Political Economy*, February, 1345–1370.

Lucas, Robert E. Jr. (1976). "Econometric policy evaluations: a critique," in *The Phillips curve and labor markets*, Karl Brunner and Allan H. Meltzer, eds. (Amsterdam: North-Holland).

Lucas, Robert E., Jr., (1972). "Expectations and the neutrality of money," *Journal of Economic Theory*, 4, April, 103–24.

Magee, Stephen P. (1973). "Currency contract, pass-through, and devaluation," *Brookings Papers on Economic Activity*, 1, 303–325.

Meade, J. (1951). *The Theory of International Economic Policy. In The Balance of Payments, I* (London: Oxford University Press).

McCallum, Bennett T. (1989). *Monetary Economics: Theory and Policy*, (New York: Macmillan Publishing Company).

Mishkin, Frederic S. (2016). *The Economics of Money, Banking, and Financial Markets*, (New York: Pearson).

Modeste, N. C. (1981). "Exchange Market Pressure during the 1970s in Argentina: An Application of the Girton-Roper Monetary Model)," *Journal of Money Credit and Banking*, 13 (2), 234–240.

Mundell, R. (1971). *Monetary Theory*, (Pacific Palisades: Goodyear).

Mundell, Robert (1963). "Capital Mobility and Stabilization Policy under Fixed and Flexible Exchange Rates," *Canadian Journal of Economics and Political Science*, XXIX (4), November, 475–485.

Mundell, Robert A. (1961). "A Theory of Optimum Currency Areas," *American Economic Review*, 51 (4), September: 657–665.

Muth, John F. (1961). "Rational expectations and the theory of price movements," *Econometrica*, 29, 315–35.

Nelson, Charles R. and Charles I. Plosser (1982). "Trends and random walks in macroeconomic time series: some evidence and implications," *Journal of Monetary Economics*, 10, September, 139–167.

Obstfeld, M. (1982). "Macroeconomic Policy in the Open Economy: Can We Sterilize? Theory and Evidence," *American Economic Review*, 72 (2), 45–50.

Okun, M. Arthur (1962). "Potential GNP: Its Measurement and Significance," Proceedings of the Business and Economic Statistics Section, American Statistical Society.

Phelps, Edmund S. (1967). "Phillips Curves, Expectations of Inflation, and Optimal Unemployment over Time," *Economica*, 34: 254–81.

Phillips, Alban W. H. (1958). "The Relation between Unemployment and the Rate of Change of Money Wage Rates in the United Kingdom, 1861–1957." *Economica*, 25: 283–300.

Polak, J.J. (1957). Monetary Analysis of Income Formation and Payments Problems. *International Monetary Fund Staff Papers*, 8, 212–226.

Robinson, J. (1937). *The Foreign Exchanges. In J. Robinson, Essays in the Theory of Employment*. (Macmillan: London).

Romer, David, (2001). *Advanced Macroeconomics*, (New York: McGraw Hill.

Salvatore, Dominick (2010). *International Economics*, (New York: John Wiley & Sons Inc.).

Sargent, Thomas, J. (1973). "Rational expectations, the real rate of interest, and the natural rate of unemployment," *Brookings Papers on Economic Activities*, 2, 429–72.

Schorderet, Y. (2001). "Revisiting Okun's law: An hysteretic perspective," unpublished manuscript, University of California, San Diego.

Shin, Y., Yu, B., and Greenwood-Nimmo, M. (2011). "Modelling asymmetric cointegration and dynamic multipliers in a nonlinear ARDL framework." SSRN Electronic Journal

Sidrauski, Miguel (1967), "Rational choice and patterns of growth in a Monetary Economy," *American Economic Review*, 57 (2), Papers and Proceedings of the 79th Annual Meeting of the American Economic Association: 534–544.

Tinbergen, J. (1952). *On the Theory of Economic Policy*, (Amsterdam: North-Holland).

Tobin, James (1956). "The interest elasticity of the transactions demand for cash". *Review of Economics and Statistics*, 38 (3): 241–247.

von Whitman, M. (1975). Global Monetarism and the Monetary Approach to the Balance of Payments. *Brookings Papers on Economic Activity*, 3, 491–555.

Walsh, Carl E. (1998). *Monetary Policy and Theory*, (New York: The MIT Press).

Weymark, D.N. (1997). Measuring the Degree of Exchange Market Intervention in a Small Open Economy. *Journal of International Money and Finance*, 16 (1), 55–79.

Wu, D.M. (1973), "Alternative tests of independence between stochastic regressors and disturbances," *Econometrica*, 41: 733–750.

Index

A
absolute PPP, 74, 75
absorption, 6, 225
accelerator principle, 144
accommodating transaction, 21
adaptive expectation, 53, 55, 171
aggregate demand (AD) curve, 154
aggregate supply curve, 176, 180
anchor currency, 239, 240
animal spirit, 145
appreciation, 34, 148, 153, 160, 196, 248–249, 258, 280
asset, 60, 81–83, 88–91
autonomous taxes, 145, 149
autonomous transaction, 21
average income, 99–100

B
balance of payments account, 13
bank deposit, 86–87
beachhead effect, 224
borrowed monetary base, 88
borrowing interest rate, 111
Brownfield investments, 20
budget constraint, 108, 111, 112
budget surplus, 7
bullion, 206
business cycle, 182

C
cambios, 32
Cambridge equation of exchange, 95–96
capital account, 13, 16, 18
capital outflow, 107
certificates of deposit, 85
changes in inventory (cinv), 144
changes in inventory stock, 3
classical dichotomy, 200
Cobb-Douglas production function, 108
cointegration, 125, 128
constancy property of parameters, 128
core inflation, 186
corner solution, 109
covered interest rate parity condition, 70
covering open position, 41

E. E. Ghartey, *International Macroeconomics and Finance*,
https://doi.org/10.1007/978-3-032-04145-6

cross exchange rates, 34
currency, 82–84, 87, 89
currency area, 259, 262
currency board, 269
currency carry trade, 248, 252
currency pass-through, 223
currency union, 251, 252, 258–259, 279
current account, 17, 18

D
debt forgiveness, 13, 18
depreciation, 2, 34, 107, 199, 220, 243, 248, 256, 257, 279
derivatives, 20
devaluation, 256–257, 279
diagnostic test results, 127
direct investments, 18
discount rate, 103, 109
disequilibrium model, 125
dollarization, 255
double-entry bookkeeping account, 24

E
economic interpretations, 115
efficient foreign exchange market, 70
elasticity approach to the BOPs, 227
emerging market economies, 258, 268
error-correction model, 125–128
error-correction term, 126
exchange market pressure, 208–212
exchange rate, 195
exchange rate overshooting, 201
exchange rate principle, 152–153
exchange rate regime, 252
exchange rate targeting, 266
expectation augmented Phillips curve, 173

F
financial account, 16, 20
financial flow, 22
financial friction, 144, 149
financial inflow, 148
Fisher's effect, 151, 160
Fisher's equation of exchange, 94
fixed exchange rate, 212–213, 258, 264
fixed exchange rate regime, 239
flexible exchange rate regime, 214, 256
float, 85
floating exchange rate, 107, 231, 264–265
foreign exchange futures, 38
foreign exchange market, 64, 68, 240
foreign exchange market intervention, 239
foreign exchange market participants, 32
foreign exchange options, 38
foreign exchange regime, 240
foreign exchange risk, 39–40
foreign exchange risk premium, 77
foreign exchange stabilization fund, 88
foreign exchange swap, 37
foreign investors, 243
forward discount, 37
free market system, 180
free-on-board, 13, 16
fundamental BOPs identity, 13

G
general consumption taxes, 4
geometric perspective, 146
gold standard, 265
government purchase shock, 145
Greenfield investments, 13
gross domestic product, 1, 2

gross fixed capital formation, 3
gross national income, 6
gross private national saving, 6

H
hedging, 41
households, 108–109, 111, 116
hysteresis, 183, 184

I
impossibility trinity, 247–250
indirect business taxes, 4
Indirect effect, 108
inflation rate, 200
inflation targeting, 253
interest arbitrage, 44
interest rate spread, 256
international currency area, 259
international market segmentation, 223
interregional currency area, 262
inter-temporal budget constraint, 108, 111
inventory rule model, 101
inverted real income equation test, 133–138
IS-LM curves, 142

J
J-curve effect, 220–222

K
Keynesian liquidity preference, 152

L
labor market, 177
Lagrangian equation, 114
law of iterated expectation, 57
law of one price, 74
leisure, 108–110, 112–115
lender of last resort, 256, 277
liabilities, 86, 87
liquidity preference money demand, 96
long-run aggregate demand curve, 189

M
marginal efficiency of capital, 144, 163
marginal productivity of capital, 144
marginal product of labor, 202
Marshallian equation, 95–96
Marshall Lerner condition, 219
martingale, 71, 77
micro-economic foundation, 105–106
monetary aggregates, 84, 85
monetary approach to exchange rate, 214
monetary base, 86–93
monetary policy autonomy, 251
monetary policy curve, 150–155
monetary policy principle, 152, 190, 200
monetary policy trilemma, 248, 252
monetary shock, 182
monetary union, 258, 279
money supply, 82, 86, 92–94
multi-period utility function, 108–109
multiplier, 146–148
mutual funds, 84–85

N
national income, 1
national income accounting, 2, 3
national income identity, 3
national saving, 7
negative shock, 179
net factor income from abroad, 1, 4

net international investment position, 15
net international reserve, 243
net national product, 3
net taxes, 6, 8
net unilateral transfer, 1, 16
neutrality property of money, 200
nominal effective exchange rate (neer or nexr), 34
nominal wage rate, 173
non-accelerating inflation rate unemployment, 195
nonlinear, 148

O
offset coefficient, 211
Okun's law, 173, 174
open-economy, 107, 114, 122
open economy market, 201
open market operation, 237
opportunity cost measure, 107, 110, 124
optimum currency areas (OCA), 247
outward direct investment, 20
over-valued exchange rate, 237

P
par value, 236–240
perfect capital mobility, 241
permanent increase in money supply, 197
phase diagram, 196
Phillips curve, 176
portfolio investments, 18
positive time preference, 109
price homogeneity, 129
price specie flow mechanism, 206
primary income, 4, 15, 17
procyclical, 95
productivity shock, 179
purchasing power parity, 66

Q
quantity theory of money, 93–95

R
random walk, 71
rational expectation, 53, 55, 72, 171
real business cycle, 145, 182
real cash balance, 97, 108, 112–113, 123
real effective exchange rate, 107, 113, 117, 124
real exchange rate, 35, 107, 113, 223
real income, 97
real interest rates, 147
real output, 174, 177, 179
real wage rate, 173
regional currency area, 247
relative PPP, 76
remittances, 5
reparation, 4
reserve currency, 33
reserves, 86–88, 109
resource, 108
response policy lag, 219
rest of the world (ROW), 241
revalue, 240

S
scale variable, 110, 124
secondary incomes, 13, 18
seigniorage, 33, 247, 257, 279
self-correction mechanism, 197, 206
shocks to taste, 182
shopping-time model, 106–107, 109, 112
short position, 43
slackness in the labor market, 177
social insurance, 2
Special Drawing Rights (SDR), 20, 86–88
speculation, 42–43, 241

speculative attacks, 279
square root formula of money demand, 97
stabilization effect, 108
stagflation, 207
sterilized exchange intervention, 234, 235
sterilized intervention, 90, –92
structural invariance, 132
structural stability test, 134–138
super-exogeneity test, 132
super-neutrality property of money, 196, 200
system of national income account, 8

T
Taylor's principle, 157, 160, 190
Taylor's rule, 151, 152, 160
technological shock, 145
technology, 179
Tequila effect, 244
threshold of tolerance, 243
tightness in the labor market, 174
total direct taxes, 7
total indirect taxes, 7
Treasury deposits, 86–88

U
unanticipated spot rate, 72
uncovered interest rate parity condition, 70
under-valued exchange rate, 240–242
unemployed, 2
unemployment, 173, 183, 195
unique solution, 116
unit real income property, 130
unsterilized intervention, 90–91, 240
utility function, 105–107, 113

V
value added, 1
vault cash, 87
vehicle currency, 31

W
wages, 190
weak exogeneity test, 130
Wu-Hausman method, 129

Z
zero lower-bound limitation, 152